Wissenschaftliche Untersuchungen
zum Neuen Testament · 2. Reihe

Herausgeber / Editor
Jörg Frey (München)

Mitherausgeber / Associate Editors
Friedrich Avemarie (Marburg)
Judith Gundry-Volf (New Haven, CT)
Hans-Josef Klauck (Chicago, IL)

229

Michael A. Daise

Feasts in John

Jewish Festivals and Jesus' 'Hour'
in the Fourth Gospel

Mohr Siebeck

MICHAEL A. DAISE, born 1956; 1993 M. Div., Philadelphia Theological Seminary; 2000 Ph. D. at Princeton Theological Seminary; Assistant Professor, College of William & Mary, Williamsburg, USA.

ISBN 978-3-16-149018-7

ISSN 0340-9570 (Wissenschaftliche Untersuchungen zum Neuen Testament, 2. Reihe)

Die Deutsche Nationalbibliothek lists this publication in the Deutsche Nationalbibliographie; detailed bibliographic data is available in the Internet at *http://dnb.d-nb.de*.

The book was printed by Laupp & Göbel in Nehren on non-aging paper and bound by Buchbinderei Nädele in Nehren.

Printed in Germany.

To Leslie

Preface

This monograph is less a revision of my dissertation than a second work spun from it. That dissertation, written under James H. Charlesworth for Princeton Theological Seminary, treated of traditio-historical and theological issues raised by the *logia* in John 7:37-39, set during the Feast of Tabernacles. Closely related to (and completed simultaneously with) it was a mémoire on formal citations in the Fourth Gospel, written under the late (and missed) Marie-Émile Boismard for the École Biblique et Archéologique Français de Jérusalem. On the subsequent advice of Professor Dr. Martin Hengel, I began to consider how to set the dissertation on John 7 in a larger framework; and, as I did, I alighted on a concept which has proven thesis enough to develop in a single monograph. Consequently, though the hypothesis I present here was conceived after the one on which I received my doctorate, I offer it first.

The gist of its method is to look at the Gospel of John through the lens of Second Temple Jewish festal protocol. From my recent research on Second Temple Jewish ritual I have begun to accrue a *halakhic* grid, of sorts, through which I have noticed features in the Fourth Gospel I had not done before. Two of them – key to this monograph – are the calendrical violation implied by the consumption of barley prior to Passover in John 6:1–15 and the possibility that the Passover in question at John 6 could be, not the First Passover, prescribed in Exodus 12, but the so-called 'Second' or 'Lesser Passover,' prescribed in Numbers 9. Drawing upon certain plausible, albeit debatable, conventions in Johannine studies (such as the prior inversion of chapters 5 and 6), I discerned a larger scenario on the feasts in the narrative that seems to yield a more fundamental purpose for which they were designed; namely, to serve the motif of Jesus' "hour" by quantifying its imminence.

For the ability and resource required to write this book I am deeply indebted to numerous people and institutions. To Professor Charlesworth and Father Boismard, for the impetus and nurture, respectively, to pursue Johannine studies. If my review of Fr. Boismard's specific theory on feasts is somewhat critical, let it also be noted that the very approach I take to the issue in this monograph – that is, as a puzzle to be solved – is *homage* to the methodology I learned from him. Further thanks are due to Professor Dr. Hengel, for counsel on developing my initial work; to series editor

Jörg Frey, for encouragement and flexibility in receiving its end result; to colleagues Christophe Rico of the University of Strasbourg/École Biblique and Crispin H.T. Fletcher-Louis of St. Mary's Bryanston Square, London, for constructive critiques of earlier drafts; and to all members of the Department of Religious Studies at the College of William and Mary, for the supportive context in which I was able to complete the work.

The Israel Antiquities Authority granted me permission to access *11QTemple Scroll* and several other Qumran fragments on 10 and 14 July, 2003; and, for that research, the College of William and Mary offered me a Faculty Summer Research Grant in the same year. Dr. Henning Ziebritzki and the editorial staff at Mohr Siebeck furnished the most careful assistance in preparing the final manuscript. The Interlibrary Loan staff of Earl Gregg Swem Library at the College of William and Mary consistently succeeded in accessing my (sometimes obscure) requests for bibliography. And David Grant Smith, a William and Mary alumnus currently at Harvard Divinity School, skillfully formatted the manuscript and prepared its indices.

My deepest debt, however, is owed my wife, Leslie, whose genuine faith in God, unfailing love for me and constant sacrifice of herself have made our home, itself, a temple "in spirit and in truth." To her I dedicate this volume.

Pentecost XVI, 2006   *M.A.E.D., Williamsburg*

Table of Contents

Tables

Chapter 1

Introduction

1.1 Further on the Feasts

In this inquiry, I will argue that the feasts in John once served a purpose yet unnoticed in Johannine scholarship.

This is not to deny what has been noticed about them. Six feasts are listed in the Fourth Gospel: a (first) Passover, introduced at 2:13; an anonymous festival at 5:1; a (second) Passover at 6:4; the Feast of Tabernacles at 7:2; the Feast of Dedication at 10:22–23; and a final Passover at 11:55. No less than nine exegetes have made proposals about the collective significance and purpose of these feasts; and, from these proposals have come several enduring insights – that they furnish commemorative symbolism for Johannine christology[1]; that, from a *halakhic*/calendrical point of view, they are of a piece with the Fourth Gospel's Sabbath episodes[2]; and, most recently, that they enjoy an interface with the motif of Jesus' 'hour' as a tandem form of periodization.[3] My contention, rather, is that, alongside these (and other) purposes served by the festivals – and in an earlier phase of the Fourth Gospel's composition history – lay a more fundamental aim, now eclipsed by the current form of the text.

---

[1] Mollat 1953; 1960; 1973.

[2] Yee 1989.

[3] Destro and Pesce 1995a; 1995b; 1997; 2000; Pesce 2001. For further detail on all three of these views, see Chapter 3, '3.1.2 'Les jalons de ce récit,' Donatien Mollat'; '3.1.4 Johannine '*Takkanot*,' Gale A. Yee'; and '3.3 Anthropological Theory: '*Tempo Sociale*' to the '*Tempo Diverso*' of Jesus' 'Hour,' Adriana Destro and Mauro Pesce,' respectively. In that chapter, these and other hypotheses are rehearsed and assessed in more detail.

1.2 Guiding Assumptions, Points of Departure and Thesis

1.2.1 Guiding Assumptions

I build my hypothesis on several *a priori* exegetical decisions. First, that, in an earlier stage of the Fourth Gospel's compositional history, chapters 5 and 6 were inverted.[4] Debate over the Gospel of John's diachronic development has generated a plethora of theories – accidental displacement, unfinished editing, the compilation of sources, a succession of editions, a final redaction[5]; and all things being equal, I share the agnosticism expressed by some about ever determining which of these hypotheses, if any, is correct.[6] I am, however, willing to entertain any proposal (or part of a proposal) if other factors from the text strongly lend themselves to it; and, with the case I am about to make below, I find such factors present for the prior inversion of John 5 and 6.

Second, I assume that, in its earlier stage(s), the Fourth Gospel was written from a perspective astutely knowledgeable about Judaism. That is, however Hellenized or theologically removed from Judaism its final editor(s) may have been or become, the Fourth Gospel's earliest author – the Evangelist – knew the religion of Judaism intimately and integrated that knowledge deeply into his narrative. James H. Charlesworth conceives this early awareness (quite plausibly) within a diachronic hypothesis of two editions, putting the turn between the earlier Judaic and later phases during the siege of Jerusalem circa 68–70 C.E.[7] But, whether the literary development of the Fourth Gospel came through successive editions or other means – and whether a turning point can be circumscribed so precisely to the end of the First Jewish War against Rome or not – I assume as my second guiding principle that, in its earlier phase(s), the Gospel of John was crafted within a Jewish/Palestinian milieu by an author intimately acquainted with Judaism.

Further, I assume that this awareness of Judaism lies latent in the narrative unless otherwise indicated; and, similarly, that it extends as much to *halakhoth* as it does to ideology. That is to say, except for cases in the text where a breach is made and stated – such as Jesus' breaking of the Sabbath

---

[4] Details on scholarly discussion about this reversal follow in Chapter 2, under '2.2 The Unnamed Feast and a Second Passover (John 5:1–6:71).'

[5] See on this the review by Werner Kümmel 1973:167–83.

[6] See Kümmel's further comments on what can(not) be concluded from transposition and redaction-critical theories; 1973:177. Cf. also the doubts expressed by Jörg Frey over the degree of disunity actually created by *aporiahs* (whatever their source), as well as over the justification for ascribing extensive passages in the Fourth Gospel to anyone but the Evangelist himself; 2002:183–86.

[7] Charlesworth 2002b:73–77, 89–94, 102–109. Charlesworth allows that both editions may have been written by the same author (p. 77).

in chapters 5 and 9 – I expect that the author has cast Jewish life more or less as Judaism prescribed it, and that this Jewish life embraces, not only belief, but praxis.

1.2.2 Points of Departure

1.2.2.1 Barley and Passover

From these assumptions I take two points of departure. The first is a temporal tension that arises in the feeding of the five thousand episode (6:1–15) when the Passover at 6:4 is read as a regular Passover, observed on 14 Nisan. As that episode begins, its Passover is introduced, not as having arrived, but as being imminent: "And the Passover, the feast of the Jews, was near" (6:4). The bread used to feed the five thousand, however, is distinctly described as having been baked from barley: unlike Synoptic counterparts to the story, which make no mention of the type of grain used, the Johannine account has Andrew specifically saying, "There is a youth here who has five barley loaves (πέντε ἄρτους κριθίνους) and two fish. But what are these for so many?" (6:9).

The problem is not agricultural – fresh barley would have been available (and in fact was harvested) in Nisan. Rather, it is *halakhic*. According to the law of *ḥadaš* (new produce), prescribed in Leviticus 23:11–15, new barley (or any new produce) could not be consumed for non-cultic purposes until its first sheaf had been offered at the temple; yet, in the Jewish liturgical year, the day of that offering – the Waving of the 'Omer – would have necessarily post-dated Passover. The Waving of the 'Omer was slated for "the day after the Sabbath" following Passover; and, though there was some debate over which precise Sabbath was in view, all possible options follow, rather than precede, 14 Nisan. Since, in John 6, barley is already being used for such non-cultic purposes (baking), yet Passover has not yet come but is only "near," a calendrical conflict emerges; and this, in turn, begs for resolution.

Several solutions present themselves (to be reviewed below); but I will suggest that the least problematic among them is to read the Passover at 6:4, not as a regular Passover, observed on 14 Nisan (the first month of the Jewish calendar), but as the Passover prescribed in Numbers 9:9–14, observed on 14 'Iyyar (the second month of the Jewish calendar). In Qumran and Rabbinic sources, this Passover is dubbed the 'Second' (פֶּסַח שֵׁנִי) or 'Lesser Passover' (Hebrew/פֶּסַח קָטָן; Aramaic/פִּסְחָא זְעֵירָא); but, in Numbers 9 (and Philo Judaeus), it is simply called 'Passover,' distinguished from the regular Passover only by the month in which it is celebrated. Reading John 6 thus pushes the date of its Passover back one month into 'Iyyar, allowing the regular Passover and the Waving of the

'Omer to have already passed and, thereby, legitimating the secular (non-cultic) use of barley at 6:9.

If this seems a thin basis on which to predicate such a novel reading, it is buttressed by three further features of the Passover in 'Iyyar that also fit snugly with the Johannine context. First, the Priestly tradition implicitly associates Passover in 'Iyyar with the manna tradition, on which John 6 largely turns: the Exodus manna episode dates the first giving of manna to Israel "on the fifteenth day of the second month from their going out from the land of Egypt" (Exodus 16:1). Second, the conditional observance of Passover in 'Iyyar accounts for the absence of any mention of Jesus making pilgrimage in John 6. Passover in 'Iyyar was a contingent festival, only to be observed if the First (regular) Passover was missed (due to impurity or distance from the cult). Rabbinic tradition, in fact, discouraged such attempts. If Jesus had already celebrated Passover in Nisan (as is readily inferred), there would be no need for him to do so again in John 6. Third – and the factor that leads to my thesis on the larger purpose of feasts – when John 5 and 6 are inverted (and 6:4 is read as Passover in 'Iyyar), the feasts in John arrange themselves into a chronological schema that implies intent. The full order of feasts (and their times) would now be: the Passover at 2:13 (14 Nisan), the Passover at 6:4 (14 'Iyyar), the unnamed feast at 5:1 (???), Tabernacles at 7:2 (15–22 Tishri), Dedication at 10:22–23 (25 Kislev) and Passover at 11:55 (14 Nisan). As for the unnamed feast at 5:1, the temporal proximity required between the events of John 5 and those of John 7 (to be elaborated below) suggests that, whatever its precise identity may have been, it is more likely than not to have occurred within the several month period that would have passed if the Tabernacles after it (Tishri) followed the Second Passover before it ('Iyyar) in the same year. This effectively puts the feasts into a chronological sequence, spanning a single year – a design, which, in turn, implies intent.

1.2.2.2 Feasts and Jesus' 'Hour'

My second point of departure is an insight made by University of Bologna professors Adriana Destro and Mauro Pesce; namely, that, in John 2–12, the temporal rhythm designated by the feasts has an interface with the temporal rhythm designated by Jesus' 'hour.' The motif of Jesus' 'hour' operates dynamically in chapters 2–12: though it arrives during the last Passover, in John 12 (12:23, 27; 13:1; 17:1), it is introduced as being imminent just before the first Passover, in John 2 (2:4); and, between the two, it is cast as growing increasingly so near as to have essentially already come (4:21–23; 5:25; cf. 16:31–32). Destro and Pesce see the relationship of this 'hour' to the feasts as part of a grand dialectic operating between the rites of the Jesus and Johannine movements, on the one hand, and those of John the Baptist, the Samaritans and, especially, the Jews, on the other.[8] In this dialectic, Jesus' 'hour' represents an "alternate time" (*tempo diverso*) to the "social time" (*tempo sociale*) of the Jewish festivals; and, as it progresses toward its culmination, this "alternate time" of Jesus' 'hour' ushers Jesus' followers away from the "social time" of the feasts into itself.[9]

I am persuaded of this interface seen by Destro and Pesce; but, given the peculiar features of the festal sequence reconstructed above, I modify it in two ways. First, since the feasts included in that sequence do not represent all (major) festivals of the Jewish calendar, the schema is better explained as a chain of temporal indicators, marking months and seasons, than as a full liturgical calendar. And second, since those festivals unfold sequentially during the same period in which Jesus' 'hour' is said to be growing ever nearer, their relationship to that 'hour' is better understood as service than as dialectic. More precisely, I will argue that, in this earlier stage of the Fourth Gospel's development (when chapters 5 and 6 were reversed), the feasts fundamentally functioned to accentuate Jesus' 'hour' by quantifying its imminence till it arrived.

1.3 Caveat and Outline

1.3.1 The Force of the Argument

It is not lost on me that many premises in this argument will prove contestable. At almost every exegetical turn I have been painfully aware that there are other options available than the ones I have chosen – not all of them so improbable (or less preferable) as to render my interpretive decisions necessary. John 5 and 6, for instance, may not have been inverted in an earlier stage. Or, to anticipate other decisions, the "nearness" of the Passover at 6:4 may connote "just passed" rather than "imminent"; the barley loaves at 6:9 may represent old rather than freshly harvested grain; John 6 may not, in fact, have Exodus 16:1 in view; and 4:35 may date the Samaritan episode to Kislev rather than 'Iyyar.

But, if my thesis is not compelling in its parts, it is suggestive as a whole; and therein, I hope, will lie some contribution to Johannine studies. Its premises may not be necessary, but neither are they implausible; and,

---

[8] Destro and Pesce 1995a:79–106; 1995b:89–99; 2000:6–24.

[9] Destro-Pesce 1995a:77–82, 100–106; 1995b:87–88; 2000:5–12, 16–21, 118–20; Pesce 2001:55–56 (cf. Destro and Pesce 1997:112–26). The full hypothesis of Destro and Pesce is treated in detail in Chapter 3, '3.3 Anthropological Theory: *'Tempo Sociale'* to the *'Tempo Diverso'* of Jesus' 'Hour,' Adriana Destro and Mauro Pesce,' and Chapter 5, '5.2.3 Destro and Pesce Revisited.'

when bound together into the scenario argued here, they may prove apt to catalyze constructive discussion.

1.3.2 The Development of the Argument

I will develop this thesis in four major steps. First, I will review the feasts themselves, as they appear in the narrative (Chapter 2). I will examine all six explicitly mentioned feasts, as well as two implicitly operative ones (the Feast of Unleavened Bread and the Waving of the 'Omer). And, for each, I will give particular attention to (a) the extent of episodes covered (that is, the duration of each feast in narrative time) and (b) the diachronic issues affecting that coverage in the current text and in putative earlier strata.

Second (Chapter 3), I will examine the array of theories thus far proposed for the purpose(s) of the feasts. Here, I will only treat efforts that have engaged all six feasts (not merely, for instance, those that deal with the feasts between John 5–12). And, as I do, I will find them to reflect three distinct conceptions of the role feasts play: (a) literary, in which the feasts are alleged to function as structuring or hermeneutical devices for the narrative; (b) liturgical, in which the feasts are thought to calibrate the narrative to Johannine worship; and (c) anthropological, in which the feasts are understood to represent and facilitate the Jewish institutional matrix from which Johannine Christianity emerged.

Third (Chapter 4), I will develop the thesis just proposed in greater detail. The temporal tension surfacing in John 6, some options for resolving it, the possibility of reading 6:4 as the Passover in 'Iyyar and the corroboration such a reading enjoys from the Johannine narrative – all will be elaborated, with particular attention given to attestations of the Second Passover in Second Temple and Tannaitic sources.

Finally (Chapter 5), I will apply the sequence reconstructed in Chapter 4 to the purpose of feasts in John as a whole. I pause to note the implication of this sequence for an issue plaguing studies in Christian Origins – the *Praedicatio Domini*: the one year span of that sequence offers a more text-critically viable hypothesis than has been done for aligning the Johannine chronology of Jesus' public ministry with the chronology implied in the Synoptics and espoused by early Christian writers. I devote the lion's share of attention, however, to working out the implications of this sequence for the purpose of feasts in John. I note their role as temporal markers, trace the motif of Jesus' 'hour,' then show the one (feasts) to have functioned in service to the other ('hour'): feasts brought Jesus' 'hour' into relief by quantifying its growing imminence in John 2–12. I end by rehearsing four ramifications this thesis carries for reading the feasts in the current state of the text: the Second Passover at 6:4 remains such in the final version; but the single year chronological sequence is now reconfigured, the feast at 5:1 no longer has moorings by which it can be identified and much of the temporal momentum that once drove the theology of Jesus' 'hour' has now been weakened.

1.4 Sources and Style

1.4.1 Israelite and Tannaitic Data

Before I begin, several notes on certain sources, editions and editorial choices.

First, on two ostensibly anachronistic sources. If the final redaction of the Fourth Gospel dates to the late first century C.E., the period in question for this work (which includes earlier strata) spans circa 60–95 CE.[10] In the course of discussion, I cite two sets of information that may seem out of range for such a span: agricultural data from Iron Age Israel[11]; and both agricultural and *halakhic* data from Tannaitic tradition. The second of these two does not typically pose a problem for Johannine studies, since it is generally accepted that John came to its final form in the first decades of the Tannaim and, further, that it was likely written in the face of their reforms. But, inasmuch as this study reaches back to earlier (pre-70) strata in John – and given that (primarily) Tannaitic literature may still postdate the late first century (and even include Amoraic tradition) – the question of relevance obtains.

On the first – agricultural data from the Iron Age – the evidence I cite by and large concerns agricultural *conditions*, not agricultural *practices*, in ancient Israel: while the latter would have changed somewhat between the tenth century B.C.E. and the first century C.E., the former would not have[12] and, so, remain relevant into the period of this inquiry. Moreover, the (relatively modest) points I make from these earlier data will all be corroborated by both Second Temple and Rabbinic sources – from direct research into primary texts and from the important work of Yehuda Feliks, *Agriculture in the Land of Israel in the Period of Mishnah and Talmud* (1963/Hebrew).

As for Tannaitic sources, four observations on their usage: (1) as just mentioned, the agricultural data I cite from them will enjoy corroboration reaching back into the Second Temple period; (2) similarly, with a few ex-

---

[10] Here I follow the dates circumscribed by Charlesworth 2002b:73–91.

[11] Specifically, from Oded Borowski's work (1987).

[12] See Zohary 1982:15, 36, 41; Borowski 1987:xxi; Scott 1993:20, 198n41. My thanks to Professor Oded Borowski for confirming this point in a personal communication, 24 May, 2005.

ceptions (for instance, references for the intercalation of a "second 'Adar"), the *halakhic* passages I cite – for the Waving of the 'Omer, the law of *ḥadaš*, the Passover in 'Iyyar – will also enjoy confirmation from Second Temple sources; (3) these *halakhic* traditions, further, will all be found to presuppose a standing temple and cult, thus, arguably predating 70 C.E.; and, (4) even if some of the passages I reference represent late second century (or Amoraic) tradition, I offer enough data for each item that the general point being made should still hold.

1.4.2 Translations and Editions

All translations of non-English texts, ancient and modern, are mine. Editions of non-biblical texts will be cited in footnotes with their first usage. And, as for editions of biblical texts, for the Masoretic text (MT), I use Elliger and Rudolph 1983; for the Septuagint (LXX), Rahlfs, Ziegler and Wevers 1931–(1993) where editions are available, Rahlfs 1979, where they are not; and, for the New Testament (NA[27]), Aland, Aland, Karavidopoulos, Martini and Metzger 1993.

1.4.3 Editing Choices

Except where passages in the Gospel of John can be confused with those of other works, I cite them only by chapter and verse. Further, though I am aware of the ambiguity and nuance attending the term οἱ ᾽Ιουδαῖοι in the Fourth Gospel, I am also persuaded that its broad usage (for Galileans [6:41, 52] or common folk, not just leaders [8:30–31]) precludes it being translated narrowly as "Judeans" or "Jewish authorities"; and, so, for the sake of consistency and clarity, I gloss it simply as "the Jews." Moreover, unless I am engaging terminology used by someone else, I have chosen to reference the feasts, not by their Hebrew titles, but by their Hellenistic or Anglicized designations: Passover for *Pesaḥ*; the Feast of Unleavened Bread (or Azyma) for *Maṣṣot*; Pentecost for *Šavu'ot*; Tabernacles for *Sukkot*; the Day of Atonement for *Yom Kippurim*; and the Feast of Dedication for *Hanukkah*. I also indicate the first of the seventh month as the Feast of Remembrance, not *Ro'š Haššanah*.

Chapter 2

Feasts in the Narrative of the Fourth Gospel

2.1 The First Passover (John 2:13–3:21)

To provide context for the ensuing discussion, I will first rehearse the Johannine feasts as they appear in the narrative. My interest is two-fold: to demarcate episodes that, in narrative time (not literary structure), occur within the observance of those feasts; and to articulate redaction-critical issues attending those episodes.[1]

The first feast to appear in the narrative is a Passover. Introduced at 2:13, it furnishes the backdrop for Jesus' activities at least through 2:13–25. While it is "near," Jesus makes pilgrimage to Jerusalem (2:13), protests vending in the temple (2:14–17) and addresses opposition to that protest (2:18–22); and while it is in process – that is, "during the feast" – he performs signs that evoke faith among many (2:23–25). This context likely penetrates further, however, into Jesus' interview with Nicodemus in chapter 3. No evident hiatus occurs between that interview and the events of chapter 2 before it; and the signs at which Nicodemus marvels in 3:2 best refer to those Jesus was said to have been doing during the feast at 2:23–25:

> And as he was in Jerusalem during the Passover, during the feast,
> many believed on his name, beholding his signs, which he was doing
> (αὐτοῦ τὰ σημεῖα ἃ ἐποίει). . . (Nicodemus) came to him by night
> and said to him, "Rabbi, we know that you have come from God
> as a teacher; for no one can do these signs which you are doing
> (ταῦτα τὰ σημεῖα. . .ἃ σὺ ποιεῖς) unless God is with him."[2]

This would mean that Jesus' observance of the Passover in Jerusalem extended to Passover proper and perhaps beyond the first day of Unleavened Bread (15 Nisan), into the seven day observance that immediately followed.

---

[1] For the full complex of recognized aporiahs in the Fourth Gospel, on which much of the discussion in this chapter depends, see the summaries by Menoud 1947:12–13; Howard 1955:111–14; and Kümmel 1973:170–71.

[2] John 2:23; 3:2.

How much further this Passover context reaches into John 3 is open to question, since Jesus' discourse to Nicodemus in 3:10–21 may at any point bleed into the Evangelist's own words to the reader[3] and, thus, be abstracted from the narrative setting. A clear end comes, however, by 3:22, where Jesus and his disciples leave the festivities in Jerusalem and depart "into the land of Judea." Consequently, in narrative time, this first Passover spans Jesus' "cleansing of the temple" (2:14–17), his answer to interrogators (2:18–22), his signs in Jerusalem (2:23–25) and his conversation with Nicodemus (3:1–21).

John Bowman would draw the beginning back earlier, to John the Baptist's declaration of Jesus as "Lamb of God" (at 1:29). He reads "the third day" in 2:1 as the third day *of the week*, then counts backwards through the succession of days at 1:29, 1:35 and 1:43 to place 1:29 on the prior Sabbath, which he further identifies as the Sabbath before the Passover at 2:13.[4] But this cannot be so, on two counts. First, Bowman's reading of "the third day" as "the third day of the week" endows the term with more than it carries. Specifically numbered days of the week do appear elsewhere in John; but, where they do, they are qualified with the modifier τῶν σαββάτων – literally, "of the Sabbaths," but perhaps more smoothly, "of the week." So, 20:1, "And on the first day of the week (τῇ δὲ μιᾷ τῶν σαββάτων), Mary Magdalene came to the tomb early, while there was still darkness"; and 20:19, "And when it was evening that day, the first of the week (τῇ μιᾷ σαββάτων)…Jesus came, stood in their midst and said to them, 'Peace to you.'" Absent such qualification at 2:1, the "third day" there might just as well be counted relative to the chronological sequence that precedes it. The use of similar relative markers for the days leading up to 2:1 (τῇ ἐπαύριον at 1:29, 35, 43) suggests this is the preferred reading. Doing so does put the wedding at Cana three days after John the Baptist's confession at 1:29. But it by no means allows that wedding to be set specifically on a "Tuesday" (or any other day[5]), nor John the Baptist's confession, thereby, on the prior "Sabbath."

Further, Bowman's reading crunches the chronology of chapter 2 beyond its limits. If the Saturday before 2:1 was the Sabbath before the Passover mentioned at 2:13, that Passover would have to fall, at the latest, on the following Friday. But, with the wedding at Cana occurring no more than three days before that Friday (on a Tuesday), the time period described at 2:12–13 becomes impossible: at 2:12, Jesus stays in Capernaum after the wedding "not many days"; and at 2:13, when he finally does as-

---

[3] On the origins of this observation, see Bousset 1909:3–4.

[4] Bowman 1975:111–12.

[5] Following Paul Billerbeck on marriage customs related to Jewish young women, for instance, Annie Jaubert suggests Wednesday; 1991:63n7.

cend to Jerusalem for the Passover, that Passover is still only "at hand" (not already come) – "And the Passover of the Jews was near and Jesus went up to Jerusalem." The duration required by Bowman simply does not fit the interval allowed in the text. And for that reason (as well as the one stated above), his extension of the Passover context back to 1:29 cannot stand. The narrative scope covered by the Passover at 2:13, thereby, is best limited to 2:13–3:21. John 2:13–22 while the feast was yet "near"; 2:23–3:21 as it transpired.

Debate has ensued over whether 2:13–3:21 obtained (or obtained in its current location) earlier in the Fourth Gospel's composition history. While some have insisted so, others have suspected the current placement derives from redactional activity: that 2:23–3:21 (or 3:1–21) initially hailed from the Tabernacles context at John 7[6]; and that 2:13–22 was either associated with the final Passover at John 12[7] or absent altogether – inserted later, contemporaneously with John 21.[8] In such scenarios, the first feast to appear in the narrative would have been either the unnamed festival at 5:1 or, if chapters 5 and 6 were reversed (see below), the Passover at 6:4. Depending on what other differences might be speculated to have existed in earlier recensions, Jesus' ministry in John would, consequently, have run for some time (3:22–4:54?) before ever being marked by a feast.[9]

2.2 The Unnamed Feast and a Second Passover (John 5:1–6:71)

The next two feasts are those just mentioned: the unnamed festival at 5:1 and the Passover at 6:4. They are considered together here because the identity of the first is partly bound up with the relationship chapters 5 and 6 have to the Fourth Gospel as a whole and to each other. The first is set in Jerusalem on a Sabbath (5:9b). In two manuscripts it is named: Azyma, or the Feast of Unleavened Bread, and Tabernacles.[10] The real issue of its

---

[6] On 2:23–3:21, see the discussion by Howard 1955:126–27; on 3:1–21, that by Bacon 1910:491–92, 510–11, 518–20, following Tatian. For a rationale behind the current placement of 3:1–21, see the insight by Jean–Marie Auwers on the maturation of Nicodemus' faith between chapters 3 and 19; 1990:481–502.

[7] So G.P. Lewis in an unpublished paper delivered at the Birmingham New Testament Seminar, 23 April, 1929; reported by Howard 1955:126–27, 303 (Appendix D). This would coordinate the passage with its Synoptic counterparts: Matt 21:12–13, 23–27; Mark 11:15–19, 27–33; Luke 19:45–46; 20:1–8.

[8] Bacon 1910:488–93.

[9] This, assuming the remaining text of an earlier recension would have appeared as it does now, John 1:35–2:12; 3:22–4:54. But see the suggestion of Benjamin Bacon (1910:493) that John 2:1–12 was "equally alien to the original context with 2:13–25."

[10] Uncial Λ and miniscule 131, respectively.

identity, however, turns on whether ἑορτή in 5:1 is anarthrous (as per the reading in NA[27]) or articular.[11] If the first – "After these things there was *a* feast of the Jews" – it might be any festival in the Jewish liturgical year[12]; if the second – "After these things there was *the* feast of the Jews" – it could be Tabernacles, customarily called גחה, "the Feast," or another feast previously designated in the text: the Passover anticipated at 6:4, for instance, if chapters 5 and 6 were at one time reversed.[13] Making pilgrimage for this feast (5:1), Jesus heals a lame man (5:2–9), provokes protest for having done so (5:10–16) and responds to his accusers with a discourse on his emulation of the Father (5:17–47).

The second feast, the Passover at 6:4, occurs in all manuscripts and versions save the thirteenth century miniscule 472.[14] Like the Passover at 2:13, it is designated as "near" (ἐγγύς) but not yet come. Throughout chapter 6, Jesus, over a minimum two day period (6:16–17, 22), miraculously feeds five thousand (6:1–15), walks on the Sea of Tiberias (6:16–21), proclaims himself the "Bread of Life" (6:22–59) and suffers a schism among his disciples (6:60–71). But, unlike the case with all other feasts introduced in John, at no point is Jesus described as making pilgrimage for this one. Chapter 7 begins with him traveling through Galilee (7:1) then attending the Feast of Tabernacles (7:2–10); but at no juncture in between is he shown (or implied) to have gone to Jerusalem for the Passover at 6:4.

Two further issues have factored into the identity and role of these feasts. One is diachronic speculation, based on two perceived aporiahs between John 5 and 6. Geographically, there is an abrupt shift of scene from Jerusalem at the end of John 5 to the Sea of Tiberias at the beginning of John 6. Thematically, the controversy and discourse begun during the feast in John 5 (5:16–18) seem vividly sustained during Tabernacles in John 7, despite the fact that, with the Passover at 6:4 between them, a minimum six months (from Nisan to Tishri) – and likely more – would have passed

---

[11] ℵ C L Δ Ψ f[1] (=1 118 131 209 1582 [these hereafter referenced as *Family* 1]) 33 892 1424.

[12] On this reading, for instance, it has been argued that 5:1 then connoted the term *Asartha* ("festal gathering"), sometimes used for Pentecost (*Ant.* 3.252; *Tg. Neof.* Deut 6:10); see van Bebber 1898:34.

[13] On both textual possibilities, see the discussion by J. Th. Ubbink, who opts for the articular reading; 1922:131–32.

[14] See the discussions by Westcott and Hort 1881–82:77–81 (Appendix); Holzmeister 1933:136 and Sutcliffe 1938:27. Several other manuscripts demarcate 6:4 with various *signa*; and debate has ensued over whether the absence of any reference to Passover at 6:4 in George of Trezibond's 1520 Latin translation of Cyril of Alexandria's *Commentarius in Joannem*, in fact, preserved (van Bebber 1898:156n1) or altered (Sutcliffe 1938:40n2) the original.

from the one to the other.[15] Indicators for this last point are numerous: (1) Jesus expects a violent reception, such as he encountered at 5:16–18, should he attend Tabernacles in chapter 7 (7:6–7); (2) before he arrives for that Tabernacles, some Jews are already seeking him with malicious intent (7:13); (3) when he does arrive and begins speaking to the crowd, he immediately raises the Sabbath controversy of John 5 as an issue, asking them why they (still) sought to kill him and comparing his healing at that time to Moses' circumcision (7:19–23); and, (4) when he is identified by other Jews later during the feast, they state outright that, as was the case in 5:16–18, some Jews had already been seeking to kill him (7:25–26). Further, on 7:14–24 specifically, it has been noticed that (5) the Jews' astonishment at Jesus' knowledge in 7:15 could readily follow the correlation he makes between his words and Moses' writings at 5:47; (6) Jesus' claim to be dependent on the Father at 5:19–23 resumes at 7:16–17; (7) references to Moses span 5:45–46 and 7:19–23; (8) Jesus' stress on the "works" (ἔργα) which the Father has shown him in 5:20, 36 find a "catchword" correspondence with his retort in 7:21, "I did one work (ἓν ἔργον) and you all marvel"; and (9) the contrast between seeking God's as opposed to one's own glory at 5:41, 44 is sustained at 7:18.[16]

Some exegetes have addressed these difficulties either by insisting John 5 and 6 are in their intended order,[17] by relocating 7:15–24 to follow (somewhere in) chapter 5[18] (ignoring the geographical problem) or by placing John 6 directly after 4:46–54, without chapter 5 before or after it (circumventing the thematic problem).[19] Many, however, have concluded that,

---

[15] Boismard and Lamouille (1987:9) put it at about ten months. Exegetes who have assumed that the Johannine chronology should follow Synoptic order have further noted that, in the current narrative, John the Baptist's death, which should immediately precede the feeding of the five thousand at 6:1–15 (Matt 14:1–21; Mark 6:14–44), occurs much earlier in the current order of John – prior to the feast at chapter 5 (5:35); cf. Mann 1733:156–61.

[16] On 5:1–47 and 7:14–24, see, particularly, Yee 1989:42. With a view toward the original inversion of John 5 and 6 (one of the proposed resolutions listed below), K.P.M. Kuzenzama adds several further factors on this aporiah, related to narrative cogency and correspondence with Synoptic gospels: notably, that the narrative of Jesus' sojourn in Galilee at 7:1 follows better on John 5 than on John 6; that Jesus' pilgrimage to Jerusalem at 5:1 follows better on John 6 than on John 4; and that the reversal of chapters 5 and 6 allows the critical turning point in Jesus' ministry at 6:60–71 to coincide chronologically with the same in the Synoptics; 1979:61–65. Kuzenzama, himself, is inclined to accept the current order of the chapters as original; see pp. 67–69.

[17] See Howard 1955:167–69; Kuzenzama 1979:65–69.

[18] See Bacon 1910:473, 473n2; 1933:197–98 (further regarding Bacon on this issue, see Smith 1981:210–12); Howard 1955:113.

[19] See Bousset 1909:10n3. Robert T. Fortna (1988:79–117, especially p. 79) argues the Evangelist inserted John 5 (at least partly [5:2–9] by relocation) into a prior text (the

in an earlier recension, John 5 (or part of it) and John 7 were contiguous. John 6, in these hypotheses, was either a later addition (yielding an original sequence of chapters 4, 5, 7)[20] or was inserted from an original placement prior to chapter 5 (giving an order of chapters 4, 6, 5, 7)[21] or later in the Fourth Gospel.[22] This latter "relocation" theory has been ascribed to a number of factors: inadvertent displacement, the awkward assimilation of sources, conscious redaction, successive editions, the age or premature death of the Evangelist[23] or some combination of the five.[24] In all of these theories, however, the geography of the passages is set right and their thematic homogeneity explained. If John 6 did not obtain in an earlier edition, Jesus would have moved – rigorously but plausibly – from Cana in Galilee (4:46–54) to Jerusalem (5:1–47) to Galilee (7:1–9) and back to Jerusalem (7:10). If chapter 6 did obtain, preceding chapter 5, Jesus would have gone, more smoothly, from Cana (4:46–54) to the Sea of Tiberias (6:1–71), remaining in Galilee (7:1–9) till he made pilgrimage once more to Jerusalem (7:10). Moreover, it becomes more plausible that Jesus' healing in chapter 5 would have remained newsworthy among Jerusalemites in chapter 7: the event either would have happened earlier that same feast (putting 7:15–24 with John 5) or would have taken place not so long before, during a feast that presumably lay some time within the six month interval that passed between the Passover at 6:4 and the Tabernacles at 7:2.

The other issue important for interpreting these feasts is the time of year implied at 4:35. Amidst the Samaritan episode that precedes chapter 5, Jesus makes a point about his mission to his disciples, saying, "Do you not say, 'There are (still) four months and the harvest comes?' Behold, I say to you, lift up your eyes and look at the fields, that they are (already) white unto harvest." The two words in parentheses signal variant and debated readings: "still" (ἔτι) obtains in most manuscripts and versions but not in

---

Signs Gospel) that went from the healing of the royal official's son at Capernaum (2:12a; 4:46–54), to (possibly) the miraculous catch of fish at the Sea of Galilee (21:1–14), to the feeding of the five thousand and walking on water on the other side of the Sea of Galilee (6:1–15), back across the Sea of Galilee to Capernaum (6:16–21).

[20] Cassel and Norris 1871:111–12; Devillers 1999:199–205; 2002:273–80.

[21] According to O.C.I. Cassel and J.P. Norris (1871:112), as well as Mary Shorter (1972–73:181), this solution was proposed as early as Ludolphus of Saxony in the fourteenth century.

[22] So, Shorter's own thesis, that John 6 has been relocated from an original placement just prior to 10:22; 1972–73:181–83.

[23] On these, as well as the proposal that John 5 and 6 are as the author intended them, see Menoud 1947:13–18; Howard 1955:116–19, 164–69; Kümmel 1973:170–83. On the age and premature death of the Evangelist, particularly, see Kümmel 1973:183.

[24] Cassel and Norris, for instance, suggested John 6 was an insertion, added with John 21 but accidentally displaced; 1871:111–12.

some[25]; "already" (ἤδη), which, in several witnesses, closes the clause at 4:35b,[26] is so punctuated in others[27] as to belong, instead, to the clause following it at 4:36. Moreover, the imagery used roughly connotes spring, at the beginning of the Jewish year (Nisan). The "harvest" in view is undoubtedly the cereal harvest: the term "harvest" (θερισμός), a cognate to "reap" (θερίζειν), is, in the LXX and elsewhere in the New Testament, typically (though not exhaustively) used in contexts that indicate or imply grain harvests[28]; "sowing" (σπείρειν) and "reaping" (θερίζειν) presume a crop that is planted and picked rather than cultivated and gathered (such as fruit from trees); and, similarly, "white" (λευκός) was a customary description of ripe grain fields.[29] Being sown between mid–Tishri and mid–Kislev (October to December), grains ripened between Nisan and Sivan (March through May) – barley first, from Nisan to 'Iyyar (first through second months); wheat later, from 'Iyyar to Sivan (second through third months).[30] Sundry variables affected those precise times in any given year: climatic, technological, calendrical,[31] methodological.[32] More or less, however, the language of 'harvest,' 'white fields,' 'sowing' and 'reaping' in 4:35 connotes the season of spring, sometime between Nisan and Sivan.[33]

---

[25] P^{75} D L 086 (apparently) f^{13} (=13 69 124 174 230 346 543 788 826 828 983 1689 1709 [these hereafter referenced as the *Ferrar* group]) 1241.

[26] P^{75} C[3] 083 *Family* 1, the *Ferrar* group and the *Majority text*.

[27] ℵ (corrected) C (original scribe) D L W (from a later addition) Ψ 33 579.

[28] Of those places where its referent is clear, LXX Gen 8:22; 30:14; Exod 23:16; 34:22; Lev 19:9; 23:10, 22; Josh 3:15 [cf. 5:10–11]; Judg 15:1; Ruth 1:22; 2:23; 1 Kgdms 6:13; 8:12 (likely); 12:17; 2 Kgdms 21:9–10; 24:15; Jdt 2:27; 8:2; Sir 24:26 (cf Josh 3:15); 51:20; Isa 16:9 (possibly); Jer 27:16; Matt 9:37–38 (possibly); 13:30, 39; Mark 4:29; Luke 10:2 (possibly); even Rev 14:15. Exceptions are LXX Job 14:7–9; 18:16 (likely); 29:19 (likely); Isa 18:4–5. With Jer 5:24 it is difficult to discern.

[29] Vogelstein 1894: 42–43, 43n36, 58.

[30] See Cladder 1919:210.

[31] Calendrical variables would result from a combination of two factors: one, the accrued gaps between festal and agricultural years arising from the lunar ephemeris of the first century Jewish calendar; two, the imprecise correction of those gaps through the intermittent intercalation of a "second 'Adar." On the first, see Daise 2005:122–23; on "second 'Adar," see *m. Meg.* 1:4; *m. Ned.* 8:5; *m. 'Ed.* 7:7; *t. Roš. Haš.* 1.14; *t. Meg.* 1.6; *t. Ned.* 4.7; *t. B. Meṣi'a* 8.31; *t. Sanh.* 2.1–15; *t. 'Ed.* 3.1; *t. 'Ohal.* 18.17; *Mek.* on Exod 12:2 (*Pisḥa* 2.53–81); *Mek.* on Exod 16:35 (*Vayassaʿ* 6.86–114); *Tg. Ket.* Esth I 9:31; *Tg. Ket.* Esth II 9:29 (for the specific manuscript testimony in both targums to Esther, see Grossfeld 1991: 89n[bbb], 194[pp]); as well as Ogg 1965:93; Schürer 1973:2.588–94; and, anticipating them both, the early but erudite discussion by Cladder 1919:209–11.

[32] See, for instance, Hermann Vogelstein's comment that the prescription to sow seventy days before Passover at *m. Menaḥ.* 8:2 and *t. Menaḥ.* 9.3 served "for the attainment of an especially good yield"; 1894:40; see also p. 58.

[33] For thorough discussions, see Feliks 1963:142–45, 189; Borowski 1987:31–44, 57–58, 88–93; cf. also Vogelstein 1894:40, 57–59; Zohary 1982:26–27; and Scott 1993:20,

In the context of John 4, it is designed to elucidate the Samaritans' immediate, *en masse* reception of Jesus, perhaps in contrast to the relatively
mixed response Jesus had thus far received from the Jews (John 3:1–2;
4:1–3): as Jesus speaks these words to his disciples, the inhabitants of Sychar are receiving the testimony of the woman with whom he had just spoken (4:27–30, 39); on that woman's testimony, they will soon invite him to
stay, then believe in him directly (4:40–42).[34]

The issue concerns which part of 4:35, if any,[35] indicates the narrative
time in which the Samaritan episode occurred. This has bearing on the
feasts at 5:1 and 6:4, since, either in the text as it stands or in a reversal of
chapters 5 and 6, one or the other of them would come soon after. If the
temporal indicator is 4:35b, "the fields are white for harvest," the Samaritan episode would date between Nisan and Sivan, the first through third
months of the Jewish calendar[36]; if that indicator is 4:35a, "four months
and the harvest comes," the episode would date roughly to Kislev, the
ninth month of the Jewish calendar, four months earlier.[37] This question,
itself, has turned on whether 4:35a was a proverb or not. If it was, its "four
months" till harvest was metaphorical, supporting the first option; if it was
not, the "four months" reflect narrative time, rendering the "fields white
for harvest" as metaphorical and supporting the second option. Favoring
4:35a as a proverb are (1) that it scans as iambic pentameter[38]; (2) that
such a proverb could have arisen, either from counting from the end of
sowing to the beginning of harvest,[39] or from the Jewish division of the

---

179, 198n42, who draws upon Borowski's dissertation. Note the varied temporal parameters suggested by G.E. Wright 1955:52–54 and, from a report based on early twentieth
century practices in Nablus, E. Hampden-Cook 1923–24:287.

[34] On this interpretation, see, for instance, Giblin 1983:99; Cullmann 1969:46; and
Cuvillier 1996:255, quoting Xavier Léon-Dufour.

[35] J. Maiworm, for instance, argued that both 4:35a and 4:35b are spiritualized and,
consequently, that, "for a determination of the time of year, John 4:31–38 is useless";
1923:93–95, quotation p. 95.

[36] So Cladder 1919:215.

[37] Brown (1966/1970:1.173–74), who does not follow this scenario, calculates
slightly later: the barley/wheat harvest to May–June (second through fourth months of
the Jewish calendar); the Samaritan incident to January–February (tenth through twelfth
months of the Jewish calendar). Further on the two options sketched here, see Maiworm
1923:94.

[38] Argyle 1971: 247–48; Collins 1986:51, 57–58; idem 1990:140–41. Argyle does not
argue 4:35a is proverbial because it is metrical but, in fact, the opposite – that, inasmuch
as it was proverbial, "such sayings were often metrical" (p. 247). For the possible Semitic quality of 4:35a, see the discussions by Rudolf Schnackenburg (1968:1.449) and
Peter W. Ensor 2000:15n13.

[39] See Schnackenburg 1968:1.449 and Beasley–Murray 1999:63.

year into six two–month (Rabbinic)[40] or three four–month (Qumran)[41] segments; and (3) that a spring date fits nicely with 4:43–45, where, two days
later (4:40), Galileans receive Jesus well, "having seen all the things he
had done in Jerusalem during the feast." The "feast" in question seems to
have been the Passover at 2:13 (cf. 2:23); and, were the Samaritan incident
dated between Nisan and Sivan, it would have occurred on the heels of that
Passover, recently enough to account for its apparent freshness in the
minds of Galileans.[42] Favoring 4:35a as an indicator of narrative time are
(1) that no proverb analogous to 4:35a has been found, as has been for the
proverb cited at 4:37[43]; (2) that the meter in 4:35a could be felicitous[44]; (3)
that, when 4:35a is read with ἔτι ("There are *still* four months"), any generic (proverbial) sense is lost; and, most especially, (4) that, in Rabbinic
literature, the stated interval of time between sowing and harvest is not
four months, but six.[45]

Given these many and complex factors, exegetical posture toward the
identity of the feast at John 5:1 has varied widely. Some have concluded
that the anonymity of the feast either precludes it being identified[46] or is a
clear signal that its identity has no hermeneutical significance for chapter
5. Others, sometimes in spite of having adopted the first view, attempt to
find that identity out.[47] A gamut of proposals have been made, all closely

---

[40] See the discussions by J.H. Bernard (1929:1.155); Leon Morris (1971:278–79);
and, more recently, P.W. Ensor (2000:15); cf. *t. Ta'an.* 1.7.

[41] Inferred by F.-M. Braun from 1QS x 7; 1955:26; see Bultmann 1971:196n4.

[42] See Brown 1966/1970:1.174. Further on 4:35a as a proverb is Charles Homer Giblin, who argued that Jesus prophetically corrected it as part of his spiritual message;
1983:99.

[43] See Hoskyns 1947:246 and Barrett 1978:241. On 4:37 as a proverb, note the observations of Wilfred G.E. Watson (1970:369–70) on its Ugaritic and (likely) biblical ante-
cedents.

[44] Bernard 1929:1.155–56.

[45] Typically cited are *t. Ta'an.* 1.1 and *y. Ta'an.* 1.2 (Vogelstein 1894:57, 57n1; Ogg
1962:729.); but Urban Holzmeister has added (inferences from) *t. Ta'an.* 1.7; *b. Ta'an*
5a; *b. Bek.* 8ab; *b. B. Meṣi'a* 106b; see 1933:144–46. In the fourth of his seven more refined premises for this view, Joseph M. Bover observed that the interval between seed-
time and harvest seems to require more than four months; he did not, however, demonstrate awareness of the Rabbinic texts supporting his point; 1922:442–44. Further against
4:35a as proverbial, Teresa Okure adds that 4:35a does not share the impersonal quality
shown in the proverb at 4:37 and, similarly, that various contextual, syntactical and lexi-
cal features of 4:32–38 require ὑμεῖς at 4:35a to be taken as directed specifically toward
disciples (not generically toward all people); 1988:148–53. As Okure's discussion shows,
the debate is more nuanced than recounted here.

[46] Kirmis 1940:14–16, 30; cf. the review of Kirmis by Joseph Blinzler 1942:203.

[47] So, for instance, Luc Devillers, who regards the identity of the feast inconsequential for the current state of the text, but significant for its prehistory; 1999: 201; 2002:15,
276n18.

tied to views on John 5 and 6: the Passover "at hand" in John 6:4 (when chapters 5 and 6 are reversed),[48] a fourth Passover,[49] Pentecost,[50] Remembrance,[51] Tabernacles[52] and Purim.[53]

2.3 The Feast of Tabernacles (John 7:2–52 [–10:21])

The next festival, the Feast of Tabernacles, covers at least John 7:2–52. It is explicitly introduced as such at John 7:2 (ἡ σκηνοπηγία), further referenced throughout the chapter (7:10, 14, 37) and likely connoted at 7:38, where the imagery of "rivers of living water" may have the feast's daily libations,[54] related biblical texts[55] or both in view. In these verses, Jesus disputes with his brothers over making pilgrimage to Jerusalem (7:2–9), makes that pilgrimage clandestinely nonetheless (7:10), provokes controversy and elicits belief while there (7:11–44) and frustrates priestly and Pharisaic attempts to arrest him (7:45–52).

Elements in chapters 8–10 suggest that, with the excision of the *pericope de adultera* (7:53–8:11), the Tabernacles context extends into them, as well. John 8–9 are replete with further allusions to the feast: the correspondence (1) between Jesus' self-identification as "light amidst darkness"

---

[48] Cassel and Norris 1871:109–12; Menoud 1947:13; Bultmann 1971:240.

[49] Ubbink 1922:134–36; Boismard and Lamouille 1987:44 (for Jean III [see *infra*]); and see the discussions by Cassel and Norris 1871:107 and Bacon 1910:490–91.

[50] Van Bebber 1898:33–34; Belser 1903:169; Klug 1906:160; Bacon 1910:397n3, 409–410, 490–91; Gärtner 1959:37; Schnackenburg 1968:2.93; Boismard and Lamouille 1987:38, 160–61 (for Jean II-B [see *infra*]); Rigato 1991:25–28.

[51] Guilding 1960:69–86; Braun 1964:80; Moreton 1959:208–13.

[52] Ogg 1962:729; and now Devillers (1999:182, 186–205; 2002:11n8, 276, backed by Boismard 1999:208–18), who considers it to have originally been part of the Tabernacles section at 7:2–10:21.

[53] Belser 1900:34–36 (prior to being persuaded by Johannes van Bebber on 6:4; see below, under '5.1 Implications for the *Praedicatio Domini*'); and Bowman 1971:43–56; 1975:35–43; cf. also pp. 99–109, 113–18, 123–26, 129–32, 231. See the discussion by Cassel and Norris 1871:107–108; and, further on various views on the feast at 5:1, Ubbink 1922:132–34; Kirmis 1940:14–30; Rigato 1991:25; and Manns 1995:117.

[54] *M. Sukkah* 4:1, 9–10.

[55] Among the many biblical texts proposed to lay back of 7:38 are several passages treating of the rock in the wilderness (Exod 17:6; Num 20:11; Deut 8:15; Isa 12:3; 41:18–20; 48:21; Pss 78:16, 20; 114:8), the eschatological temple (Ezek 47:1–12; Joel 4:18; Zech 14:8) or their combination, as per the merger of the two motifs in relation to the Tabernacles libation at *t. Sukkah* 3.3–13. On the relation of these themes to John 7:37–38 – with Jewish and Christian traditions contemporary with the Fourth Gospel particularly in view – see the important mid-twentieth century debate between Marie-Émile Boismard (1958:544–45), André Feuillet (1962:108–13, building on José Comblin 1953:33–36) and Pierre Grelot (1959:371–74; 1963:44–47, 49–50).

and the Tabernacles illumination rite[56]; (2) between the debate over Abra-hamic pedigree and the association given Tabernacles with Isaac's birth in *Jubilees*[57]; and (3) between the healing of the man born blind and the Pool of Siloam, the source from which the aforementioned libation was drawn.[58] Moreover, no temporal marker between 7:52–10:21 suggests the events unfolding in them (had to) occur(red) anytime after "the last great day of the feast" referenced at 7:37–38.[59] And the discourse begun at 9:35 runs, without temporal interruption, through 10:21.[60] Reading the passages this way would mean that, further at the Feast of Tabernacles, Jesus exacer-bated the controversy begun in 7:2–52 (8:12–59), healed the man born blind (9:1–34), allegorized that healing (9:35–41) and proclaimed himself the "Good Shepherd" (10:1–21).

2.4 The Feast of Dedication (John 10:22–39)

Next in sequence is the Feast of Dedication, or Hanukkah (10:22–23).

> There was the feast of Dedication in Jerusalem;
> it was winter and Jesus was walking about in the temple,
> in the Portico of Solomon.

On its face, Jesus' activity in Jerusalem for this feast is small: a further discourse on shepherding (10:22–30; cf. 10:1–18) and another altercation with the Jews over his identity. As in 5:17–47, he makes an implicit claim to deity that provokes an unsuccessful attempt to stone him (10:31–39), after which, at 10:40, he departs across the Jordan to the place where John was first baptizing. Two factors, however, have, for some, implied other-wise. First, alternate readings for the conjunction opening 10:22 imply dif-ferent relationships between the introduction to the Dedication and what

---

[56] John 8:12; 9:4–5; *m. Sukkah* 5.2–4.

[57] John 8:31–59; *Jub.* 16:10–31.

[58] John 9:1–7; *m. Sukkah* 4:9. A review of Tabernacles motifs in 7:1–8:59 can be found in Kerr 2002:226–50.

[59] Jesus' declaration "I am the light of the world" (8:12) picks up where he had left off at 7:37–38; 8:20 pauses to locate Jesus at the temple treasury, but has him continue his discourse, unabated; Jesus flees the temple at 8:59 but immediately heals the man born blind while "passing by" at 9:1. John 9:14 puts that healing on a Sabbath but noth-ing precludes a Sabbath overlapping the last day of Tabernacles referenced at 7:37 – the same happens for the first day of the Feast of Unleavened Bread after the crucifixion at 19:31. And, though 9:34–35 has Jesus find the healed man after that man had been ex-communicated, nothing in the text prohibits such a meeting from still having occurred on the same day as the healing.

[60] A recent argument for this extended Tabernacles context has been offered by Devillers 2002:16–18, 273–80, 383–85, 389–94, 477–79, 505–508.

came before: while some witnesses read only ἐγένετο (as translated above)[61] and others read ἐγένετο δέ ("*And* there was the Feast of Dedication"),[62] a number read, ἐγένετο τότε, "*At that time* (it) was the Feast of Dedication " or "It was the Feast of Dedication *at that time*."[63] Second, this introduction as a whole appears without geographic or temporal transition in the narrative. Unlike other introductions to the feasts,[64] this one appears *ex machina*, amidst two dialogues that could just as well be of a piece without it. In fact, were 10:22–23 excised, the Jews' question to Jesus about messiahship at 10:24 could easily read as an immediate follow-up to their dispute among themselves at 10:19–21, suggesting 10:1–21 could flow logically into 10:24–39 as a single, homogeneous episode:

John 10:19   A schism again emerged among the Jews because of these words.
John 10:20   Many of them were saying, "He has a demon and is mad.
             Why do you listen to him?"
John 10:21   Others were saying, "These words are not from a demon-possessed
             person. A demon cannot open the eyes of the blind, can it?"
John 10:24   Therefore the Jews gathered round him and were saying to him,
             "How long will you keep us in suspense?
             If you are the Christ, tell us openly!"

While some exegetes find the text plausible as it stands,[65] others have proposed text- and redaction-critical ways of making 10:1–21 one and the same with 10:22–39. Brooke Foss Westcott, followed by J.R. Lancaster and R.L. Overstreet, has read τότε at 10:22 to make the introduction embrace everything from 9:1 to 10:39[66] – that is, "It was the Feast of Dedication *at that time*" means *at the time* Jesus both healed the man born blind

---

[61] *Family* 1 and 565.

[62] *P*[66] (original scribe) ℵ A D Θ, the *Ferrar* group and the *Majority text*.

[63] *P*[66] (corrected) *P*[75] B L W Ψ 33 579.

[64] Other feasts in John invariably follow geographical and temporal transitions: Jesus comes to Jerusalem for the first Passover from Capernaum, having stayed there "not many days" (2:12); for the feast at 5:1, he comes, again, from Galilee – either from Cana (if John 5 follows 4:46–54), having spent at least one day there, or from Capernaum (if John 5 follows John 6), following at least two days at the Sea of Tiberias (see 6:1–3, 22, 59); for Tabernacles, likewise, Jesus travels from Galilee, having "gone about" there for some time (7:1), then delaying his pilgrimage until the middle of the feast (7:10,14); and, for the last Passover, Jesus arrives in Jerusalem from Bethany, where he had come "six days before" (12:1,12–19). The Passover at 6:4, as noted above, does not occasion a pilgrimage; but even here a geographic transition is articulated, from Cana (4:46–54/6:1–71) or Jerusalem (5:1–47/6:1–71) to the other side of the Sea of Tiberias (6:1).

[65] Some have maintained the plausibility of the current order by regarding 10:1–21 as a transitional passage, bridging the preceding Tabernacles section and the subsequent Dedication section; cf. Du Rand 1991:95. Along similar lines, Frédéric Manns has argued the literary integrity of 10:1–30; 1986:135–45.

[66] Westcott 1954:2.30; Lancaster and Overstreet 1995:328–32, 328n40.

(9:1–41) and issued the "Good Shepherd" discourse (10:1–39). Others have reconfigured or diachronically reconstructed the way 10:1–39 (or various sections of it) would have originally followed 9:41. Benjamin Bacon, for instance, rearranged thus: 10:22–25/10:11–18/10:1–5/10:26–39/10:40–42 (with 10:6–10 as an ill-conceived editorial insertion)[67]; G.H.C. MacGregor and J.H. Bernard have it as 10:19–29; 10:1–18; 10:30–42[68]; Hans H. Wendt suggested an original discourse of 9:4–5, 39–41; 10:1–18, 24–38, expanded by the Evangelist with 9:1–3, 6–38; 10:19–23, 39–42[69]; and, more recently, Wolfgang Langbrandtner has argued that an original 10:19–21, 24–25, 30–42 was expanded by the redactor with 10:1–18, 26–29.[70] If these renderings or reconfigurations are factored, Jesus' activity during the Dedication would have originally included matters now slated under Tabernacles: the first part of the "Good Shepherd" discourse, if not the entirety of his healing the man born blind.

Further questions have been raised by the anomalous language used to introduce the feast. Elsewhere in John, festivals are introduced with a somewhat formulaic vocabulary and syntax:

a feast/the feast/the feast of X/the X
+ of the Jews [+ X]
+ was near.

Moreover, in most of these cases, Jesus is said to "go up" (ἀναβαίνειν) to the feast listed[71]:

First Passover (2:13)	And the Passover of the Jews was near, and Jesus went up (ἀνέβη) to Jerusalem.
Unnamed Feast (5:1)	After these things, there was a/the feast of the Jews, and Jesus went up (ἀνέβη) to Jerusalem.
Tabernacles (7:2, 6, 8, 10)	And the feast of the Jews, Tabernacles, was near... Therefore Jesus said to (his brothers), "You go up (ἀνάβητε) to the feast; I do not go up (οὐκ ἀναβαίνω) to this feast, for my time has not yet been fulfilled." But when his brothers went up (ἀνέβησαν) to the feast, then he himself went up (αὐτὸς ἀνέβη) – not openly; but, as it were, in secret.

---

[67] Bacon 1933:202–208.

[68] MacGregor 1929:231–44; Bernard 1929:1.xxiv–xxv.

[69] Wendt 1902:150–53.

[70] Langbrandtner 1977:46–50. These views are found recounted (though not necessarily followed) by Donald D. Williford 1981:174–75 and Ulrich Busse 1991:6–7. In the face of these diachronic theories, note the observation of Busse that, despite its redaction-critical history, John 10 is now "firmly integrated" into the narrative and discourses that precede and follow it; 1991:7–9, quotation p. 7.

[71] The exception is the Passover at 6:4, where, as noted above, Jesus remains in Galilee.

Final Passover (11:55; 12:1)   And the Passover of the Jews was near.
                                 And many went up (ἀνέβησαν) to Jerusalem from
                                 the country before the Passover, to purify them-
                                 selves...Therefore Jesus, six days before the Pass-
                                 over, came (ἦλθεν) to Bethany, where Lazarus was,
                                 whom he raised from the dead. [72]

By contrast, the Feast of Dedication is introduced, "There was (at that time) the feast of Dedication in Jerusalem; it was winter" (ἐγένετο [τότε] τὰ ἐγκαίνια ἐν τοῖς Ἱεροσολύμοις, χειμὼν ἦν). No explicit mention is made of Jesus "going up" to Jerusalem: he is, rather, found already there, "walking in the temple, in the Portico of Solomon."

Some have taken this to mean Jesus' pilgrimage is to be inferred; others, that he simply had remained in Jerusalem since Tabernacles at 7:2.[73] More recently, Luc Devillers has suggested that it reflects a recognition that the Feast of Dedication was not one of the three pilgrimage feasts prescribed at Deuteronomy 16:16 – Passover, Pentecost and Tabernacles.[74] Except for the Feast of Dedication, the named feasts in John are either the first or the third of these; and Devillers is persuaded that, in an earlier recension, the unnamed festival at 5:1 was part of the Feast of Tabernacles now placed at 7:2.[75] For Devillers, then, the Dedication is the only non-pilgrimage feast appearing in John; and he contends that the variant language by which it is introduced reflects this difference in status.[76] The same argument could apply to any of the theories that identify the feast at 5:1 as one of the pilgrimage feasts.

In response to this, however, one might ask whether there is anything inherent in the language of Johannine festal introductions that signals the distinction Devillers wishes to make. That is to say, apart from the name of the feast itself, there is nothing in a clause such as, "And the (feast) of the

---

[72] Though the language of "going up" is not explicitly applied to Jesus for the final Passover, it is certainly implied, since, as he "comes" (ἦλθεν) to Bethany six days before the feast, many are simultaneously "going up" (ἀνέβησαν) to Jerusalem to purify them-selves before it (11:55).

[73] Kümmel 1973: 166; Yee 1989:89. For Kümmel, Jesus remained in Jerusalem from Tabernacles through the last Passover. On the (similar) grounds that the feast at 5:1 is introduced simply as "being" (ἦν [5:1]/ἐγένετο [10:22]), rather than "being near" (ἐγγύς), Friedrich Kirmis contended that Jesus might have already been in Jerusalem before that feast began, as well – this despite the following clause, which reads, "and Jesus went up (ἀνέβη) to Jerusalem"; 1940:30.

[74] In an unpublished dissertation written for Johns Hopkins University, William R. Scott argues that, though pilgrimage is not a necessary component of the event denoted by חג in the Hebrew Bible, it is nonetheless part of the dimension given that term at Deut 16:16; 1993:26–29.

[75] Devillers 1999:182,186–205.

[76] Devillers 2002:17n35.

Jews was near" (and its variants) that identifies the feasts at 2:13; 6:4; 7:2; and 11:55 as pilgrimage festivals; nor, conversely, is there anything in the language, "There was (at that time) the feast of Dedication in Jerusalem," that identifies the Dedication as not being so.

2.5 The Final Passover (John 11:55–19:42)

The last feast to appear is another Passover. It is anticipated with the arrival of pilgrims at Jerusalem (and Jesus at Bethany) six days beforehand (11:55; 12:1); and it ends with the crucifixion itself, during the afternoon of what is termed "the Preparation of the Passover" (παρασκευὴ τοῦ πάσχα), "the Preparation of the Jews" (τὴν παρασκευὴν τῶν Ἰουδαίων) or simply "the Preparation" (παρασκευή; 19:14, 31, 42). Debate has been waged – too vast and detailed even to summarize here – over whether this day of "Preparation" represents 14 Nisan, as various cues suggest,[77] or 15 Nisan, as per the Synoptics[78]; and, if the former, how to account for or reconcile the two with one another and with the historical life of Jesus.[79] Were it the first (as I am inclined to think), Jesus' activity on this final Passover culminates on that Passover day, itself; were it the second, it extends into the first day of the Feast of Unleavened Bread.

To summarize that activity, six days prior to this final Passover (12:1) Jesus is anointed by Mary for burial (12:1–8); and five days prior to it (12:12) he enters Jerusalem (12:12–19), demurs from an audience with the Greeks (12:20–26), receives a voice from heaven forecasting his death/glorification (12:27–36) and, after a narrative commentary on the Jews' unbelief (12:37–43), reiterates a final plea for faith (12:44–50). The night before "the Preparation of the Passover" he washes his disciples' feet (13:1–20), launches Judas' betrayal (13:21–30), issues a Farewell Dis-

---

[77] For instance, (1) taken as an objective genitive, the phrase "Preparation *for* the Passover," itself, implies the day on which lambs were slaughtered, homes consecrated and food prepared for the pascal meal (Exod 12:6–9); (2) during the Johannine last meal, Jesus' disciples think he sends Judas to purchase items still needed for the feast (13:27–29); (3) in the morning of the crucifixion, the cohort leading Jesus to Pilate refuses to enter the Praetorium, "that they would not be defiled but might (rather) eat the Passover" (18:28; cf. 18:3, 12); and, (4) at Pilate's sentencing of Jesus sometime later, he had not yet released the prisoner he customarily did ἐν τῷ πάσχα, "during the Passover" (18:39).

[78] Matt 26:17–30; Mark 14:12–26; Luke 22:7–39.

[79] For reviews of hypotheses on the Johannine Passion chronology (together with their own theses), see Ogg 1940:205–42; 1962:729–30; and Donfried 1992:1.1015–16. The issues are also rehearsed by Joachim Jeremias, in his classic argument that the Last Supper was a Passover meal; 1966:15–88.

course to (and final prayer for) his disciples (13:31–17:26), is arrested (18:1–11), brought to trials before Annas and Caiaphas (18:12–14, 19–24) and denied by Peter (18:15–18, 25–27). And on that day of Preparation, itself, he is interrogated by Pilate (18:28–19:11), brought again to trial (19:12–16) and, finally, crucified (19:17–42).

2.6 Azyma and the Waving of the 'Omer

2.6.1 Azyma

At least two more feasts should be mentioned, though they are not named in the narrative: the Feast of Unleavened Bread (hereafter called Azyma, from the Greek τὰ ἄζυμα) and the Waving of the 'Omer. Azyma follows immediately on the heels of Passover, either as a six-day extension of it (with solemn assembly; Deut 16:1–8) or as a discrete, seven-day feast juxtaposed to it (Lev 23:6–8; Num 28:17–25).[80] As such, it may be assumed to be in progress during Jesus' activity at two *loci* in the Fourth Gospel. Certainly his burial and first resurrection appearances at 20:1–23. If Jesus was crucified on 14 Nisan, then the next day, on which he lay buried, would be the first day of Azyma; and the day following, on which he arose, the second day of Azyma.[81] This likely explains the comment at 19:31 that the Sabbath on the day following Friday's crucifixion was "great" (μεγάλη) – "for the day of that Sabbath was great" (ἦν γὰρ μεγάλη ἡ ἡμέρα ἐκείνου τοῦ σαββάτου). According to Leviticus and Numbers, the first and last days of Azyma were, themselves, Sabbaths: like the regular seventh-day Sabbaths, Israel was told that, on them, "you shall have a holy assembly: you shall not do any work of service."[82] If the Sabbath of the first day of Azyma fell on a regular weekly Sabbath, as the Johannine chronology implies, the two would have dovetailed, accounting for the intensified significance given that Sabbath by the Evangelist.

Azyma may also lay back of 2:23–25, where we are told that many pilgrims beheld Jesus' signs and believed in his name "when he was in Jerusalem during Passover, during the feast" (ἐν τῷ πάσχα ἐν τῇ ἑορτῇ). Within this period Jesus performs multiple signs, is believed by many who see them and is approached by Nicodemus "at night" (3:1–2) – all suggest-

---

[80] See Auerbach (1958:3–5), who reads the Deuteronomist's Azyma as temporally removed from Passover. The Synoptics use "Azyma" for the day on which the Passover lambs were slaughtered (Luke 22:7–13), the separate feast juxtaposed to that day (Mark 14:1 [though not in D]) or the entire pascal octave (Matt 26:17–19; Mark 14:12–16).

[81] The same would apply, albeit set ahead one day, were Jesus crucified on 15 Nisan, as some have argued for John.

[82] Lev 23:7–8; Num 28:18, 25.

ing an interval beyond the single day of 14 Nisan.[83] Johannes van Bebber restricted 2:23–25 to 15 Nisan only, the first day of Azyma. He contended that, when set in relation to τὸ πάσχα (2:23; 13:1), ἡ ἑορτή designates a single festal day within the larger Pascal octave.[84] And, on the basis of four factors, he argued that this single day could only have been the day following Passover: (1) that 15 Nisan was a Sabbath, distinguished both from the Passover that precedes it and the six remaining days of Azyma that follow it (Lev 23:6; Num 28:16–25); (2) that, in Scripture, 15 Nisan is, itself, called a "feast" (גֹח/ἑορτή); (3) that 15 Nisan was also called "the feast" in first century Judaism, as reflected in the Gospel of Matthew, where the Jewish leaders' attempts to avoid killing Jesus "during the feast" (μὴ ἐν τῇ ἑορτῇ; Matt 26:4–5) are foiled by Jesus' precise prophecy to the contrary (Matt 26:2)[85]; and (4) that the Sabbath character (and thus 15 Nisan date) of 2:23–25 is indicated later at 5:16, where the customary sense of the imperfect, "because he used to do these things on the Sabbath," could only refer back to the signs Jesus was doing "when he was in Jerusalem during Passover, during the feast" (ἐν τῷ πάσχα ἐν τῇ ἑορτῇ).[86]

Van Bebber's argument, however, is quite ill-informed. Regarding (1), that 15 Nisan was a Sabbath, distinct from the days before and after it: as mentioned above, Leviticus and Numbers list two such days, the first (15 Nisan) and last (21 Nisan) days of Azyma, with neither of them elevated over the other in importance.[87] And, though Deuteronomy lists only one such Sabbath, it designates that Sabbath to be the last (20 Nisan), not first day of the sequence.[88] For (2), that 15 Nisan was a "feast" in its own right: Leviticus 23:6 and Numbers 28:17 do ostensibly identify it as such; but the immediately subsequent clauses in each verse clarify further that this "feast" consists in seven full days of abstinence from unleavened bread, and that 15 Nisan in the previous clause is introduced only as the first of them:

---

[83] That Nicodemus approached Jesus during Passover week was suggested by Hermann J. Cladder 1919:214.

[84] Van Bebber 1898:24–25.

[85] That is, since the Jewish leaders' wish *not* to crucify Jesus "during the feast" was precisely overturned by the divine plan – and, since that crucifixion took place on one day (in van Bebber's view, the first day of Azyma) within the pascal octave – the "feast" to which the Jewish leaders referred had to have been the first day of Azyma.

[86] Van Bebber 1898:24–26; see also idem 1904:74, as well as Belser 1903:171.

[87] Lev 23:7–8; Num 28:18, 25. Cf. also *Cairo Geniza Targum* F on Lev 23:7–8, which labels both the first and last days of Azyma as *Yom Tov* (טֹב יוֹם); text: Kahle 1927–30:2.49–62.

[88] Deut 16:8.

> And on the fifteenth day of this (first) month
> is the festival of Unleavened Bread to the Lord;
> seven days you shall eat unleavened bread.[89]

With regard to (3), Matthew's use of ἡ ἑορτή: if the Jewish leaders' plan that Jesus not be killed "during the feast" (Matt 26:4–5) is an ironic foil to Jesus' prophecy that he would be killed on 15 Nisan (Matt 26:2), it must also be noted that this same day which the leaders call "the feast" (μὴ ἐν τῇ ἑορτῇ) is designated by Jesus in his prophecy to be "the Passover" – "You know that, after two days, the Passover comes" (τὸ πάσχα γίνεται). If "the feast" at Matthew 26:5 refers to a single day, as van Bebber argued, so too does "the Passover" at Matthew 26:2, breaking down van Bebber's distinction between the two terms. Finally, (4) on the notion that ἐποίει at 5:16 refers to a previous episode, in which Jesus had healed on the Sabbath: van Bebber's inference fails to appreciate the other imperfects associated with that verb in 5:16–18. Besides informing us that Jesus "was doing these things (ταῦτα ἐποίει) on the Sabbath" (5:16) – and, similarly, that he "was loosening (ἔλυεν) the Sabbath" (5:18) – the passage also states that the Jews "were persecuting" (ἐδίωκον) him for doing so, that Jesus "was calling (ἔλεγεν) God his own Father" and that, accordingly, the Jews "were seeking to kill him" (ἐζήτουν αὐτόν...ἀποκτεῖναι) for making such a claim.[90] If one of these imperfects connotes customary action reported previously in the narrative, the others should do the same. But, though this is the case with Jesus calling God his Father (at 2:16), it is not so with the other two: the Jews are not provoked to kill Jesus in John until chapter 5; and, though they (the Pharisees) do persecute Jesus early on, it was not because he was working on the Sabbath, as 5:16 asserts, but because he had protested the temple apparatus without evident credentials (2:18) and was baptizing more disciples than John (4:1–2).

More fundamentally, van Bebber's notion that ἡ ἑορτή designates a single day within the Passover octave of τὸ πάσχα cannot be sustained if equally applied to the Tabernacles octave of ἡ σκηνοπηγία. The term "the feast" appears relative to "Tabernacles" at two places in van Bebber's reading of John: at 7:2, in apposition – "And the feast of the Jews was near, Tabernacles" (ἦν δὲ ἐγγὺς ἡ ἑορτὴ τῶν Ἰουδαίων ἡ σκηνοπηγία); and at 6:4, where, in van Bebber's view, the original absence of τὸ πάσχα makes the clause "and the feast of the Jews was near" (ἦν δὲ ἐγγὺς ἡ

---

[89] Lev 23:6; cf. Num 28:17.

[90] Several witnesses to 5:16 have the Jews also seeking to kill Jesus for working on the Sabbath: A Θ Ψ, the *Ferrar* group and the *Majority text*.

ἑορτὴ τῶν Ἰουδαίων) anticipate Tabernacles at 7:2.[91] If the term "the feast" in John designates a single day within a larger festal octave, one might ask what day that might be within the octave of Tabernacles. It cannot be "the last great day" noted at 7:37, since the full phrase puts that day as one of many within the feast: "the last great day *of the feast*" (ἐν δὲ τῇ ἐσχάτῃ ἡμέρᾳ τῇ μεγάλῃ τῆς ἑορτῆς). Similarly, at 7:14, Jesus goes up to the temple and teaches "when it was already the middle of the feast" (ἤδη δὲ τῆς ἑορτῆς μεσούσης).[92] It is clear, then, that, at 7:2, 7:14 and 7:37, the term "the feast" is tantamount to the entire span of Tabernacles; and, if such is the case for that festival, no less can be assumed for Passover.

In sum, Jesus' activity in Jerusalem at 2:23–25 probably extended into the days of Azyma that directly follow Passover. Restricting that activity to the first of those days (15 Nisan), as van Bebber argued, finds little or no textual support.

2.6.2 The Waving of the 'Omer

The Waving of the 'Omer was the offering of the first fruits of the grain harvest. Leviticus slates it cultically, as both the day following the first Sabbath after Passover and the day from which the pentecontad till Pentecost was to be counted:

> He shall wave the 'omer before the Lord for your acceptance;
> on the day after the Sabbath (ממחרת השבת) the priest shall wave it.
> You shall count for yourselves,
> (beginning) on the day after the Sabbath (ממחרת השבת),
> from the day you bring the 'omer for the wave offering,
> seven Sabbaths; they will be complete (Sabbaths).[93]

Deuteronomy identifies it agriculturally, as "the beginning of the sickle upon the standing grain" (Deut 16:9); but several targums conflate the two, so as to show them one and the same:

> Seven weeks shall you count for yourself, from the beginning of the sickle
> upon the harvest for the 'omer of the wave offering (בחצד עומרא דארמותא)
> you shall begin to count seven weeks.[94]

---

[91] Van Bebber 1898:33–34, 154–72 (Appendix II). A fuller discussion of van Bebber's position on 6:4 comes in Chapter 5 below, under '5.1 Implications for the *Praedicatio Domini*.'

[92] At 7:10, "the feast" can signify either reading.

[93] Lev 23:11, 15.

[94] *Tg. Onq.* on Deut 16:9; text: Sperber 1959a.

On the first day (after 15 Nisan) you shall offer the 'omer (יח עומרא)
and shall eat unleavened bread from the old harvest...
Seven weeks you shall count for yourselves,
from the time you begin to send forth the sickle to harvest the field;
after the harvest of the 'omer (בתר חצר עומרא)
you shall begin to count seven weeks.[95]

My people, sons of Israel, seven weeks of days shall you count for yourselves
from beginning the sickle for the harvest,
to harvest the 'omer for the wave offering (למחצד בעומרא דאנפותה);
you shall begin to count seven weeks of days.[96]

The precise day of the Waving of the 'Omer was interpreted differently, depending on how the Sabbath immediately preceding it was conceived: the day following the first (Sabbath) day of Azyma, 16 Nisan[97]; the first Sunday following Passover, if the Sabbath was considered to be the first weekly Sabbath after Passover[98]; the day following the last (Sabbath) day of Azyma, 22 Nisan[99]; the first Sunday after the end of Azyma, if that Sabbath was considered to be the first Sabbath after Azyma had ended.[100] If

---

[95] *Tg. Ps.-J.* on Deut 16:8–9; text: Clarke 1984.

[96] *Tg. Neof.* on Deut 16:9; text: Díez Macho 1971. Further on the identity of the two days, see Auerbach 1958:10.

[97] LXX Lev 23:11; Philo, *Spec.* 2.162; Josephus *Ant.* 3.250; *m. Menaḥ.* 10:3; *Sifra* on Lev 23:9–14 (*Emor* §231/Parashah 10); *Sifra* on Lev 23:15–16 (*Emor* §232/Pereq 12); *Tg. Onq.* on Lev 23:11, 15 (cf. Grossfeld 1988:51n4); *Tg. Ps.-J.* on Lev 23:11, 15; so also, apparently, *Cairo Geniza Targum* F on Lev 23:11 (cf. F on Lev 23:7–8).

[98] The Boethusians/Sadducees: *m. Menaḥ.* 10:3; *t. Menaḥ.* 10.23.

[99] So the Falashas, as well as the community behind the Syriac version of Leviticus 23; see the discussion by Charles, cited in the next note.

[100] This was deduced for the book of *Jubilees* by Dominique Barthélemy by counting a pentecontad backward from a Feast of Weeks apparently dated to the fifteenth of the third month (*Jub.* 15:1; 44:4–5); Barthélemy 1952:200–201; see also VanderKam 1998:30–31, 53. The same is more explicitly attested for the Qumran sectarians: 4Q320 4 iv 8; 4 v 2, 11; 4 vi 7; 4Q321 v 4, 9 (frg. 4); vi 7 (frgs. 4-5); 4Q325 1 3; 4Q326 4 (partially reconstructed); and possibly 11Q19 xi 10; xviii 10–11. The sectarian dates of both the "Feast of Barley" (as it is called in 4Q325–326) and, especially, the "Waving of the 'Omer" (in 4Q320–321) become apparent when their placements in these texts are calculated according to the solar ephemeris and cycles into which they are plotted; see Talmon with Ben-Dov 2001a:3–36; 2001b:39–41; 2001c:66–68; 2001d:125; and 2001e:133–34. For a fuller discussion of these views, see Charles 1902:106–107; van Goudoever 1961:18–29; and VanderKam 1998:30–32. In light of recent research, Charles's view that *Jubilees* represents the third of the above-mentioned positions, the Waving of the 'Omer on the day following the completion of Azyma (p. 106), must be corrected; see Vander-Kam (as cited above). Moreover, in his (forced) argument that the final redactor of John intended the "next day" of 1:29 to indicate 15 Nisan (and, therefore, the orthodox/anti-Quartodeciman Holy Week), Karel Hanhart mistakenly associates the rubric for "the day after the Sabbath" (ממחרת השבת) at Lev 23:11, 15 with the temporal note on "the day

the first of these views regulated the cult by the first century (as seems likely),[101] the Waving of the 'Omer would have actually been observed on 16 Nisan, two days after Passover.

In the Gospel of John, this date may be in view at one, possibly two, *loci*. Perhaps during Jesus' stay in Jerusalem at 2:23–25, if the clause, "when he was in Jerusalem...during the feast," covers at least two days beyond Passover. More clearly, however, on the day of resurrection at 20:1–23. If the Johannine crucifixion occurred on 14 Nisan, the resurrection two days later would have dated to 16 Nisan, the day following the first day of Azyma.[102]

In sum, at least two further feasts figure (albeit tacitly) in the Fourth Gospel: Azyma, at 2:23–3:21 and 20:1–23; and the Waving of the 'Omer, at least at 20:1–23. The first would have been of a piece with the first Passover, in which Jesus performed faith-evoking signs and interviewed Nicodemus; both would have furnished the festal context for Jesus' earliest resurrection appearances.[103]

---

after Passover" (ממחרת הפסח) in MT (though not LXX) Josh 5:11; see Hanhart 1977:341–43.

[101] See, for instance, Cladder (1919:210), as well as the (unpublished) view of E. Rivkin that this date for the Waving of the 'Omer was adopted during the reign of Herod Agrippa; in Hanhart 1977:343n30.

[102] The phrase "the first (day) of the Sabbaths" (τῇ [δὲ ἡμέρᾳ ἐκείνῃ τῇ] μιᾷ [τῶν] σαββάτων), by which the resurrection day is designated (20:1, 19), could ostensibly signal the Waving of the 'Omer: since Lev 23:15–16 counts the pentecontad between it and Pentecost as "seven Sabbaths" (שבע שבתות) – and numbers the last as the "seventh" (השבת השביעית) – one could surmise that the "first day of the Sabbaths" was 16 Nisan, the first day of that fifty day period. But, since the same turn of phrase is used for the Synoptic resurrection (Matt 28:1; Mark 16:2; Luke 24:1), in which the crucifixion occurs on 15 Nisan and the resurrection on 17 Nisan, such an interpretation would depend on ascribing to the Synoptic Evangelists the second (Sadducean/Boethusian) view of the Waving of the 'Omer listed above, as apparently did G.H. Trench (1918:xxix); cf. van Goudoever 1961:225–26.

[103] Neither feast would apply to the Passover at John 6, nor Azyma to Jesus' appearance to Thomas "after eight days" in 20:26–29. The events in John 6 span a two day period (6:1–4, 16–17, 22) that begins when Passover was "near" but not yet come. And Jesus' appearance to Thomas "after eight days" from the first resurrection appearance would have occurred one day after the second (not first) Sabbath following Passover, either two (with the crucifixion at 14 Nisan) or three days (with the crucifixion at 15 Nisan) after Azyma had ended. This date would fit the Qumran sectarian calculation for the Waving of the 'Omer; but on the unlikelihood of John using such a calendar, see Chapter 5, under '5.3.2 The Chronology of the Festal Sequence.'

2.7 Summary

Six feasts appear in the Fourth Gospel, in the following order: a Passover (2:13), an unnamed festival (5:1), another Passover (6:4), the Feast of Tabernacles (7:2), the Feast of Dedication (10:22–23) and a final Passover (11:55). At least four of these feasts may have undergone relocation or reconfiguration in the gospel's composition history: the first Passover, the unnamed feast, the second Passover and the Dedication. And five of the feasts see Jesus making pilgrimage to and/or engaging in ministry within Jerusalem: all but the Passover at 6:4. In two (the feast at 5:1; the final Passover), possibly three (Tabernacles), of those five, that activity lasts till the introduction of the next feast (or, for the final Passover, till the end of that feast). In two others, however (the first Passover and the Dedication), that activity ends substantially before the next feast is introduced, apparently leaving the intervening episodes outside any festal context: for the first Passover, Jesus' activity in Jerusalem lasts from 2:13–3:21, leaving the episodes of 3:22–4:54 outside the coverage of any feast; and, for the Dedication, his activity spans from 10:22–39, leaving 10:40–11:54, also, outside the coverage of any feast.[104] Moreover, at two junctures, 2:23–3:21 and 20:1–23, the unmentioned feasts of Azyma and/or the Waving of the 'Omer were likely operative.

---

[104] This factor will prove important in assessing several views on the function of the feasts in Chapter 3.

Chapter 3

The Role of the Feasts in the Fourth Gospel: Previous Hypotheses

3.1 Narrative Theories

No less than nine exegetes (some working in pairs) have ventured hypotheses on the role these feasts play in the Fourth Gospel (or, for some, the signals they once gave to the Johannine community).[1] Of these, five (among them, one pair) have treated the feasts as literary devices structuring the narrative: Marie-Émile Boismard with Arnaud Lamouille, Donatien Mollat, Donald D. Williford and Gale A. Yee. Two have assumed the feasts are liturgical cues calibrated to Johannine praxis: Aileen Guilding and Michael D. Goulder. And, most recently, two (working together) have regarded the feasts as representatives and facilitators of the Jewish institutional matrix from which Johannine Christianity emerged: Adriana Destro and Mauro Pesce.

In this chapter, I will rehearse these theories, with a view toward determining a point of departure for my own proposal on the issue. I will give particular attention to assessing the strengths and weaknesses of their respective inferential structures and will conclude that, though some labor under significant difficulties (in whole or in part), others offer significant contributions on which further work can build – specifically, (1) the argument by Mollat that feasts furnish commemorative symbolism for Johannine christology, including his suggestion that they can just as well function as facilitators as they can foils to that christology; (2) the observation by Yee that the feasts enjoy a calendrical rapport with Johannine Sabbaths; and, most relevantly for this inquiry, (3) the insight of Destro and Pesce that the feasts in the Fourth Gospel engage the Johannine motif of Jesus'

---

[1] Though some exegetes have found cohesive design (only) in the festivals listed from John 5–12 (cf. Bacon 1933:166–75, 185n5, 188–89, 192–215 [esp. p. 203]; Lowry 1954:85–89), the number cited here reflects (and the following review is limited to) theories that treat of all six feasts. To these theories could have been added the discussion by Alan R. Kerr (2002:67–101, 205–67), otherwise cited throughout this work in other contexts. Kerr's primary interest centers on the feasts' implications for the Johannine temple motif; but in so doing he does engage all six of them.

'hour.' As mentioned above, this last observation, in particular, will furnish an important point of departure for my own thesis on the matter.

3.1.1 Foil to 'la Pâque du Christ': M.-É. Boismard and A. Lamouille

In modern scholarship, the narrative approach to feasts in John was arguably begun by Marie-Émile Boismard, in part with his co-commentator, Arnaud Lamouille. Boismard presented his views in two works, the second diverging somewhat from the first. In his 1951 article, "L'Évangile à Quatre Dimensions," he contended the feasts served a septenary structure that casts Christ as perfect messiah and new creator[2]; and, in his 1977 commentary, *L'Évangile de Jean*, written with Lamouille and published in a new edition in 1987, he argued, somewhat differently, that the feasts furnish an imperfect foil to the perfect "Passover of Christ."

In the 1951 article, Boismard saw the feasts in John to have been woven into a multivalent septenary structure that permeated the entire gospel. His driving question concerned the thematic criteria by which the author selected its contents: if 20:30–31 betrays selectivity (as it does), then "what motifs have been able to guide Saint John in the choices he made?"[3] Boismard's answer was three-fold: Christ in dramatic struggle with Jerusalem; Christ as agent of the new creation; and Christ as mediator of the new covenant. Of these three, it was the second – Christ as agent of the new creation – in which he presented his initial understanding of the feasts.[4]

Fundamental to this understanding was Boismard's observation that the author of John rhetorically structured Jesus' public ministry on the number seven. Lacing the story are seven great discourses,[5] seven principal miracles,[6] seven mass responses of faith,[7] seven (different) expressions of Je-

---

[2] In his brief review of liturgical approaches to structuring the Fourth Gospel, Giuseppe Segalla omits treatment of Boismard's 1951 article and (thus, incorrectly) gives priority in this approach to Donatien Mollat (1953; 1960; 1973); Segalla 1992:274–75.

[3] Boismard 1951:94.

[4] The first and third portray Jesus, respectively, as new Jerusalem and new Moses/Tabernacle; Boismard 1951:95–99, 105–13.

[5] The interview with Nicodemus (3:3–21); the interview with the Samaritan woman (4:5–27); the discourse that follows the healing of the paralytic (5:19–47); the sermon on the Bread of Life (6:27–71); the discourse on the origin of the Messiah at the Feast of Tabernacles (chapters 7–8); the discourse on the Good Shepherd (10:1–39); the discourse after the Supper (14:1–17:26).

[6] The changing of water into wine (2:1–11); the healing of the royal official's son (4:53–57); the multiplication of the loaves (6:1–13); walking on water (6:17–21); the healing of the paralytic (5:1–15); the healing of the man born blind (9:1–7); the resurrection of Lazarus (11:1–44). On these seven signs, see also Saxby 1992:11–12.

[7] John 2:23; 4:39; 7:31; 8:30; 10:42; 11:45; 12:37 (?; for this last, perhaps 12:42).

sus' messianically salvific relation to humankind[8] and seven names for Jesus in the first week of his public ministry.[9] Moreover, shaping "the entire life of Christ" within that story are "seven different periods...of which several count exactly one week" (that is, *seven* days): (1) the first week of the messianic ministry; (2) the events which gravitate around the first Passover (2:13–4:54); (3) those which gravitate around the second Passover (chapters 5–6); (4) the seven days of the feast of Tabernacles (chapters 7–9); (5) the discourse held by Christ during the feast of the Dedication, with the healing of Lazarus (chapters 10–11); (6) Holy Week, ending with the death of Christ during the third Passover (chapters 12–19); and (7) the Paschal week (chapter 20).[10]

John structured his gospel thus, contended Boismard, for two christological reasons. Since seven was the ancient (and Semitic) number for perfection, these heptads first signify Christ's messianic perfection and, thereby, serve to authenticate his messianic work.[11] But further, since seven was also the number of days spanned in the Genesis creation story, the seven-fold structure of the narrative (of which some components were, themselves, seven-day feasts) casts Jesus' public ministry as an act of new creation. More specifically: as in the first three days of the Genesis creation God separated the elements and their effects one from another, so in the first three periods of Christ's public ministry does Jesus separate the old covenant from the new; and, as in the fourth through sixth days of the Genesis creation God furnished and populated the heavens and the earth, so in the fourth through sixth periods of Christ's public ministry does he reveal himself as the great luminary that gives light to the world (8:12; 9:4–5, 39, 41), as well as "le maître de la vie" that gives life to the world (9:9–10; 11:25) and birth to new humanity (7:39; 16:21; 19:34 [with Gen 2:18–24]). Moreover, as in the seventh day of the Genesis creation God rested, so in the seventh period of Christ's ministry does he repose "dans la gloire de la Résurrection."[12] "The intention of John is therefore clear," concludes Boismard:

---

[8] "I am the bread of life" (6:35–56); "I am the light of the world" (8:12); "I am the door" (10:7); "I am the Good Shepherd" (10:11–14); "I am the resurrection" (11:25); "I am the way, the truth and the life" (14:6); "I am the true vine" (15:1–5).

[9] Six names are messianic: "Lamb of God" (1:29, 35–36), "Rabbi" (1:38), "Messiah" (1:41), "Son of God" (1:49), "King of Israel" (1:49) and "Son of Man" (1:51); one, "Jesus of Nazareth" (1:45), "seems, unlike (the others), to be opposed to Jesus' messianic character," given scriptural testimony that the Messiah was to come from Bethlehem. For all these sevenfold lists, see Boismard 1951:99–100.

[10] Boismard 1951:101.

[11] Boismard 1951:99.

[12] Boismard 1951:102–105; quotation p. 104.

by the symbolism of the number seven, he wishes to present
the work of the Messiah as a new creation, resuming,
or more exactly, restarting the first creation.[13]

The purpose of the feasts, then, is to serve the Fourth Gospel's theology of
Christ's messianic perfection and new creation. The feasts do not number
seven themselves (and nothing is made here of the fact they are six). But,
by virtue of their overlap with most of the narrative's seven divisions, and
on the assumption that some of them spanned seven-day periods, they are
understood to have interlocked with the Fourth Gospel's septenary format
and, so, to have enhanced its numerological presentation of Jesus as perfect messiah and new creator.

In his later commentary, Boismard with Lamouille developed his well-
known, elaborate theory of the Fourth Gospel's composition history. According to Boismard and Lamouille, that history unfolded in four phases,
labeled Document C (ca. 50 CE in Palestine), Jean II-A (60–65 CE in Palestine), Jean II-B (ca. 95 CE in Asia Minor/Ephesus) and Jean III – the
current form of the text (early 2nd century in Ephesus).[14] With regard to
the feasts, the first two of these phases carried only one or two, each em-
bracing (parts of) verses from what are now various *loci* in the narrative: in
Document C, there was only the Feast of Tabernacles[15]; in Jean II-A, both
the Feast of Tabernacles (now more elaborate) and, prior to it in the narrative, the unnamed feast later to be associated with John 5.[16] The full six
feasts do not appear until strata Jean II-B and Jean III. Jean II-B diffused

---

[13] Boismard 1951:104.

[14] Boismard and Lamouille 1987:67–70.

[15] The Feast of Tabernacles is listed, with five sub-headings, under the general title
'At Jerusalem, The Feast of Tabernacles': Entrance of Jesus to Jerusalem (7:2, 10;
12:12–13); Expulsion of the Temple Vendors (7:14; 2:14–16); The Greeks Wish to See
Jesus (12:20–23, 31–32, 48); Healing of a Blind Man (8:59; 9:1, 6–7); The Plot Against
Jesus (11:47; 12:19; 11:53–54); see Boismard and Lamouille 1987:17–18, 22–25. Verses
here and in the other strata recounted below would have appeared in the order listed. Except for instances in which Boismard and Lamouille have explicitly designated them as
such, their numbering does not account for partial and modified texts within each verse.
For these details, consult the page numbers listed for each stratum.

[16] In Jean II-A, the unnamed feast has two sub-headings, listed under the general title,
'In Galilee': Healing of an Infirm Man (5:1, 5–6, 8–9; 2:23); Interview with Nicodemus
(3:1–3, 9–10, 31–34; 5:24, 30–32, 37). The Tabernacles section, still under the title, 'At
Jerusalem,' is extended to ten sub-headings: The Entrance of Jesus to Jerusalem (7:2, 10;
12:12–15); Discussion within the Crowd (7:40–43); Dialogues with Jesus (8:14–15, 54–
55, 42, 20–24); Expulsion of the Temple Vendors (7:14; 2:14–16); Jesus, Bread of Life
and Living Water, (2:18; 6:31–32, 49–51, 41, 43, 35, 37–39; 7:37–38); The Jews are of
the Devil (8:25–26, 43, 40–42, 44, 46–48, 59); The Greeks Wish to See Jesus (12:20–23,
31; 3:14, 16, 18; 12:34); Healing of a Blind Man (8:59; 9:1–3, 6–7, 15, 17–21, 24, 26–30,
33–37); Incredulity of the Jews (12:37, 39–40); and The Plot Against Jesus (11:47;
12:19; 11:53–54); Boismard and Lamouille 1987:27–29, 32–35.

Jean II-A's Tabernacles into three Passovers, put the unnamed feast after the second of those Passovers (tacitly understanding it as Pentecost), added the Feast of Dedication and subsumed everything under a structure of eight "weeks" (a convenient designation drawn from the seven or eight days spanned by some of these units[17]) – all bracketed by the Prologue and a Conclusion.[18] The structure is charted in Table 1[19]:

Table 1. Marie-Émile Boismard & Arnaud Lamouille: Outline of Jean II-B

Weeks/Feasts	Episodes
Prologue	Prologue, 1:1–18
First Week/No Feast	Testimony of John, 1:19–34 Calling of the First Disciples, 1:35–51 Wedding at Cana, 2:1–12
Second Week/First Passover (2:13)	Expulsion of the Temple Vendors, 2:13–22 Signs Accomplished by Jesus, 2:23–25 Interview with Nicodemus, 3:1–13 Discourse on Judgment, 3:14, 16, 18–21, 35–36 John Baptizes at Aenon, 3:22–30 Jesus & the Samaritan Woman, 4:1–10, 15, 13–14, 16–42 Jesus Departs for Galilee, 4:43–45 The Son of the Royal Official, 4:46–54
Third Week/Second Passover (6:4)	The Multiplication of the Loaves, 6:1–15 The Walk on the Sea, 6:16–21 Dialogue on the Bread of Life, 6:22–51a Dialogue on the Eucharist, 6:51b–59 The Profession of Peter's Faith, 6:60–69 The Announcement of Judas' Betrayal, 6:70–71

[17] Particularly, Boismard and Lamouille note the days of the first week of Jesus' ministry (1:19–2:11), the Feast of Tabernacles (7:2, 14, 37), the Passion week (12:1, 12; 19:31, 42) and the week of the resurrection appearances (20:1, 26); 1987:39.

[18] Boismard and Lamouille 1987:35–44, 160–61.

[19] Some passages listed in this table are absent certain (parts of) verses in Jean II-B: for 'Dialogue on the Bread of Life' (6:22–51a), 6:27b, 39 are absent; for 'The Jews are of the Devil' (8:44–59), 8:46b–47, 54b–55; for 'Healing of a Blind Man' (9:1–37), 9:5; for 'Parables on the Pastor' (10:1–21), 10:9, 13, 16; for 'The Resurrection of Lazarus' (11:1–46), 11:13, 25b–26a; for 'The Washing of the Feet' (13:1–17), 13:16; for 'The Announcement of Judas' Betrayal' (13:18–30), 13:20; for 'The Coming of Three Persons' (14:13–26), 14:14; for 'The Prayer of Jesus' (17:1–26), 17:3, 12b, 19–21.

Weeks/Feasts	Episodes
Fourth Week/Pentecost (5:1)	Healing of an Infirm Man, 5:1–16 Discussions on Jesus, 7:11–13 Jesus is Justified, 7:19–24 The Pharisees Wish to Arrest Jesus, 7:31–32, 44–52 Discourse on Judgment, 5:19, 21–26, 30 Discourse on the Witnesses, 5:31–47

Fifth Week/Tabernacles (7:2, 14, 37)	Jesus Goes Up for Tabernacles, 7:1–10
	Jesus Teaches in the Temple, 7:14–18
	Discussions on Jesus, 7:25–28a, 24a,
	    28b–30
	Jesus Announces His Departure,
	    7:33–36; 8:23–24, 28–29
	Rivers of Living Water, 7:37–39; 8:30
	Jesus Makes Us Free, 8:31–39
	The Jews are of the Devil, 8:44–59
	Healing of a Blind Man, 9:1–37
	Blindness of the Pharisees, 9:39–41; 8:12,
	    15–16a, 14b, 13, 14a, 16b–19
	Parables on the Pastor, 10:1–21

Sixth Week/Dedication (10:22)	Jesus, Christ & Son of God, 10:22–39 Jesus Withdraws Beyond the Jordan, 10:40–42 The Resurrection of Lazarus, 11:1–46 The Plot Against Jesus, 11:47–54

Weeks/Feasts	Episodes
Seventh Week/Third Passover (11:55; 12:1; 13:1)	The Approach of the Passover, 11:55–57 The Anointing at Bethany, 12:1–11 The Entrance of Jesus to Jerusalem, 12:12–19 The Greeks Wish to See Jesus, 12:20–30 The Judgment of This World, 12:31–33, 44, 46–50, 35–36 The Incredulity of the Jews, 12:37–43 The Washing of the Feet, 13:1–17 The Announcement of Judas' Betrayal, 13:18–30 Jesus Announces His Departure, 13:31–35 The Announcement of Peter's Renunciation, 13:36–38 Jesus Announces His Departure, 14:1–12 Coming of Three Persons, 14:13–26 The Gift of Peace, 14:27–31 The True Vine, 15:1–6 The Love of the Disciples, 15:7–17 The Hatred of the World, 15:18, 20; 16:2; 15:21, 26–27; 16:1 Jesus Will Send the Paraclete, 16:4b–15 Jesus Announces His Return, 16:16–22 Last Words to the Disciples, 16:23a, 25, 23b–24, 29–33 The Prayer of Jesus, 17:1–26 Passion Accounts, 18:1–19:42
Eighth Week/No Feast (though Azyma coincides)	Resurrection Accounts, 20:1–31
Conclusion/No Feast	The Miraculous Catch, 21:1–14 Peter Instituted as Pastor, 21:15–19 The Destiny of the Beloved Disciple, 21:20–22 Epilogue, 21:24–25

Jean III, the last stratum, maintained this eight week structure but, with final rearrangements and supplements, inverted the Passover at 6:4 and the unnamed feast at 5:1 into their present order.[20]

---

[20] Boismard and Lamouille 1987:44–45. Further major redactions of Jean II-B in this final phase were (1) incorporating the discourse and dialogue material that followed the healing at the unnamed feast (5:1–16) into the Feast of Tabernacles context (7:11–13, 19–23, 31–32, 44–52); (2) relocating 12:44–50 from before 12:35 to after 12:43; (3) joining Jesus' words in 3:31–34 (Jean II-A) with his words in 3:35–36 (Jean II-B) and, after

In this more elaborate schema (as is evident from Table 1), Boismard and Lamouille expanded Boismard's earlier sevenfold structure into an eightfold one. Perhaps because he had painted with such broad strokes in his 1951 article, Boismard sometimes demarcated sections at imprecise junctures. Two of these were inconsequential for the total number of sections in his outline.[21] His third section, however, the "events which gravitate around the second Passover" (5–6), in fact, circumscribed events that gravitate around two feasts: the second Passover (6:1–71) and the unnamed feast at 5:1 (5:1–47). Boismard and Lamouille corrected this misallocation in Jean II-B and Jean III (albeit with John 5 and 6 inverted in Jean II-B), dividing Boismard's third section into two and, thus, increasing the overall number of segments from seven to eight.

Moreover, Boismard and Lamouille also expanded the number of numerological constructs they perceived in the narrative – specifically, in the narrative of Jean II-B. To the list of "sevens" mentioned above they added the sevenfold use of "healthy" (ὑγιής) in the healing of the lame man[22]; the sevenfold use of the clause "to open the eyes" (ἀνοίγειν [τοὺς] ὀφθαλμούς) in the healing of the man born blind[23]; the sevenfold use of the verb "to wash" (νίπτειν) in the washing of the disciples' feet[24]; Jesus' sevenfold use of "I am" ([ἐγώ] εἰμι) in the discourse following 7:28[25]; the sevenfold use of Martha's name in the resurrection of Lazarus,[26] as well as the use of Thomas's name in the whole gospel[27]; the sevenfold use of the phrase "to bear fruit" (φέρειν καρπόν) in 15:1–16 (all accounted for in Jean II-B); the sevenfold use of the phrase "to give testimony" at 5:31–47 (all accounted for in Jean II-B); the sevenfold appearance of the adverb "a little" ([τὸ] μικρόν) at 16:16–22 (all accounted for in Jean II-B); the men-

---

putting them on the lips of John the Baptist, relocating them from before 3:22–30 (as was 3:35–36 in Jean II-B) to after those verses; (4) rearranging, supplementing and transferring verses from what are now 8:12–19, 23–24, 28–30, 31–39, 44–59 to their current location; and (5) adding various explanatory and corrective glosses.

[21] John 10:1–21, which Boismard categorized under the Feast of Dedication and Raising of Lazarus (10–11), comes before the Dedication is introduced (10:22–23) and, thus, is better placed with the Feast of Tabernacles, beginning at 7:2; and 11:55–57, which Boismard similarly classified under the Dedication and Raising of Lazarus, itself, introduces the final Passover and, so, is more aptly associated with "Holy Week" that follows in chapters 12–19.

[22] In Jean II-B, within 5:1–16; 7:11–13, 19–24, 31–32, 44–52; 5:19, 21–26, 30 with some omissions, the seventh time modified with "whole" (ὅλος).

[23] The seventh time, again, modified with "whole."

[24] In Jean II-B, within 13:1-15, 17, modified, again, with "whole" (7:10).

[25] In Jean II-B, 7:28b–30, 33–36; 8:23–24, 28–29 with some omissions. On the seven uses of "I am" statements, see also Saxby 1992:11.

[26] In Jean II-B, 11:1–46 except 11:13, 25b–26a.

[27] John 11:16; 14:5; 20:24, 26, 27, 28; 21:2; all verses present in Jean II-B.

tion of seven disciples at 21:2; the reference to "the seventh hour" at 4:52; and – quite significantly for their understanding of the feasts – the seven appearances of the term "Passover" (πάσχα) during the final Passover at 11:55–19:42.

Further, Boismard and Lamouille noted the appearance of two more significant numbers: one hundred and fifty three (of the fish at 21:11), which they interpreted to be a configuration of the numbers seven and ten; and, more importantly, six – the sixth hour[28]; the six-fold designation of Jesus as "this man" throughout the gospel[29]; the six purification jars at 2:6; six uses of the verb "to believe" (πιστεύειν) in John 5:31–47 (all accounted for in Jean II-B); and, of course, the six feasts that span the gospel.[30] According to Boismard and Lamouille, six symbolized imperfection and, thus, cast the items so numbered as imperfect foils to the perfect items numbered at seven.

With regard to the feasts, Boismard and Lamouille, in part, sustained Boismard's earlier interpretation of their significance: by more or less spanning seven to eight day periods, the feasts joined the Fourth Gospel's other septenary symbols in underscoring Christ's messianic perfection; and, by dovetailing the second through seventh of Jesus' seven–week public ministry, they helped structure that ministry into an act of new creation.[31] Further, however, Boismard and Lamouille drew upon the numerology of the number six to interpret those feasts as a flawed contrast to a christianized Passover established at Christ's resurrection. Inasmuch as six is the number for imperfection, they reasoned, the six Jewish feasts in John represent the inadequate character of the Jewish festal system. But, since the final Passover, in which Jesus passes "from this world to the Father," employs the word "Passover" seven times (the number of perfection[32]), the juxtaposition of the two is meant to show that the inept system of Jewish festivals has been trumped by the superior nature of the Christian Passover. The festivals in John, thus, serve as a foil, contrasting the obsolete, imperfect feasts of the Jews with the newly created, perfect "Pâque du Christ":

---

[28] At 4:6 and 19:14.

[29] John 7:46; 9:16, 24; 11:47; 18:17, 29.

[30] Boismard and Lamouille 1987:61–62.

[31] Boismard and Lamouille 1987:38–39, 61; cf. Boismard 1951:99–105.

[32] John 11:55 (twice); 12:1; 13:1; 18:28, 39; 19:14 (all included in Jean II-B).

> The intention of John, then, is to demonstrate that the Christian Passover,
> that of Christ, has replaced the cycle of Jewish liturgical feasts...
> The Jewish cult is replaced by the Christian cult,
> centered on the only true Passover, the "passage" from this world
> to the Father effected by Jesus, then by his disciples.[33]

Debate wages over whether or not the Gospel of John is as numerologi-
cally potent as Boismard and Lamouille assume.[34] But, even were their
premise granted, several broader aspects of their argument bring their larger thesis about the feasts into question. It should first be noted that not all
of the sextenary and septenary constructs they list for the Fourth Gospel
actually obtain. Some of the discrepancies can be ascribed to minor, usually textual grounds and are of little consequence.[35] Others, however, are
more substantive and alter the number of those constructs by some degree.
For those alleged in the 1987 commentary, there are two, possibly three.
The verb "to wash" (νίπτειν) in the washing of the disciples' feet[36] occurs
eight, not seven times,[37] as does the name "Martha" in the raising of Lazarus episode.[38] And, with respect to the seven uses of πάσχα in 11:55–
19:42, though that term does not appear more times than Boismard and
Lamouille counted, the Passover, itself, is referred to as "the feast"
(ἑορτή) twice more[39]; and, since one of the appearances of πάσχα occurs
in the phrase "the Preparation of the Passover" (παρασκευὴ τοῦ πάσχα)
at 19:14, reference to the Passover might realistically be inferred in the ab-

---

[33] Boismard and Lamouille 1987:38–39, 42, 61; quotation pages 38, 61.

[34] For biblical scholarship on the use of numerological techniques in John, see Richard Bauckham (2002:79–80, 86–87; especially the bibliographical summaries cited on p.
79n12). Bauckham, himself, draws upon this assumption to argue the authorial unity of
John 21 with John 1–20 (2002:77–87); but note, also, his comments on the general lack
of interest exegetes have shown in the dissertation of Martin J.J. Menken on the numerological significance of word and syllable counts in select Johannine passages (Menken
1985:12–27, 269–74).

[35] Particularly, in Bezae (original hand) one of the occurrences of the clause "to bear
fruit" (φέρειν καρπόν) in 15:1–16 is omitted (at 15:4) and another (at 15:2) reads the
related καρποφόρον. In ℵ (second corrector) D (from a later addition) L Δ Ψ 844, the
"sixth hour" at 19:14 reads "third hour." In P[66] (corrected) P[75] ℵ (second corrector) B L
T W, the sixth of the sixfold designation of Jesus as *this* man" (at 7:46; cf. 9:16, 24;
11:47; 18:17, 29) does not appear. And at 21:2, the count of the disciples is seven only if
one assumes the unnamed "sons of Zebedee" numbered two.

[36] In Jean II-B, 13:1–17 (without 13:16).

[37] John 13:5, 6, 8 (2x), 10, 12, 14 (2x). Alternate readings to the NA[27] εἰ μὴ τοὺς
πόδας νίψασθαι at 13:10 all read νίψασθαι: cf. (1) ℵ; (2) D; (3) P[66] Θ 1424; (4) P[75] A
C (third corrector) *Family* 1, and the *Majority text*.

[38] In Jean II-B, 11:1–46 (except 11:13, 25b–26a): see 11:1, 5, 19, 20, 21, 24, 30, 39.

[39] John 12:20; 13:29 (both included in Jean II-B).

breviated references to "the Preparation (of the Jews)" at 19:31 and 19:42.[40]

For Boismard's 1951 article, there are more. With regard to the seven large discourses, two of them arguably divide further: Jesus' discourse at the Feast of Tabernacles, which Boismard ascribes to John 7–8, is significantly interrupted by the account of Nicodemus before the chief priests and Pharisees at 7:45–52 – given that 7:14–44, itself, consists in Jesus' intermittent dialogue with the crowd over a period of at least two days, even this two-fold division may break down further. Moreover, Jesus' Good Shepherd discourse at 10:1–39 arguably spans two festal contexts: the Feast of Tabernacles (begun at 7:2) from 10:1–21, and the Feast of Dedication (begun at 10:22–23) from 10:22–39.[41] This brings the number of large discourses from seven to at least nine. Furthermore, Boismard does not consider in his list Jesus' response to the Greeks and final warning at 12:20–36, 44–50. And, given that John 17 is Jesus' prayer to the Father, it is not implausible that it should be considered separate from chapters 14–16 (not part of them, as Boismard has it), increasing the number of large discourses by that much more.

For the seven mass responses of faith – where it is said that, after such and such an action of Christ, "many believed in him" – Boismard missed that this sentiment is also expressed at 4:41, of the Samaritans after Jesus stayed with them two days, and at 12:11, as a reason the chief priests planned to kill Lazarus.[42] The comments to this effect in these verses do not precisely follow one of Jesus' deeds, as Boismard suggested. But neither do some of those he listed among the "seven": the mass response of faith at 4:39 came after the Samaritan woman's testimony; those at 7:31 and 8:30 came in the wake of Jesus' discourses (not a sign); that at 10:42 is a result of John the Baptist's (much earlier) testimony; and that of the authorities at 12:42 follows after the whole of Jesus' ministry. Moreover, one might ask whether the sentiment that "many (from the Jews) believed" differs so substantively from the sentiment that Jesus' own disciples believed[43] that the latter should be excluded from the count, as Boismard has it.

On the seven expressions of Christ's messianically salvific relation to humankind, Boismard arrives at seven, in part, because he lists Jesus as "the truth" and "the life" at 14:6, along with Jesus as "the way," under a

---

[40] Both included in Jean II-B.

[41] See the discussions in Chapter 2, under '2.3 The Feast of Tabernacles (John 7:2-52 [-10:21])' and '2.4 The Feast of Dedication (John 10:22-39).'

[42] See also the speculative fear of the Sanhedrin at 11:48 that, if they permitted Jesus to continue, "all will believe in him."

[43] John 2:11, 22; 17:8; cf. 6:39; 16:27, 30–31.

single heading. They arguably should be listed separately, however, making nine expressions – especially since Jesus as "life" appears independently of the other two (with "resurrection") at 11:25. Moreover, if by these expressions Boismard has in mind Jesus' "I am" statements, does not Jesus' plain self-ascription as "I am" at 8:58 also show that he was "aware of being in relation to men, in the relation of messianic salvation?" [44] Or if, by contrast, Boismard has in view metaphorical expressions of Jesus' messianic purpose, do not other metaphors appear elsewhere in the gospel: Jesus as the temple at 2:19; as the serpent lifted up in the wilderness at 3:14–15; as Jacob's ladder (albeit implicitly) at 1:51; and, if the pronoun αὐτοῦ is taken to be Jesus, as the rock in the wilderness or eschatological temple at 7:38? Moreover, with regard to the seven different names used for Jesus in 1:29–51, Boismard seems to have missed that, at 1:45, an eighth title, "Son of Joseph," appears in apposition to "Jesus of Nazareth."

Further on Boismard and Lamouille, the correlation they perceive between the Fourth Gospel and the Genesis creation story, on which much of their understanding of the feasts turns, breaks down upon closer examination. How that correlation works out in the 1987 commentary is difficult to discern. As noted above, Boismard and Lamouille (rightly) expand Boismard's initial sevenfold structure into an eightfold one; and, in so doing, they reduce the correspondence between the Fourth Gospel and the seven days of creation from spanning the entire body of the Fourth Gospel (1:19–20:31), as it was in Boismard's 1951 article, to covering only the first seven of the eight weeks by which it was organized in 1987 (1:19–19:42). This raises questions, however, since John 20, which, in the 1951 outline corresponded to the seventh day of creation, in the 1987 outline corresponds to none of those days; and since John 5 and 6, which in the earlier outline correlated to the single third day of creation, in the latter outline are split into two separate units.

In any case, the correlation Boismard proposed in his 1951 outline is, itself, fraught with problems; and there is little the 1987 outline offers that could rectify them. More elaborately stated, that correlation was argued to be threefold: (1) to certain separations God makes in the first three days of the Genesis creation correspond several replacements that Christ effects in the first three weeks of his ministry (1:19–6:71); (2) to the luminaries and creatures God furnishes in the fourth through sixth days of the Genesis creation correspond several cosmic and life-giving features ascribed to (or enacted by) Christ in the fourth through sixth weeks of his ministry (7:1–19:42); and (3) to the rest God takes on the seventh day of creation corre-

---

[44] Boismard 1951:100.

sponds Christ's repose during the (seventh) week of his resurrection (20:1–31).[45] Details are as follows:

Table 2. Marie-Émile Boismard: Creation in Genesis & Jesus' Public Ministry in John

The Genesis Creation Story	The Public Ministry of Jesus in John
1st – 3rd Days: Separation	1st – 3rd Weeks (1:19–6:71): Replacement
• First day: light & darkness	• First week (1:19–2:12) § Baptism of water with baptism of spirit (1:29–34) § Water of ancient purifications with wine of new economy (2:1–11)
• Second day: lower & upper waters	• Second week (2:13–4:54) § Temple with resurrected body of Christ (2:13–21) § Natural birth w/new birth in spirit & in truth (3:3–8) § Cults at Jerusalem & Gerizim w/cult in spirit & in truth (4:20–24)
• Third day: land & water	• Third week (5:1–6:71) § Sabbath with life–giving work of Messiah (5:1–47) § Manna from heaven with Christ's body (6:41–71)
4th – 6th Days	4th – 6th Weeks (7:1–19:42)
• Fourth day: luminaries	• Fourth week (7:1–9:41): dominated by light § Occurs during Tabernacles, the "Feast of Light" § Jesus declares himself "light of the world" (8:12) § Jesus opens soul of man born blind to his light (9:4–5, 39–41)
• Fifth day: living beings/ birds & fish	• Fifth week (10:1–11:57): God's creative action makes life appear in the world § Jesus, as Good Shepherd, leads sheep to abundant life (10:9–10) § Jesus proclaims himself "the resurrection & the life" (11:25) § Jesus raises Lazarus from the dead (11:1–44)
• Sixth day: land animals & humankind § Eve comes out of side of Adam (Gen 2:18–24)	• Sixth week (12:1–19:42): the great birth pangs of new humanity (16:21) § Humankind is regenerated in the blood of Christ § Water, as symbol of the new life of the church (7:39), comes out of the pierced side of Christ (19:34)

---

[45] Boismard 1951:102–105. In their 1987 commentary, which moves the seventh week back to the final Passover (11:55–19:42), Boismard and Lamouille add that, in this week, Jesus performs no sign; 1987:39.

The Genesis Creation Story	The Public Ministry of Jesus in John
Seventh Day	Seventh Week ([11:55–19:42[46]]/ 20:1–31)

• Seventh day: God rested	• Seventh Week
	§ Christ rests in the glory of the resurrection
	   (20:1–31/1951 article)
	§ Jesus performs no sign (11:55–19:42/1987
	   commentary)

Some of the corollaries Boismard sees between the fourth and fifth days of creation and the fourth and fifth weeks of Jesus' ministry are quite suggestive: particularly, the creation of luminaries with Christ as light (fourth day/week); and the first creation of life with the resurrection of Lazarus (fifth day/week). By and large, however, the correspondences are problematic, on several counts. Some of them are simply tenuous: the Feast of Tabernacles, for instance, included a festival of illumination among its rites,[47] but it was not identified as a festival of light, itself; and the water flowing from Jesus' side is only by a stretch analogous to Eve coming from Adam's side. Further, each week of Christ's ministry (even where the parallels are plausible) contains material not mentioned by Boismard which does not readily align (if it does not altogether conflict) with the themes of its respective day of creation. The fourth week (John 7–9), for example, which Boismard calibrates to the fourth day of creation on the motifs of light and luminaries (8:12; 9:4–5), also contains discourses on the Jews' attempt to stone Jesus (7:14–24), messianic origins (7:25–52) and Abrahamic pedigree (8:31–59). And the fifth week (John 10–11), which Boismard connects to the fifth day of creation through the theme of life-giving creation (10:9–10; 11:25), also contains the episode of the Jews' second attempt to stone Jesus (10:31–39) and the Sanhedrin's plot to assassinate him (11:45–53).

Moreover, there is nothing in the character of the first three weeks of Jesus' ministry that requires the "replacements" that occur within them to be tied to the specific days of creation Boismard alleges. One might ask, for instance: How is the replacement of purification water with new wine (2:1–11) more reflective of the separation of light and darkness (first day of creation) than it is of the separation of the upper and lower waters (second day of creation)? Or, how is the replacement of manna with Christ's body (6:1–71) more reflective of the separation of land and water (third day of creation) than it is of the separation of light and darkness (first day of creation)? Pushing the point further, it is simply difficult to work out how *replacements* in the first three weeks of Christ's ministry are at all

---

[46] This represents the 1987 structure.

[47] As discussed above, *m. Sukkah* 5:2–4, possibly alluded to at John 8:12; 9:4–5.

analogous to *separations* in the first three days of creation: in the first, one reality voids another; in the second, one entity is removed from another, but both continue to exist.

Further, at points Boismard ascribes some dynamics to one part of Christ's ministry that are also to be found elsewhere in that ministry, blurring the pristine classification on which his theory depends. An example is the motif of Jesus as (bringer of) light (8:12; 9:4–5, 39–41): Boismard connects it to the creation of luminaries on the fourth day of creation; but it also appears at 3:19–21, which Boismard aligns, instead, with the separation of upper and lower waters on the second day of creation. Again, the theme of the life-giving work of Christ having precedence over the Sabbath (5:1–47): Boismard aligns it to the separation of land and water on the third day of creation; but it appears again at the healing of the man born blind on the Sabbath at 9:1–41, which Boismard, instead, calibrates to the creation of stars to govern day and night on the fourth day of creation.

Finally on the hypothesis of Boismard and Lamouille – their supersessionist argument that the six feasts in John are trumped by the seven uses of πάσχα is just as easily belied by the mathematics on which it is built as it is supported by them. One might first note that, by some interpretations (though not advocated here), the feasts in John did not originally number six, but five. As reviewed earlier, if John 5 and 6 were at one time inverted and the feast at 5:1 was read with the articular ἡ ἑορτή, that ostensibly anonymous feast (at 5:1) would arguably have been the Passover introduced (earlier) at 6:4.[48] Two references to feasts would have combined into one, reducing their total number by as much. But even excluding that scenario as a possibility, there remains the problematic inference Boismard and Lamouille make from the juxtaposition of six feasts in the narrative to seven uses of πάσχα in the final Passover. Specifically, it is difficult to see how seven references to πάσχα between 11:55–19:42 have any bearing on six references to feasts between 2:13–19:42, all the more so when the contrast between them is to connote the sweeping theological claim that the Christian Passover renders the Jewish festal system obsolete. And it is equally hard to grasp why those numbers are set over against one another in the first place, since the final Passover, which is christianized into perfection, is also the feast which brings the Jewish festal sequence in John to six, the number of imperfection. Could it not also be reasoned that, since the sixth and last Jewish feast in which Christ secured redemption contains its own name seven times, the Evangelist intended to declare that, by his death and resurrection, Christ established (rather than abolished) the Jewish festal system?

---

[48] See Chapter 2, under '2.2 The Unnamed Feast and a Second Passover (John 5:1–6:71).'

Adding to the confusion is the further contention by Boismard and Lamouille that the supersession of the Christian Passover over the six Jewish
feasts parallels the supersession of the resurrection over the six signs Jesus
had earlier done during his public ministry. In both Jean II-B and Jean III
(final form) of their schema, Jesus performs six signs during his public
ministry, followed by the resurrection. Each are done on a separate "week"
within Jesus' ministry: the first week/the wine of the wedding at Cana
(2:1–11); the second week/the healing of an official's son at Capernaum
(4:46–54); the third week/the multiplication of the loaves (6:1–13); the
fourth week/the healing of an infirm man (5:2–16); the fifth week/the healing of the man born blind (9:1–7); and the sixth week/the resurrection of
Lazarus (11:1–44). Though Jesus performs one further sign after his resurrection (the miraculous catch of fish [21:1–14]), the actual seventh sign
was the resurrection, itself, "which John considers implicitly as the seventh
'sign.'"[49] According to Boismard and Lamouille, these six signs function
in relation to the resurrection (the implicit seventh sign) in the same way
the six feasts do in relation to the final Passover: as the six feasts juxtaposed to the seven uses of "Passover" connote the imperfect Jewish festal
cycle trumped by the perfect Passover of Christ, so the six signs preceding
the seventh sign of the resurrection connote the imperfect manifestation of
Jesus' glory through signs trumped by the perfect manifestation of that
glory in Jesus' rising from the dead.[50] The problem that arises, however, is
that the way these signs signify supersessionism with respect to Christ's
glory does not, in fact, match the way the feasts do so with respect to Jewish and Christian festal liturgy. With the latter, the feasts number six and
the sixth doubles as both the feast that trumps and one of the feasts that is
trumped; with the former, the signs number seven and the seventh trumps
the previous six without being counted among their number.

In sum, the numerological theory of feasts in John espoused by Boismard and Lamouille lies open to serious question. Even were it granted
that the number of festivals has symbolic significance, other aspects of the
argument render the hypothesis on the whole weak: many of the numerical
constructs on which it turns – particularly the seven references to "Pass-

---

[49] Boismard and Lamouille 1987:38–39, 42; quotation p. 39. In Document C and Jean
II-A, the miraculous catch of fish (now 21:1–14) had also been placed within Jesus'
earthly ministry: in Document C, it followed Jesus' discourse with his brothers in Galilee
(7:1, 3–4, 6, 9); in Jean II-A, still following that discourse, it was placed after the healing
of the infirm man (5:1, 5–6, 8–9; 2:23) and the interview with Nicodemus (3:1–3, 9–10,
31–34; 5:24, 30–32, 37), during the unnamed feast. But, in order to reduce the number of
signs in Jesus' public ministry from seven (which it would otherwise have been) to six,
Jean II-B transformed it into a resurrection appearance and transplanted it to chapter 21,
thus leaving the remaining number of signs in Jesus' pre-resurrection ministry at six.

[50] Boismard and Lamouille 1987:17, 27, 38–39, 42.

over" – are arguably not septenary; most of the alleged correlations between the Johannine narrative and the Genesis creation story are tenuous;
and the logic by which the six feasts play their christological role ultimately turns in on itself.

3.1.2 'Les jalons de ce récit': Donatien Mollat

Soon after Boismard's first article, Donatien Mollat proposed his own theory on feasts in John, in the introduction to his French translation of the
Fourth Gospel for *La Sainte Bible*. He maintained that theory, unchanged,
through the first and second editions of that work[51] but modified it quite
dramatically in the third.[52] In his first two editions, Mollat argued that the
Johannine feasts provide the structural medium into which all other features of the gospel fit; and, as such, they furnish the hermeneutical context
in which its miracles and discourses gain their meaning.[53] After surveying
nine devices by which exegetes have sought to organize the Johannine narrative,[54] Mollat contended that, though each of them captures some aspects
of Johannine thought, none grasps all. John's overall message exceeds all
these motifs and features; and the broader framework that accommodates
that message is the feasts that lace its narrative. The Jewish festivals,
claimed Mollat, are the "milestones" ("les jalons") of Johannine *kerygma,*
which, in distinction to the Synoptics, center Jesus' activity in Jerusalem;
further, they are the contexts in which the *semeia* and discourses of that
kerygma receive their significance:

> These feasts, it seems, represent the essential joints (les articulations essentielles)
> of the Johannine Gospel. We can consider them as fundamental elements
> of its plan. They do more than frame the miracles and discourses;
> they determine the sense.[55]

Mollat then structured the Fourth Gospel on its feasts, commenting
(somewhat) on just how they inform the episodes they cover. Bracketing
the Prologue and chapter 21 (as an Appendix), he divided the body of the
gospel eightfold. Six of these sections follow the sequence of festivals –
some items of note: (1) the first section, titled 'The Events that Revolve
around the *1st Passover* or *the Passover of the New Temple*,' divides into

---

[51] Mollat 1953:27–36; 1960:27–36.

[52] Mollat 1973:27–41; on Mollat, see also the reviews by Caba (1974:338–39) and
Mlakuzhyil (1987:19–21).

[53] Mollat 1953:32–33; 1960:32.

[54] Chronology, geography, drama, logic, themes, cycles, numbers, symbols and "un
plan organique," Mollat's label for Maurice Goguel's idea that the Fourth Gospel is "une
collection d'épisodes qui illustrent différents aspects de la vie chrétienne"; Mollatt
1953:28; 1960:28, quoting Goguel.

[55] Mollat 1953:27–33; quotation pp. 32–33; 1960:27–33; quotation p. 32 (in the 1960
edition, Mollat omits the adjective "essentielles").

four subsections; (2) in the label Mollat gives chapter 5, the festival at 5:1 is not identified with a feast *per se*, but with the Sabbath – '*The Sabbath of the Paralytic*'; (3) the section covering '*The Feast of Tabernacles*' is similarly associated with the Sabbath mentioned at chapter 9 – '*The Feast of Tabernacles and the Sabbath of the Man Born Blind.*' A further section, covering 3:22–4:54 and titled '*Journey in Samaria and Galilee,*' comes between the sections on the 1st Passover and '*The Sabbath of the Paralytic*' mentioned above and, itself, divides into three subsections. The eighth section, covering chapter 20, is titled, '*The Resurrection.*'[56]

In the second edition, Mollat condensed the four subsections under the 1st Passover into three; he removed the section '*Journey in Samaria and Galilee*' as a major heading and consolidated and subsumed its three subsections under the 1st Passover as the fourth of its subsections; and he expanded the title '*The Resurrection*' to '*the Day of the Resurrection*' in what now became the seventh section.[57] By this "septénaire de fêtes," Mollat concluded, the author of the Fourth Gospel meant to signify Jesus' life and ministry as the realization of messianic perfection and fullness.[58] The outlines for Mollat's first two editions appear in Table 3, with his remarks on the interpretive significance of the feasts aligned with their respective sections[59]:

---

[56] Mollat 1953: 35–36; italics, here and below, are as per Mollat.

[57] Mollat 1960:35–36.

[58] Mollat 1953:36; 1960:36; cf. also 1973:40.

[59] Except for the outline and minor (e.g., punctuation) changes, the text of Mollat's introduction is the same in both 1st and 2nd editions. For the outline and comments, see Mollat 1953:32–36; 1960:32–36.

Table 3. Donatien Mollat: Feasts & the Fourth Gospel, 1st – 2nd Editions

Outline: 1st Edition	Outline: 2nd Edition	Hermeneutical Significance
Prologue (1:1–18) I. The Events that Revolve around *the 1st Passover* or *the Passover of the New Temple* (1:19–4:54) • 1:19–2:11, First Week of Messianic Ministry • 2:12–22, Jesus chases vendors from temple & announces his risen body to be new Temple • 2:23–25, Jesus' ministry at Jerusalem during feast	*Prologue* (1:1–18) I. The Events that Revolve around *the 1st Passover* or *the Passover of the New Temple* (1:19–4:54) • The Inaugural Week (1:19–2:12) • The Feast of the First Passover at Jerusalem (2:13–25)	 • Jesus purifies the temple as a sign of the new temple of his risen body
• 3:1–21, Discussion with Nicodemus	• Revelation of New Birth in the Spirit (3:1–21)	• Jesus announces spiritual regeneration in the Spirit
II. *Journey through Samaria & Galilee* (3:22–4:54) • 3:22–36, Stay in Judea • 4:1–42, Interlude in Samaria • 4:43–54, Arrival in Galilee/Second Miracle in Cana	• Journey through Samaria & Galilee (3:22–4:54)	 • Jesus announces cult in Spirit & in truth • Jesus, Savior of the world
III. *The Sabbath of the Paralytic* (5:1–47)	II. *The Sabbath of the Paralytic* (5:1–47)	• Jesus demonstrates that the Sabbath is fulfilled in the life-giving work of the Son of God
IV. *The Passover of the Bread of Life* (6:1–71)	III. *The Passover of the Bread of Life* (6:1–71)	• Passover context (6:4) gives miracle & bread of life discourse "a pascal character"

Outline: 1st Edition	Outline: 2nd Edition	Hermeneutical Significance
V. *The Feast of Tabernacles & the Sabbath of the Man Born Blind* (7:2–10:21)	IV. *The Feast of Tabernacles & the Sabbath of the Man Born Blind* (7:2–10:21)	• Jesus' words tied to rites & ideas characteristic of Tabernacles: rivers of living water (7:37–39) w/liturgy of water; light of the world (8:12; 9:1–41) w/procession to Siloam; true descent from Abraham (8:31–59) w/*Jubilees* tradition that Tabernacles commemorates announcement of Isaac's birth (Gen 17:17; 21:6; *Jub.* 16:20–31); claim to be source of messianic joy (8:56) w/joy of the feast (Deut 16:13–15).
VI. *The Feast of the Dedication* (10:22–11:54)	V. *The Feast of the Dedication* (10:22–11:54)	• In the political & religious spirit of the restoration of the temple desecrated by Antiochus Epiphanes the Sanhedrin decides on the death of Jesus, lest "the Romans come & destroy our holy place & our nation" (11:48); the feast of the temple's consecration illumines the designation of Jesus as "the one whom the Father consecrated & sent into the world" (10:36).
VII. *The Passover of the Crucifixion* (11:55–19:42)	VI. *The Passover of the Crucifixion* (11:55–19:42)	• As with the lamb of the old Passover, so with Jesus, the Lamb of the new Passover: he dies with no bone being broken (19:36).
VIII. *The Resurrection* (20:1–29)	VII. *The Day of the Resurrection* (20:1–29)	• The resurrection is not tied to a feast: Jesus' death closes an epoch (19:30) & his resurrection signals the commencement of the new time announced to the Samaritan woman, "the true worshippers will worship in spirit & in truth" (4:23).
Appendix (21:1–25)	*Appendix* (21:1–25)	

In his first two editions, Mollat concluded, similarly to Boismard and Lamouille, that, overall, these feasts in John function as foils for a christological supersessionism. Permeating the entire festal structure of the
Fourth Gospel, he maintained, is the notion that, by fulfilling what each
feast signified, Jesus put an end both to them and to all other Jewish institutions (connoted by them):

> In any case, one idea emerges from this plan;
> that is, that Jesus puts an end to Jewish institutions by fulfilling them.
> Represented by its temple of stone, its Sabbaths, its feasts, its rites, its sacrifices,
> Judaism culminates in Jesus into a cult in spirit and truth,
> which he embodies in his person and to which one attains by a rebirth.
> The old economy ends in the radiance of the glory of the Son of God.[60]

In his third edition, Mollat altered this hypothesis in two ways. First, he
developed the second outline into a more elaborate scheme. He kept the
Prologue (1:1–18) and Appendix (21:1–25) separate from the body of the
narrative and still had the six feasts figure as structural elements. But he
significantly changed the roles these units play, as well as the language by
which they are described: (1) he re-titled the *Appendix* as *Epilogue* and
subdivided it into four units; (2) he renamed the first major unit of the
1953/1960 outline ('Events that Revolve around the *1st Passover*') to 'Announcement of the New Economy' and divided it more minutely into seven
units (from four), partitioning the third further into three smaller sections;
(3) he listed the four feasts spanning from the unnamed festival (5:1–47) to
the Dedication (10:22–11:54) together with the aforementioned unit, 'Announcement of the New Economy,' under the broader subheading '*The
Ministry of Jesus*' (1:19–12:50); (4) he separated John 11:55–12:50, originally part of the '*Passover of the Crucifixion*' (11:55–19:42), from John
13:1–19:42, titling it 'The End of Jesus' Public Ministry and Preliminaries
of the Last Passover' and making it a sixth unit – also under the subheading '*The Ministry of Jesus*'; (5) he re-titled the remainder of the original
'*Passover of the Crucifixion*' (13:1–19:42) as '*The Hour of Jesus: the
Passover of the Lamb of God*' and made it the second major heading of the
narrative body (with '*The Ministry of Jesus*' as the first), further dividing it
into four major sub-sections, with nine more minor subdivisions under the
first; (6) he split the '*Day of the Resurrection*' (John 20) from the
1953/1960 editions into two, 'Resurrection Stories and the Blessedness of
Faith' (20:1–29) and 'The First Conclusion of the Gospel' (20:30–31),
subsuming them as the last two of the four major sub-sections under '*The
Hour of Jesus: the Passover of the Lamb of God*'; and, (7) with the excep-

---

[60] Mollat 1953:36; 1960:36. On this view (based on Mollat's 2nd edition), see the critique by Caba (1974:338–39).

tion of the '*Day of the Resurrection*,' he split (2:13–25) or subdivided (the rest) all festal sections from his first outline.[61]

Table 4 graphs the comparison. Mollat's more elaborate 1973 outline is summarized rather than represented in its entirety; but none of his comments on the interpretive relevance of the feasts for the Johannine narrative have been omitted:

Table 4. Donatien Mollat: Feasts & the Fourth Gospel, 1st – 3rd Editions

1st & 2nd Editions	3rd Edition
Prologue (1:1–18)	*Prologue* (1:1–18)
	The Ministry of Jesus (1:19–12:50)
I. The Events that Revolve around *the 1st Passover* or *the Passover of the New Temple* (1:19–4:54)	I. Announcement of the New Economy (1:19–4:54)
A. The Inaugural Week (1:19–2:12)	1. The Inaugural Week (1:19–2:11)
	2. Transition: Jesus at Capernaum (2:12)
B. The Feast of the First Passover at Jerusalem (2:13–25)	3. The First Passover (2:13–3:21)
	a) Jesus presents himself in the temple (2:13–22)
	b) Transition: stay in Jerusalem (2:23–25)
C. The Revelation to Nicodemus of the New Birth in the Spirit (3:1–21)	c) Jesus reveals to Nicodemus the necessity of birth from above by the Spirit with true faith (3:1–21)
D. Journey through Samaria and Galilee (3:22–4:54)	4. Transition: Jesus' ministry in Judea (3:22–36)
	5. Jesus is revealed in Samaria as the founder of worship in Spirit and in truth (4:1–42)
	6. Jesus on the return to Galilee (4:43–45)
	7. At Cana Jesus heals a royal official's son (4:46–54)
II. *The Sabbath of the Paralytic* (5:1–47)	II. The Second Feast: a Sabbath Day in Jerusalem (5:1–47)
	1. Jesus heals a disabled man at Bethesda on the Sabbath (5:1–18)
	2. Discourse on the work of the Son (5:19–47)

---

[61] Mollat 1973:32–40.

1st & 2nd Editions	3rd Edition
III. *The Passover of the Bread of Life* (6:1–71)	III. In Galilee, Second Passover (6:1–71) 1. Multiplication of the loaves (6:1–15) 2. Jesus returns to his disciples, walking on the sea (6:16–21) 3. At the synagogue in Capernaum: revelation of Jesus as Bread of Life, defection of many disciples and faithfulness of the Twelve (6:22–66) 4. Peter's profession of faith (6:67–71)
IV. *The Feast of Tabernacles and the Sabbath of the Man Born Blind* (7:2–10:21)	IV. The Feast of Tabernacles (7:1–10:21) 1. Jesus ascends "in secret" to the feast and teaches in the temple (7:1–36) 2. On the last day of the feast, Jesus makes an appeal to come to him and drink the living water of divine revelation (7:37–53) 3. Episode of the adulterous woman (8:1–11) 4. Jesus proclaims himself light of the world (8:12–30) 5. Jesus gives himself as Son, liberator of people, by his promissory word of truth (8:31–59) 6. Healing and coming to faith of the man born blind (9:1–41) 7. Jesus, the Good Shepherd, leads his sheep from the wall of Judaism and, with the coming of non-Jews, announces the establishment of one flock led by one shepherd.
V. *The Feast of the Dedication* (10:22–11:54)	V. The Feast of the Dedication (10:22–11:54) 1. Jesus affirms himself "one" with Father & Son of God (10:22–39) 2. Transition: Jesus returns "where John was baptizing" (10:40–42) 3. The resurrection of Lazarus (11:1–44) 4. Meeting of the Sanhedrin (11:45–53) 5. Transition: Jesus retires to the desert (11:54)

1st & 2nd Editions	3rd Edition
VI. *The Passover of the Crucifixion* (11:55–19:42)	VI. The End of Jesus' Public Ministry and Preliminaries of the Last Passover (11:55–12:50)
	1. The question: "Will he come to the feast?" (11:55–57)
	2. The anointing at Bethany (12:1–11)
	3. Messianic entry into Jerusalem (12:12–19)
	4. Coming of the Greeks (12:20–36)
	5. Conclusion of Jesus' ministry (12:37–50)
	The Hour of Jesus: The Passover of the Lamb of God (13:1–20:31)
	I. Last Supper with disciples (13:1–17:26)
	1. Introduction to the hour (13:1)
	2. The washing of the feet (13:2–20)
	3. Declaration of Judas' betrayal (13:21–30)
	4. Transition: glorification of the Son of Man and of God in him (13:31–32)
	5. 1st farewell discourse (13:33-14:31)
	6. Jesus is the true vine (15:1–17)
	7. The disciples & world (15:18–16:4) & assistance of Spirit (16:4b–15)
	8. Conclusion (16:16–33)
	9. The prayer of the hour (17:1–26)
	II. The Passion (18–19)
VII. *The Day of the Resurrection* (20)	III. Resurrection Stories and the Blessedness of Faith (20:1–29)
	IV. First Conclusion of the Gospel (20:30–31)
Appendix (21)	*Epilogue* (21:1–25)
	1. Jesus appears on bank of lake/ the miraculous fish (21:1–14)
	2. Investiture of Peter and announcement of his martyrdom (21:15–19)
	3. Calling of "the other disciple" (21:20–23)
	4. Second conclusion of the gospel (21:24–25)

More significantly in his third edition, Mollat dramatically recast the relationship he had espoused between the feasts and Johannine christology. He explicitly retracted his earlier supersessionism: "Nevertheless, the distinct goal of the Johannine gospel is not to signify that Jesus came to put an end to the liturgy of the old covenant."[62] And, in its place, he ascribed to the feasts two different functions. One, that they facilitate (rather than contrast with) the Fourth Gospel's christology:

> But specifically, there was not a more appropriate context for the manifestation
> of the mystery of Christ than the great, Jewish liturgical celebrations,
> during which the people of God, gathered from all parts of the world,
> revived the consciousness of their calling.[63]

And two, that the feasts bring into relief the grave issue of the Fourth Gospel and underscore the scope of rejection Jesus met:

> On the other hand, this tie between the revelation and the Jewish feasts
> singularly reinforces the dramatic character of the Gospel of John.
> It underlines the gravity of (what is at) stake
> and the import of the rejection with which Jesus collided.[64]

Important in Mollat's hypothesis is his third edition retraction of festal supersessionism. Not only does it show religious sensitivity, it reflects better logic. That feasts in John typify Jesus' person by no means requires those feasts to become obsolete once that connection has been made. One might, in fact, infer the other way round that, if festal symbolism does typify features of Jesus, those feasts ought be retained rather than discarded, so as to insure that christological import stays alive in liturgical life.

A disparity obtains, however, between Mollat's prolegomena (including the outline in which they are expressed) and the text. Mollat organizes the Fourth Gospel (particularly in his 1st and 2nd editions) on the sweeping assumption that the feasts in John furnish the interpretive contexts by which all the gospel's signs and discourses gain their meaning. That is, the Jewish festivals are "les articulations de l'évangile johannique"; and so, the Fourth Gospel can be so structured as to tie each episode hermeneutically to one of them: 'The Events that Revolve around *the 1st Passover*' (1:19–4:54); '*The Sabbath of the Paralytic*' (5:1–47); '*The Passover of the Bread of Life*' (6:1–71); '*The Feast of Tabernacles and the Sabbath of the Man Born Blind*' (7:2–10:21); '*The Feast of the Dedication*' (10:22–11:54); and '*The Passover of the Crucifixion*' (11:55–19:42).

---

[62] Mollat 1973:40.

[63] Mollat 1973:40.

[64] Mollat 1973:40–41.

The Johannine narrative, however, does not bear this notion out, in two ways. First (as noted in Chapter 2), in narrative time, not all episodes occur within feasts. This is clearly the case for the events of 1:19–2:12, which Mollat identifies as "revolving around" the Passover at 2:13. The Passover in question is not introduced until 2:13; and, though Bowman tried to date 1:29 to the beginning of pascal activities on the Sabbath prior to 2:13, neither the reference to "the third day" at 2:1 nor the time span designated by 1:29, 35, 43; 2:1, 12–13 permit such a move.[65] But this is also the case through the rest of the narrative: not all episodes that appear between one feast and the next (clearly) occur within the observance of the first. For four feasts they do: the events following the feast at 5:1, the Passover at 6:4, Tabernacles at 7:2 (if taken to 10:21) and the final Passover at 11:55 (to 19:42). But for the Passover at 2:13 and the Dedication at 10:22–23 this is not necessarily the case. At 3:22 Jesus ends his observance of the Passover at 2:13 by departing Jerusalem into Judea, then returning (through Samaria) to Galilee. Some of that time might be ascribed to lingering days of Azyma, but not all, since Jesus' reception among the Galileans at 4:45 indicates that, by the time he had arrived there, the feast had ended:

> When, therefore, (Jesus) came into Galilee, the Galileans received him,
> having seen everything he had done in Jerusalem during the feast,
> for they, themselves, went to the feast.

Likewise for the Dedication at 10:22–23. Jesus leaves Jerusalem for the Trans-Jordan at 10:40–42, where, after hearing Lazarus was ill (11:3–4), he waits two more days (11:5) and does not go to Bethany until Lazarus had been buried four days (11:17). Since the Feast of Dedication lasted eight days, it is conceivable that all of these events could have occurred within its span – if Jesus left Jerusalem after the first day of Dedication; and if he heard about Lazarus' ill health immediately upon his arrival in the Trans-Jordan. The more likely chronology, however, is that the Lazarus incident (11:1–54) occurred later, after the Feast of Dedication had ended.[66] By extending the hermeneutical reach of the Dedication to 11:54 – as well as the Passover at 2:13 to 4:54 – Mollat's assumptions take a liberty that narrative time cautions against.

---

[65] See the discussion in Chapter 2, under '2.1 The First Passover (John 2:13–3:21).'

[66] At the conclusion of the episode of raising Lazarus (and after the plot to kill Jesus had been launched), 11:55 notes that the next and final Passover "was near." But, though this could indicate that the raising of Lazarus took place closer to the upcoming Nisan (Passover) than to the previous Kislev (Dedication), the commentary between them that Jesus "was no longer walking openly among the Jews" and had gone from Bethany to Ephraim (11:54) allows otherwise.

Second, not all feasts in John provide commemorative or symbolic significance to the narrative.[67] Tabernacles (7:2–10:21), the final Passover (11:55–19:42) and the Passover at 6:4 (6:1–71) clearly do. And the first Passover (2:13–3:21), as well as the Dedication (10:22–39), arguably do: the former, perhaps, through the motifs of "consuming" (Jesus as) the paschal sacrifice (2:17)[68] or "cleansing" – homes from leaven (Exodus 12:15) and the "Father's house" from merchandise (2:16)[69]; the latter, as Mollat contends, through its association with "consecration" (10:36) and foreign encroachment (11:48).[70] The correlations of these last two, however, are tenuous and arbitrary: that which consumes Jesus according to 2:17 is zeal for the temple (not future opposition leading to crucifixion); Jesus' aggression toward corrupting vendors at 2:14–16 can just as aptly (if not better) be traced to the Feast of Dedication as to Passover[71]; the dominant motif in the Dedication narrative (10:22–39) is not, in fact, "consecration," but "shepherding" – a metaphor, which, if it is not altogether unrelated to the Dedication,[72] in any case spans both the Dedication and Tabernacles sections (10:1–21); and fear of foreign reprisal at 11:48 is not specific enough a sentiment to connote the Feast of Dedication unmistakably – on the basis of the same outlook in the next two verses (11:49–50) Johannes van Bebber read Caiaphas' prophecy that "one man die for the nation" to indicate the foreign aggression of Haman and connote Purim.[73]

But, even were commemorative symbolism for the Passover at 2:13 and the Dedication conceded, it is impossible to argue the same for the feast at 5:1, since it is unnamed. As noted above, exegetes have taken cues in the narrative to suggest it might be a number of festivals: Passover, Pentecost, Tabernacles, Remembrance, Purim.[74] But this very exercise proves the point being made here: for, if the feast at 5:1 can only be identified by first consulting its narrative, it can hardly be said (as Mollat argues) that its

---

[67] One can, also, argue conversely (from a broader vantage point than is done here) that not all episodes in John derive their meaning from the feasts in which they occur or under which they are categorized.

[68] Kerr 2002:85–86, 101, 207.

[69] Westcott 1954:1.90; followed by Donald D. Williford 1981:21–22.

[70] Further on the themes of consecration and nationalism in relation to the Feast of Dedication, see VanderKam 1990:205-207.

[71] See 1 Macc 4:36–59; 2 Macc 10:1–8.

[72] Perhaps on these grounds Robert Kysar declares that Jesus' pascal discourse at this juncture "explodes beyond the confines of the narrative setting"; 1989:66–67 (quotation p. 67). Regarding the motif of "consecration," Jean Giblet is more explicit: "certainly it is said (at 10:36) that the Father sanctified Jesus; but the allusion, if there is an allusion, is quite discrete and the entire immediate context does not favor it"; 1965:24.

[73] Van Bebber 1898:35–36; and, with Belser, 1907:10–12.

[74] See Chapter 2, under '2.2 The Unnamed Feast and a Second Passover (John 5:1–6:71).'

purpose was to provide an *a priori* symbolism that would help unlock the meaning of that narrative. As much is (implicitly) conceded by Mollat, himself, when he identifies John 5, not with the feast at which its events occur (5:1), but with the Sabbath that coincides with it (5:9). This is clear from the labels Mollat gives the chapter: *'The Sabbath of the Paralytic'* in his 1st and 2nd editions; 'The Second Feast: A Sabbath Day in Jerusalem,' in his 3rd. It is also manifest in the further remarks he makes in his commentary and outline: in the 1st and 2nd editions his notes focus on how, in John 5, "Jesus demonstrates that the Sabbath is fulfilled in the life-giving work of the Son of God"; and, though, in the 3rd edition, he more mechanically outlines the chapter under two sub-sections, he essentially conveys the same emphasis – the second sub-section is benignly titled, 'Discourse on the Work of the Son' (5:19–47); but the first is given the heading, 'Jesus heals a disabled man at Bethesda on the Sabbath' (5:1–18).[75]

Perhaps most telling about Mollat's hypothesis is that, in the outline of his 3rd edition, he effectively abandons it. Not in every aspect. He is, in fact, more consistent with that hypothesis – and more accurate to the narrative – when he transfers the resurrection day (chapter 20) from being a chief heading in its own right to being a subordinate category (with Jesus' Last Supper and the Passion) under the major heading *'The Hour of Jesus: The Passover of the Lamb of God'* (13:1–20:31). As noted above, Passover, broadly conceived to include Azyma, would, indeed, cover the events of that day. Apart from this, however, Mollat not only (a) maintains his identification of John 5 (only) with the Sabbath, but also (b) subordinates the first Passover (2:13–3:21), with six other subheadings, under a new chief heading, whose title has little or nothing to do with feasts – 'Announcement of the New Economy' (1:19–4:54); and (c) severs 11:55–12:50 from its previous association with the final Passover (*'The Passover of the Crucifixion'* [11:55–19:42]), re-labeling it with a title only tenuously related to feasts ('The End of Jesus' Public Ministry and Preliminaries of the Last Passover') and lifting it to equal status with the previous feasts (as well as with the 'Announcement of the New Economy') as one of six major headings dividing 1:19–12:50. By restructuring thus, Mollat diminishes the role of feasts as structural and hermeneutical factors to the narrative. Ironically, what began as "milestones" ("les jalons") of Johannine *kerygma* are now reduced to one group of elements among many, no more determi-

---

[75] The Sabbath at 9:14 also shares the heading with the Tabernacles section in Mollat's 1st and 2nd editions: *'The Feast of Tabernacles and the Sabbath of the Man Born Blind'* (7:2–10:21). Mollat's comments on that segment in those editions, however, as well as his more elaborate outline in the 3rd edition, make it clear that he perceives the narrative primarily to be inspired, not by that Sabbath (of 9:14), but by the motifs associated with the Feast of Tabernacles; see his comments in Table 3 and his outline under heading IV. 'The Feast of Tabernacles' (7:1–10:21) in Table 4.

native for the Fourth Gospel's structure and interpretation than the nine techniques he first criticized.

In sum, Mollat has rightly shown how some of the feasts in John furnish commemorative symbolism for christology and has further noticed that, as such, they may function as enduring facilitators to that christology rather than supersessionist foils to it. His sweeping idea that all the feasts operate this way, however, clashes with significant portions of the text: not all events occur during feasts in narrative time; not all feasts self evidently furnish imagery to the signs and discourses done within them; and Mollat, himself, did not interpret John 5 this way.

3.1.3 Symbols of 'the Final Reality Revealed in Jesus': Donald Williford

Mollat's thesis was taken up with more exegetical rigor by Donald D. Williford in an unpublished dissertation completed for Southwest Baptist Theological Seminary. Williford assumes the symbolic, christological role of feasts espoused by Mollat but goes further by bringing that role more consciously into the service of the Evangelist's stated purpose at 20:30–31. If the Evangelist's aim was to present Jesus as the promised messiah, the feasts furnish both the "organizational motif" on which that aim is structured and the symbolic context by which it is elucidated[76]:

> John's avowed intent is to present evidence which will convince men that
> Jesus is "the Christ, the Son of God" so that they might have eternal life.
> The Jewish religious feasts lend themselves as an appropriate means by which
> John can best accomplish his purpose...Each of these feasts offers a significant
> historical reference to the Jewish worship of God. In addition, each contains symbols
> which can be utilized in directing readers' minds to the divine involvement
> in the person and work of Jesus. The salvation and the blessings bestowed by God,
> in the events commemorated by these festivals, provide a context for seeing
> and understanding the salvation and blessings provided in Jesus.[77]

Pressing further, Williford defines this relationship between Johannine feasts and Jesus as decidedly supersessionist. "John sets out to establish Jesus' messiahship," he continues, "by showing how Jesus fulfills or replaces Jewish expectations or institutions."[78] And, more explicitly:

---

[76] Williford 1981:5–13, 234–36. For Williford's reliance on Mollat, see pages 6, 8, 12, 235.

[77] Williford 1981:235–236. His reference to Mollat is from Mollat 1973:40, quoted above.

[78] Williford 1981:11.

> The significance of the Jewish religious feasts to the interpretation
> of John is of primary importance. The person and ministry of Jesus
> represent the fulfillment and supercession of the greatest truths found
> in the feasts…The truths contained in the ritual of the Jewish feasts
> are symbolic of the final reality revealed in Jesus.[79]

On these assumptions Williford endeavors to identify just what it is the Johannine feasts convey about Jesus as the Christ. In a manner similar to Mollat's 2nd edition outline, he structures all the episodes from 2:13–21:25 around the six feasts: I. The First Passover (2:13–4:54); II. The Unnamed Feast (5:1–47); III. The Second Passover (6:1–71); IV. The Feast of Tabernacles (7:1–10:21); V. The Feast of Dedication (10:22–11:54); and VI. The Final Passover (11:55–21:25).[80] And on this structure, he works through the text in sequence, reviewing the background of each feast represented,[81] then noticing features in the narrative, which, in his judgment, allude to or reflect elements of the feasts under which they are categorized.

Williford's findings are numerous and located *passim* throughout his work. Their gist, however, can be assessed through two more manageable lines of inquiry. The first is to chart synopses of his reasoning and conclusions for the two sections that, according to the critique of Mollat (above), present some of the greatest challenges to such a hypothesis: the first Passover (2:13–4:54) and the Feast of Dedication (10:1–11:54). If it is alleged that all feasts in the Fourth Gospel serve to provide symbolism for christology, it is more difficult to demonstrate that for these two feasts than it is for the second Passover, Tabernacles and the final Passover. Targeting Williford's discussion of the first Passover and the Dedication, then, will allow us to test the strength of his theory at two of its most potentially vulnerable areas. The second line of inquiry is to review Williford's treatment of the feast at 5:1, which represents a departure from the approach he establishes for himself at the start (and which he otherwise follows consistently).

Regarding the first line of inquiry, Williford's treatments of the first Passover and the Feast of Dedication are graphed in Tables 5 and 6, respectively, below. The tables have three columns: the first (left column) lists the narrative units Williford treats for each feast; the second (middle column) indicates the festal features Williford perceives in each of those narrative units; and the third (right column) correlates those festal features

---

[79] Williford 1981:236.

[80] Unlike Mollat, Williford begins at 2:13 and does not treat 1:1–2:12; moreover, he includes Mollat's '*The Day of Resurrection*' (John 20) and '*Appendix*' (John 21) with 11:55–19:42, under the final Passover.

[81] Williford 1981:14–20, 124–33, 177–80.

(from the middle column) to aspects of the actual feasts to which they allegedly allude[82]:

Table 5: Donald D. Williford: The Passover at John 2:13–4:54

Episode in John	Feature in Text	Aspect/Element of Feast
• Temple Cleansing (2:13–25)	• Cleansing temple from corruptions on eve of Passover (2:14–17)	• Cleansing leaven from homes on eve of Passover (Exod 12:15; cf. 1 Cor 5:7)
	• The "strong messianic overtones of Jesus' actions & words"[83]	• Due to its association w/sundry redemptions, Passover in Rabbinic literature has a "messianic aspect"
	• Intimation of Jesus' redemptive death as pascal lamb (2:19)	• Slaughter of the pascal lamb
	• Intimation of resurrection (2:19): temple metaphor replaced by crop metaphor at 12:24; resurrection occurs on day first fruits of harvest were waved before God (20:1–23)	• Harvest begun & first fruits offered at Azyma
	• Jesus' miracles at feast (2:23–25)	• People's untrustworthy belief (2:24–25) reflects temporal messianic expectations

---

[82] See Williford 1981:20–65. In the following tables, all passages from John are referenced (whether done by Williford or not). Citations from Jewish Scriptures and other Jewish literature, by contrast, are noted only where Williford gives them. Repeated and formulaic items under 'Aspect/Element of Feast' express what appear to be Williford's unstated assumptions about parallels.

[83] The Lord "suddenly coming to his temple" (Mal 3:1–3); the quotation of messianic Psalm 69 (2:17; Ps 69:9); the Sonship implied in Jesus' reference to his "Father's house" (2:17); the allusion to "the Day of the Lord" (2:17; Zech 14:21); Jesus' implied intent to replace the cultic sacrificial system; the messianic test issued by the authorities' question (2:18); Jesus' two-fold response that (a) the authorities continue to destroy the current temple/his body and that (b) he would replace it with a messianic temple/risen body (2:19); Williford 1981:22–35.

Episode in John	Feature in Text	Aspect/Element of Feast
• Interview w/Nicodemus (2:23–3:21)	• Spiritual birth required to see or enter Kingdom of God (3:3–8)	• Birth from Abraham was the criterion for first deliverance from Egypt
	• Son of Man must be "lifted up" (3:14–15): belief brings eternal life	• Moses lifted up serpent in wilderness (Num 21:8–9): looking brings healing
	• Jesus' death (being "lifted up" [3:14]) allows participation in Kingdom of God	• Death of pascal lamb establishes Israelites as a community
	• God, like Abraham (Gen 22), gave his only-begotten Son (3:16)	• In *Jubilees*, Abraham offers Isaac during Passover
	• Darkness & light imagery (3:19–21)	• In *Mishnah*, God is praised because at Passover he brought Jews out of darkness into light
	• Judgment for unbelief (3:18–20)	• Destruction if pascal rubrics not obeyed during first Passover
• Witness of John (3:22–36)	• John's appearance as Elijah (Matt 17:11–13)	• In Jewish tradition Elijah will return (Mal 4:5) on Passover
	• John confirms Jesus' words to Nicodemus on eternal life by believing (3:33, 36)	• Passover commemorates deliverance from Egypt
• Interview w/Samaritan Woman (4:1–42)	• Living water – Jesus' teaching, Holy Spirit or (likely) both – is an offer of spiritual deliverance (4:10–15)	• Passover commemorates deliverance from Egypt
	• "Salvation (that is, the Messiah) is from the Jews" (4:22)	• Due to its association w/sundry redemptions, Passover in Rabbinic literature has a "messianic aspect"
	• Jesus' proverb of "messianic harvest" (4:35; Amos 9:13)	• Due to its association w/sundry redemptions, Passover in Rabbinic literature has a "messianic aspect"

Episode in John	Feature in Text	Aspect/Element of Feast
• Interview w/Samaritan Woman (4:1–42) (continued)	• John is among those who had previously "sown" (4:37–38)	• In Jewish tradition Elijah will return (Mal 4:5) on Passover
	• Jesus' weariness, thirst & determination to fulfill Father's will (4:6–7, 32) have linguistic & thematic parallels in Passion	• Allusion to pascal death in Passion episode
	• Jesus as "Savior of the world" (4:42)	• Due to its association w/sundry redemptions, Passover in Rabbinic literature has a "messianic aspect"
• Healing Son of Nobleman (4:43–54)	• Reference to earlier feast (4:45)	• Healing of nobleman's son can be interpreted in light of Jesus' temple cleansing & discourse at 1st Passover (2:13–22)
	• Nobleman & his house believe (4:50, 53)	• Israelites obey during first Passover at exodus
	• Jesus' healing of son at point of death (4:47) connotes messianic deliverance from sin & death	• Passover commemorates deliverance from Egypt

With respect to the Feast of Dedication, Williford circumscribes it on the whole to 10:22–11:54 but tentatively includes 10:1–21, due to an ambiguity he perceives in the motifs and structure of this section. On the one hand, 10:1–21 betrays literary and thematic ties to the healing of the man born blind (9:1–41) and, by its criticism of bad shepherds, connotes a motif of judgment redolent of Tabernacles, the preceding feast (7:2). On the other hand, it abruptly changes the metaphors of sight/blindness in chapter 9 to those of sheep/shepherding, finds those shepherding metaphors sustained into the Feast of Dedication section at 10:26–29 and, by virtue of those same shepherding metaphors, reflects readings slated for the Feast of Dedication in the Jewish lectionary.[84] Williford arbitrates this ambiguity by treating 10:1–21 as a transitional passage, at once looking "backward to

---

[84] Williford 1981:171–76, 181–186.

the preceding Tabernacles material" and looking "forward to the Dedication following it."[85]

Table 6: Donald D. Williford: The Feast of Dedication at John 10:1–11:54

Episode in John	Feature in Text	Aspect/Element of Feast
• Shepherd Discourse (10:1–21)	• Jesus uses shepherd metaphors to define his messiahship over against Pharisees (10:1–21)[86]	• Commemoration of Maccabees incited nationalist hopes among Jews for political messiah
• Shepherd Discourse (10:22–42)	• Jesus uses shepherd metaphors to disabuse Jews' nationalist notion of his messiahship (10:24–30)	• Lectionary readings for Dedication contain themes of sheep/shepherding (Gen 46:28–47:31; Ezek 34:1–31; 37:16–24). • Commemoration of Maccabees incited nationalist hopes among Jews for political messiah
	• Jesus tells Jews they do not belong to his sheep & that none of his sheep will perish from out of his or his Father's hands (10:25–30)	• Lectionary reading for Dedication contains themes of the Lord seeking his flock, God judging the sheep & Shepherd–Messiah of God's flock (Ezek 34:1–31)
	• Jesus speaks of himself & the Father as "one" (10:27–30)	• Lectionary reading for Dedication contains theme of "the unity of the prophet w/ God" (Ezek 37:16–24)

---

[85] Williford 1981:175. For Table 6, see Williford 1981:169–76, 180–89. Question marks in parentheses (?) indicate my own uncertain inferences about connections Williford makes in his discussion. Also, in view of the critique to follow, references to lectionary readings in the right hand column (of Tables 6 and 7) represent Williford's dependence on the work of Aileen Guilding.

[86] On the premise that 10:1–21 relates as much to the Feast of Dedication (introduced after it) as it does to Tabernacles (before it), Williford here interprets 10:1–21 in light of the question about Jesus' messiahship at 10:24; cf. 1981:183.

Episode in John	Feature in Text	Aspect/Element of Feast
• Shepherd Discourse (10:22–42) (continued)	• Jesus refers to himself as "the one whom the Father sanctified" (10:36)	• The verb "sanctified" is a synonym of the word used for "the Dedication"; Jesus has already been cast as the true temple (2:19) and tabernacle (1:14)
	• Jews charge Jesus w/ blasphemy (10:31–33)	• Lectionary reading for Dedication is *locus classicus* for blasphemy (Lev 24:1– 25:13)
• Raising of Lazarus (11:1–44)	• [Lazarus' death & resurrection (11:11–15, 38–44)]	• ["The themes of death and resurrection have already been shown to be appropriate to Passover"][87]
	• Jesus calls Lazarus from tomb (11:43–44); Lazarus as sheep who hears Jesus' voice & follows him (10:4–5, 27)	• Lectionary readings for Dedication apply (?), containing themes of sheep/shepherding (Gen 46:28–47:31; Ezek 34:1–31; 37:16–24)
	• Jesus risks/lays down his own life to raise Lazarus (11:8–16, 45–52) as Good Shepherd, laying down his life for the sheep (10:11–18)	• Lectionary readings for Dedication apply (?), containing themes of sheep/shepherding (Gen 46:28–47:31; Ezek 34:1–31; 37:16–24)

---

[87] Here Williford allows the raising of Lazarus possibly to be identified with the final Passover at 11:55; 1981:186–87. In his earlier discussions of the first and second Passovers Williford had associated Passover with the themes of death and resurrection through (a) the required slaughter of the pascal lamb; (b) the deliverance from death offered by the serpent lifted up in the wilderness (Num 21:8–9); (c) Abraham's offering of Isaac on Passover in *Jubilees*; (d) the stress on mortality evident in first year Passover lectionary readings (Gen 2; Isa 51); (e) the motif of deliverance celebrated in the exodus story; (f) the association of resurrection with the grain harvest, begun at Azyma (12:24; 20:1–23); and (g) the eschatological messianic banquet (Isa 25:6–8, 19; 55:1–3; 65:11–13) anticipated in the celebration of Passover. See 1981:37–38, 41–46, 60–61, 63–64, 96, 99–104, 115–16.

Episode in John	Feature in Text	Aspect/Element of Feast
• Raising of Lazarus (11:1–44) (continued)	• Jesus' resurrection of Lazarus is sign that answers to Jesus' declaration that he will give his sheep life & they will never perish (10:27–28)	• Lectionary reading for Dedication applies (?), which contains themes of the Lord seeking his flock, God judging the sheep & Shepherd-Messiah of God's flock (Ezek 34:1–31)
• Plot to Kill Jesus (11:45–54)	• Pharisees fear Rome's reprisal for Jesus upon temple & nation (11:47–48)	• Feast of Dedication generates spirit of "liberation politique et religieuse" (citing Mollat)
	• Caiaphas prophesies it was expedient for Jesus to die for people (11:49–50); Jesus cast as Good Shepherd, laying down his life for the sheep (10:11–18)	• Lectionary readings for Dedication apply (?), containing themes of sheep/shepherding (Gen 46:28–47:31; Ezek 34:1–31; 37:16–24)
	• Commentary on Caiaphas' prophecy declares Jesus' death would gather children of God scattered abroad into one (11:51–52); Jesus cast as Shepherd who gathers sheep into one unified flock (10:16)	• Lectionary readings for Dedication apply (?), containing themes of sheep/shepherding (Gen 46:28–47:31; Ezek 34:1–31; 37:16–24)

As for the second line of inquiry into Williford's work – his treatment of the feast at 5:1 – Williford does invest effort in deducing that feast's christological implications; but, perhaps out of necessity, he devotes just as much attention to determining its identity. After reviewing a plethora of arguments (that it is Passover, Tabernacles, Pentecost, Purim and/or Trumpets/Remembrance) – and after rehearsing several themes attached to the sign and discourse of John 5 – he makes a two-fold judgment, the second part of which effectively eclipses the first. First, he concludes that, though all the feasts reviewed are possible, the themes in John 5 render only two likely: Passover and Trumpets. Details of the connections he sees are charted below[88]:

---

[88] Williford 1981: 67–90.

Table 7: Donald D. Williford: The Anonymous Feast at John 5:1–47

Episode in John	Feature in Text	Aspect/Element of Feast
• The Sign (5:1–18)	• Healing of lame man was "a messianic sign" of deliverance	• Passover: due to its association w/sundry redemptions, Passover in Rabbinic literature has a "messianic aspect"; Passover commemorates deliverance from Egypt
	• By healing on Sabbath (5:9), Jesus shows himself Lord over it (Mark 2:28) & suggests Sabbath of Messianic age has begun	• (Possibly Pentecost: [inferior] giving of law [& therefore Sabbath] associated w/Pentecost)
	• Jesus' defense that he was working as his Father was working (5:17) claims messiahship as Son of God	• Passover: due to its association w/sundry redemptions, Passover in Rabbinic literature has "messianic aspect"
• The Discourse (5:19–47)	• Jesus' working w/his Father (5:17, 19–23, 26–27, 30) forms "an intimate unity" that implies Messiahship	• Passover: due to its association w/sundry redemptions, Passover in Rabbinic literature has "messianic aspect"
	• As Son of God & Son of Man, Jesus messianically gives life & brings judgment (5:21–22, 24–29)	• Passover: *Mishnah* associates Passover w/judgment
		• Trumpets: *Mishnah* also ties judgment to Trumpets (*Roš. Haš.*); Jewish lectionary readings for this date stress judgment (Deut 1; 30:17–19; 32:36; Jer 30:11,18; Ezek 18:30), sometimes in conjunction w/life-giving (Isa 26:19; Hos 13:14)
		• (Possibly Pentecost: *Mishnah* also ties judgment to Pentecost)
		• (Possibly Tabernacles: *lulab* connotes ideas of immortality & victory; *Mishnah* ties judgment to Tabernacles)

Episode in John	Feature in Text	Aspect/Element of Feast
• The Discourse (5:19–47) (continued)	• Jesus is attested to be messiah by John, his own signs, the Father (in the law) & Moses (in the law)	• Passover: in Jewish tradition Elijah (John) will return (Mal 4:5) on Passover; Moses led people to celebrate Passover as com-memoration of deliv-erance • Trumpets: *Mishnah* discusses validity of father/son witnesses for establishing new moon (on which Trumpets would fall); lectionary readings for this date show a "wit-ness" theme – Moses testifies against Israel (Deut 31:19, 21, 26, 28) • (Possibly Tabernacles: law read every seventh year)

Second (and conversely) for 5:1, Williford concludes that, since John 5 betrays features relevant to several feasts (and since some exegetes are convinced that the identity of its feast cannot be determined anyway), the purpose of the feast at 5:1 may only have been to show how festivals coming later in the narrative would, themselves, inform the Fourth Gospel's christology:

> In light of the introductory nature of chapter 5 and the ability
> to find significance for this chapter in several identifications of the feast,
> it is possible that John's reference to this feast was intentionally vague.
> The purpose for this vagueness may have been that he might suggest
> the appropriateness of finding significance in each of the religious feasts
> to Jesus' person and work. This solution is one possible reason why
> the identity of the unnamed feast is difficult. The unnamed feast then
> contains items of significance to Jesus' ministry appropriate to a number of feasts.
> In the chapters that follow, John specifies the significance of some
> of the particular feasts to Jesus' person and work.[89]

---

[89] Williford 1981: 89–90, quotation p. 90. A similar conclusion has more recently been made by Kerr 2002:207.

Williford leaves himself open to several basic criticisms. First, his posture toward lectionary approaches is inconsistent. In his introduction he states that his "emphasis" will not be "upon Jesus' sermons or upon a system of lectionary readings," such as that advocated by Aileen Guilding.[90] In the body of his exegesis, however, he generously appeals to Guilding's lections, particularly when they support his supposition that every episode in the gospel is informed by the feast under which it is categorized.[91] Second, Williford's dependence on Mollat's 3rd edition for his supersessionism is ill-informed. In partial support of his supersessionist starting point, Williford cites the 3rd edition passage quoted above, under the treatment of Mollat:

> But specifically, there was not a more appropriate context for the manifestation
> of the mystery of Christ than the great, Jewish liturgical celebrations,
> during which the people of God, gathered from all parts of the world,
> revived the consciousness of their calling.[92]

As has already been noted, however, this passage from Mollat's 3rd edition does not articulate a supersessionist position but, in fact, represents Mollat's correction of his earlier supersessionism, espoused in his 1st and 2nd editions.[93] Finally, Williford's association of John the Baptist with Elijah in John[94] is mistaken. He is correct that such an identification exists among the Synoptics[95]; but he seems unaware that, in the Fourth Gospel, the figure of John denies such an association, without correction (1:21, 24–25).

Further – and more important to the issue at hand – inasmuch as Williford shares Mollat's thesis that all feasts in John furnish christological symbolism for all parts of the narrative, his work displays the same two problems as did that of Mollat. First, he associates elements of 3:22–4:54 and 10:40–11:54 with feasts that, in narrative time, had likely ended.[96] The first Passover at 2:13 in all probability covered only the events of 2:13–3:21; yet, to it Williford ascribes no less than eleven items from the events in 3:22–4:54. Similarly, the Feast of Dedication probably covered only the activities of 10:22–39; yet, to it Williford ascribes no less than eight items from the events in 10:40–11:54 (and 10:1–21).

---

[90] Williford 1981:6.

[91] Cf. Williford 1981:86–89, 96, 113–15, 139–40, 149–50, 162–64, 166–69, 184–86; cf. the references to lectionary readings in Tables 6 and 7 above.

[92] Mollat 1973:40; cf. Williford 1981:235.

[93] See above, under '3.1.2 'Les jalons de ce récit,' Donatien Mollat.'

[94] Williford 1981:48–49, 60, 84, 237.

[95] For his point, Williford cites Matt 17:11–13; see also Matt 11:13–14; Mark 9:11–13; Luke 1:16–17.

[96] Here again see above, under '3.1.2 'Les jalons de ce récit,' Donatien Mollat.'

Second, as was at points the case with Mollat, so with Williford: he connects feasts to episodes on forced deductions. Indeed, more so than Mollat. Because Williford works this theory out by close exegesis of the text (where Mollat stated it abstractly in prolegomena), Williford throughout finds himself compelled into inferences that are altogether tenuous and circuitous. Using his treatment of the Passover at 2:13 (Table 5) as an example – to that Passover he ties the following verses on the following bases: (1) 3:3–8, on the grounds that the spiritual rebirth of which these verses speak answers to the natural birth from Abraham required for participation in the exodus Passover; (2) 3:14, on the idea that Jesus' crucifixion (to which that verse alludes) would allow participation in the Kingdom of God in the same way the death of the pascal lamb had done for membership in Israel; (3) 3:16, on the premise that its sentiment of God giving his only-begotten son draws upon the *Jubilees* '*Aqedah* (*Jub.* 17:15–18:18), which dates to Passover[97]; (4) 3:18–20, on the notion that its predication of judgment for unbelief parallels the exodus threat of death to the first-born for any Israelite who did not observe Passover rubrics in Egypt; (5) 4:43–54 (the healing of the official's son), on the premise that the faith of the official and his household reflects the obedience of Israelites coming out of Egypt; (6) 4:6–7, 32 on the grounds that this expression of Jesus' fatigue, thirst and determination to do his Father's will in the Samaritan episode anticipates his similar suffering and resolve during the final Passover (at 19:28–30); and – most labyrinthine – (7) 2:19, on the two-fold premise that (a) its intimation of Jesus' death under the metaphor of the destroyed temple anticipates his death under the metaphor of the pascal lamb during the final Passover at 11:55 and (b) its tandem intimation of Jesus' resurrection under the metaphor of the rebuilt temple anticipates his resurrection during the Feast of Azyma (20:1–23) – this through the intervening association of resurrection with grain harvest at 12:24.

On this same assumption (that all feasts in John furnish symbolism for all parts of the narrative), Williford arrives at a quite problematic position on the unnamed feast at 5:1. Unable to decide which festival it is, he argues that its many possibilities render it an undefined, generic paradigm for how subsequent feasts will more precisely inform their narratives – specifically, those from chapters 5–10.[98] But, even were that idea accepted, the question arises as to why such an instructional paradigm would come at this juncture in the Fourth Gospel. That is, if the purpose of the feast at 5:1 is to demonstrate how the hermeneutical connection between feasts and text works, why is it placed after the first instance of such a connection has already occurred, the Passover at 2:13?

---

[97] Here Williford follows van Goudoever 1961:68; cf. Williford 1981:45–46.
[98] Williford 1981:89–90.

Further, Williford makes many of his correlations between feasts and texts on motifs, which, in themselves, are too broad to be considered peculiarly festal themes. Particularly does he do this with "messianism" and "deliverance." He ties 2:13–22; 2:23–25; 4:22, 35, 42 to the Passover at 2:13 on the premise that, in Rabbinic literature, the "messianic aspect" found in them is associated with Passover[99]; he joins 10:1–21, 24–30 to the Feast of Dedication at 10:22–23 on the (similar) grounds that the pastoral messianism expressed through those verses corrected the political messianism incited by memory of the Maccabees; he links 3:33, 36; 4:10–15, 47 to the Passover at 2:13 on the premise that the soteriological aspects of those verses allude to Passover's commemoration of deliverance from Egypt; and he connects 11:47–48 to the Feast of Dedication on the (like) grounds that the soteriological aspects in those verses allude to the spirit of political and religious liberation recalled in the Maccabean Revolt. While such themes could have been assimilated into the symbolism of any one or more Jewish feasts,[100] they, themselves, were not exclusively festal ideas. They circulated (and could be expressed) as much outside festal contexts as they did (could) within them; and, as such, their presence in the narrative ought not be taken *ipso facto* (as Williford does) to indicate festal connotations.

Williford, in fact, effectively undermines his own hypothesis by ascribing these broad themes to several feasts at once. A wider review of his work shows that he assigns both "messianism" and "deliverance," not only to Passover[101] and the Dedication,[102] but also to Tabernacles.[103] Inasmuch as, on Williford's terms, each of these themes can indicate any of the feasts just listed, their presence in one passage can theoretically associate that

---

[99] For 2:23–25 Williford adds the more tenuous idea that the untrustworthiness of those who believed Jesus in these verses reflected temporal messianic expectations; 1981:38–39.

[100] See, for instance, the possible messianic connotation implied in the connection between the "sanctification" (ἡγίασεν) of Jesus at John 10:36 and the language of "sanctification" (LXX ἡγίασεν), "dedication" (חָנֻכָּה) and "anointing" (מָשַׁח) in Num 7:1, 10, 84, 88), noticed by James C. VanderKam (1990:206–207). VanderKam inadvertently references Leviticus in his second mention of the chapter (p. 207).

[101] For "messianism" and Passover: the first Passover (Williford 1981:22–36, 38–39, 57–59, 61); Passover as an option for the unnamed feast at 5:1 (1981:73–84); the second Passover (1981:99–107, 116); and the last Passover (1981:193–95, 197–99, 218–22). For "deliverance" and Passover: the first Passover (1981:49–57, 62–64); Passover as an option for the unnamed feast at 5:1 (1981:73–84); the second Passover (1981:115–16); and the last Passover (1981:197–99, 207–208, 230–31).

[102] For "messianism" and the Dedication (Williford 1981:181–83); for "deliverance" and the Dedication (1981:187–89).

[103] For "messianism" and Tabernacles (Williford 1981:134–36, 140–45, 152–56, 159–64, 166, 169–71), including Tabernacles as an option for the unnamed feast at 5:1 (1981:73–82, 84–85). For "deliverance" and Tabernacles (1981:158–59).

locus with a feast quite remote from it (rather than the one just prior to it) in the narrative. Williford, in fact, admits as much, when he notes that the themes of death and resurrection in the Lazarus story, which in his outline fall under the Feast of Dedication (10:22–11:54), "have already been shown to be appropriate to Passover."[104]

In all, Williford's exegesis exemplifies (and amplifies) some of the problems at the heart of Mollat's prolegomena. On the assumption that all feasts symbolically inform the whole (or most) of the Johannine narrative, he ascribes elements in 3:22–4:54 and 10:40–11:54 to feasts that, in narrative time, had already ended; he joins festal features to textual elements on criteria that are dubious, circuitous or overly broad; he offers no plausible way of integrating John 5 into his guiding assumptions; and, by virtue of his close exegetical approach, he magnifies these difficulties in number and degree.

3.1.4 Johannine 'Takkanot': Gale A. Yee

Gale A. Yee has offered no new hypothesis for the feasts: for her, as for her predecessors, feasts appear in the Fourth Gospel so that, in the course of the narrative, the symbolism and ideas attached to them may be transferred to Jesus.[105] Yee's contribution, rather, lies in two related matters: her more nuanced understanding of the milieu in which this purpose would have been wrought; and her choice to broach the relevant texts topically rather than sequentially, including among them passages on the Sabbath.

In her introduction, Yee argues that the motive driving the Fourth Gospel's use of feasts was the Johannine community's need to craft its identity in the wake of the temple's destruction and over against Tannaitic modifications. She notes that, among the *takkanot* of Joḥanan ben Zakkai were synagogal adaptations of Passover, Tabernacles, the Sabbath and the New Moon; and, referencing J. Louis Martyn's thesis that the Fourth Gospel was written in response to the *Birkat Hamminim*,[106] she infers that this 'Blessing Regarding the Sects' would have presented the Johannine community with a peculiar challenge regarding those same feasts. How would Johannine Christians adapt Jewish festivals to their own community now, given their *de facto* expulsion from the synagogue?[107]

---

[104] Williford 1981:186–87.

[105] Yee 1989:27, 30.

[106] Martyn 1979.

[107] Yee 1989:16–26. Being abreast of refinements to Louis Martyn's thesis, Yee notes that this challenge would have come more from Johannine perceptions than it did from Tannaitic ill will; see 1989:22–24 and, for the critique of J. Louis Martyn on which Yee relies, the bibliography on p. 23n8.

The Johannine Christians responded to that challenge, argues Yee, by endowing the feasts with a "replacement theology"; that is, by applying them to Christ analogously to the way the Tannaim adapted them to the synagogue:

> Just as the Pharisees under Yoḥanan ben Zakkai respond to the destruction
> of the temple by adapting its liturgical feasts to the synagogue,
> so does John respond to the loss of the synagogue by reinterpreting
> the Jewish liturgical calendar in light of the person Jesus.[108]

Unfortunately, Yee continues, this was done (as was the *Birkat Hamminim* among the Tannaim) to separate rather than reintegrate themselves into the community with which they were in conflict:

> Sadly, the model of self-definition behind both these adaptations is formulated in
> terms of "in distinction from." In the case of Pharisaic Judaism, liturgical changes
> are made "in distinction from" the *minim* (heretics), which included Jewish
> Christianity. In the case of John and the Johannine community, reinterpretation of the
> Jewish liturgical calendar is made "in distinction from" the Jewish community.
> For John, Jesus replaces and abrogates the traditional feasts of the Jews. [109]

The body of Yee's work addresses the substance of this replacement theology, treating successively of the Sabbath (5:1–47; 7:14–24; 9:1–41), the Feast of Passover (2:13–25; 6:1–71; 13:1–19:42), the Feast of Tabernacles (7:1–8:59) and the Feast of Dedication (10:22–42). For each – similar to, but more insightfully than, Williford – she rehearses the biblical/early Judaic background, then demonstrates how the Johannine narrative transfers something from that background to the person of Jesus.

For the Sabbath, (1) Jesus' claim in chapter 5 to have broken it because he was emulating the Father's work of giving life and judgment (5:21–23) transfers to him the Pharisaic/Rabbinic idea that, on Sabbath, God does not cease from moral governance.[110] (2) In 7:14–24, Jesus' teaching in the temple (7:14), as well as his argument that Sabbath observance should be waived as much for healing as for circumcision (7:23), apply to him the Pharisaic/Rabbinic tradition that priestly work and circumcision, respectively, "took priority even over the Sabbath."[111] And (3) in 9:1–41, Jesus' two Sabbath violations – healing someone whose life was in no immediate danger and "kneading" spittle and clay – are sanctioned as divinely

---

[108] Yee 1989:16, 26–27; quotation p. 27.

[109] Yee 1989:27.

[110] *B. Ta'an.* 2a; *Gen. Rab.* 11.10 (on Gen 2:3); Yee 1989:38, 41.

[111] For priestly work, *m. Tem.* 2:1; for circumcision, *m. Šabb.* 18:3; 19:1. Yee 1989:36–37, 42–43; quotation p. 36.

wrought by the catchword language of "work" (ἔργον/ἔργα) at 9:3–4 (and, by recollection, 5:17 and 7:21)[112]:

Table 8. Gale A. Yee: 'Work' in the Sabbaths of John 5 and 9

John 5:17	John 7:21	John 9:3–4
But Jesus answered them, "My Father is working (ἐργάζεται) until now; and I, myself, am working (ἐργάζομαι)."	Jesus answered and said to them, "One work (ἓν ἔργον) I did and you all marvel."	Jesus answered, "Neither this man sinned nor his parents; but (this occurred) that God's *works* (τὰ ἔργα) might be manifest in him. We must *work* the *works* (ἐργάζεσθαι τὰ ἔργα) of him who sent me as long as it is day. Night comes when no one can *work* (ἐργάζεσθαι)."

Regarding Passover, in the first of the three to appear (2:13), Jesus replaces the temple, both by using Zechariah 14:21 to criticize its animals as "merchandise" (οἶκον ἐμπορίου; 2:16) and by predicting his resurrected body to constitute a temple in and of itself (2:19).[113] In the second Passover (6:4), Jesus replaces Moses (and manna) by replicating Mosaic acts and experiences: ascending a mountain[114]; encountering a need beyond resource[115]; providing miraculously in the face of that need – including the offer of himself as the new bread from heaven[116]; being regarded as "the prophet" like Moses[117]; crossing the Sea of Tiberias as Moses did the Sea of Reeds[118]; and facing "murmuring" from both crowd and disciples.[119] And, in the third Passover (chapters 13–19), Jesus replaces the pascal lambs by being crucified on the day those lambs were slaughtered[120]; by receiving vinegar on hyssop, the branch prescribed for applying the blood

---

[112] For healing someone not in immediate mortal danger, *b. Yoma* 85b; cf. *Mek.* on Exod 31:13 [*Šabbata'* 1.17-19]; for "kneading," *m. Šabb.* 7:2; Yee 1989:36–37, 43–46. Italics in 9:3–4 in Table 8 are as per Yee, p. 44.

[113] Yee 1989:60–63.

[114] John 6:3; cf. Exod 19:3, 20; 24:9–13.

[115] John 6:5; cf. Num 11:13.

[116] Manna/bread; 6:35–40, 49–50.

[117] John 6:14; cf. Deut 18:15–22.

[118] John 6:16–21; cf. Yee correctly quotes Ps 77:20–21 but mistakenly cites 77:18–19 as the reference.

[119] John 6:41, 61; Exod 16:2, 7–8; on these replacements in the second Passover, Yee 1989:64–67.

[120] John 18:28; cf. 1:29.

of Passover lambs to doorposts[121]; by being spared the breaking of his bones, as was prescribed for the preparation of the Passover lambs[122]; and by having blood and water pour out of his side, as the blood of pascal lambs would do onto the altar (19:34).[123]

For Tabernacles – as one would expect – Jesus' pronouncements of himself as the source of living waters (so taking 7:38) and light of the world (8:12) associate him with the libation and illumination rites,[124] as well as the eschatological and exodus symbolism associated with them – specifically, symbolism of the eschatological new temple[125] and the rock in the wilderness.[126] Also, the messianic discourse and deliberations that occur in the middle (7:25–31) and on the last day (7:40–43) of Tabernacles similarly apply to Jesus certain eschatological and exodus messianic expectations associated with that feast.[127] And, finally, for the Dedication. Yee admits that, "unlike the other feasts we have studied in the Fourth Gospel, the connections between Jesus' discourses and (this) feast are not so readily apparent."[128] Nonetheless she finds two: first, the scene's setting in the temple (10:23), as well as Jesus' claim to have been the one "whom the Father consecrated" (10:36), recall Judas Maccabee's rededication of the temple[129]; second, the ostensible idolatry effected by Jesus' self-identification as "one" with the Father (10:30–31) brings to mind Antiochus Epiphanes' institution of false worship in that same temple.[130]

Charted, Yee's conclusions are as follows:

---

[121] John 19:29; cf. Exod 12:22.

[122] John 19:36; cf. Exod 12:46.

[123] On these replacements in the third Passover, Yee 1989:67–68.

[124] *M. Sukk.* 4:9; 5:2–4.

[125] Zech 14:6–9; Ezek 47:1–5; Ps 118:27; *m. Šeqal.* 6:3; *m. Mid.* 2:6; *m. Sukk* 5:2–4; cf. *t. Sukk* 3.3–9.

[126] Exod 17:1–7; Num 20:8–13; *t. Sukk* 3.11–12; *Qoh. Rab.* 1:9 §1 (though Yee cites 1:8); Yee 1989:73–77, 79–81.

[127] Zech 14:16–19; *Qoh. Rab.* 1:9 §1; Yee 1989:73, 78–79, 81.

[128] Yee 1989:88.

[129] 1 Macc 4:36–59; 2 Macc 10:1–8.

[130] Yee 1989:83–86, 89–91. On this point Yee was anticipated by VanderKam 1990:210–14; and now see the more elaborate parallels between Antiochus IV and John 10–11 suggested by Kerr 2002:252–53.

Table 9. Gale A. Yee: Sabbath, Passover, Tabernacles & Dedication in John

Feast/Holy Day	Biblical/Early Judaic Background	Replacement in Christ
Sabbath	• God's moral governance on Sabbath (*b. Ta'an.* 2a; *Gen. Rab.* 11.10 [on Gen 2:3]) • Priority of priestly duties (*m. Tem.* 2:1) and circumcision (*m. Šabb.* 18:3; 19:1) to Sabbath • Prohibitions against healing someone in no immediate mortal danger (*b. Yoma* 85b; cf. *Mek.* on Exod 31:13 [*Šabbata'* 1.17-19]) and kneading (*m. Šabb.* 7:2) on Sabbath	• Jesus breaks Sabbath to emulate Father's work of giving life and judgment (5:21–23) • Jesus teaches in the temple (7:14) • Jesus argues for priority of healing to Sabbath on precedent of circumcision (7:23) • Jesus' healing by kneading spittle & clay on Sabbath is authorized as divinely sanctioned "work" (9:3–4; cf. 5:17; 7:21)
Passover	• Temple and its animal sacrifices • Moses § Ascends mountain (Exod 19:3,20; 24:9–13) § Encounters need beyond resource (Num 11:13) § Provides manna	• 1st Passover : § Jesus criticizes sacrificial animals as "merchandise" (2:16; cf. Zech 14:21) § Jesus defines his resurrected body as a new temple (2:19) • 2nd Passover: Jesus replicates Moses § Ascends mountain (6:3) § Encounters need beyond resource (6:5) § Provides (bread & fish) miraculously in the face of that need; offers himself as new bread from heaven (6:35–40, 49–50)

Feast/Holy Day	Biblical/Early Judaic Background	Replacement in Christ
Passover (continued)	• Moses (continued)	• 2nd Passover: Jesus replicates Moses (continued)
	§ Similar prophet predicted (Deut 18:15–22)	§ Regarded as prophet like Moses (6:14)
	§ Crosses Sea of Reeds (Ps 77:20–21)	§ Crosses the Sea of Tiberias as Moses did the Sea of Reeds (6:16–21)
	§ Faces "murmuring" from people (Exod 16:2, 7–8)	§ Faces "murmuring" from crowd & disciples (6:41, 61)
	• Pascal lambs	• 3rd Passover: Jesus replicates pascal lambs
	§ Slaughtered 14 Nisan (cf. Exod 12:6)	§ Crucified on 14 Nisan (18:28)
	§ Blood applied with hyssop (Exod 12:22)	§ Receives vinegar on hyssop (19:29)
	§ Bones not to be broken (Exod 12:46)	§ Spared the breaking of bones (19:36)
	§ Blood poured out onto altar	§ Blood & water pour out of side (19:34)
Tabernacles	• Libation (*m.Sukk* 4:9) § Eschatological new temple symbolism (Zech 14:6–9; Ezek 47:1–5; Ps 118:27; *m. Šeqal.* 6:3; *m. Mid.* 2:6; *m. Sukk.* 5:2–4; cf. *t. Sukk* 3.3–9) § Exodus rock in the wilderness symbolism (Exod 17:1–7; Num 20:8–13; *t. Sukk* 3.11–12; *Qoh. Rab.* 1:9 §1)	• Jesus declares himself the source of living waters (7:38)
	• Illumination rite (*m. Sukk* 5:2–4): eschatological new temple symbolism	• Jesus proclaims himself light of the world (8:12)
	• Eschatological (Zech 14:16–19) and exodus (*Qoh. Rab.* 1:9 §1) messianic expectations	• Discourse & deliberations on Jesus as messiah (7:25–31, 40–43)

Feast/Holy Day	Biblical/Early Judaic Background	Replacement in Christ
Dedication	• Rededication of temple by Judas Maccabee (1 Macc 4:36–59; 2 Macc 10:1–8) • Idolatry in temple by Antiochus Epiphanes	• Jesus walking "in Solomon's Portico" (10:23) • Jesus claims to be the one "whom the Father consecrated" (10:36) • Jesus identifies himself as one with the Father (10:30–31)

Yee's study is cautious, informed and insightful; and her inclusion of Sabbath texts, besides enjoying biblical support (as she notes),[131] enhances the *halakhic* and typological contexts in which the Johannine feasts can ultimately be understood.[132] That said, however, her discussion falters on at least three points. The first has already been said of Mollat and, especially, Williford: her assumption that all feasts in John function to render commemorative symbolism to Johannine christology causes many of the key connections she makes between that symbolism and the Johannine Jesus to be tenuous or confused. This comes especially to the fore in her treatment of the first and second Passovers, Tabernacles and the Feast of Dedication.[133] Regarding her treatment of the first Passover (2:13–22): as a feast, Passover is not so peculiarly tied to temple and cult as to lend festal connotations self-evidently to Jesus' critique (and forecasted replacement) of the temple at 2:16, 19. If Passover was a pilgrimage festival, requiring presence at the temple, so also were Pentecost and Tabernacles (Deut 16:16). Moreover, if any festival did have an intimate affiliation with temple and cult, it was not Passover but Tabernacles. As Yee is well aware,[134] Tabernacles is the feast on which the first and second temples were consecrated[135]; and, at least in the conception of 2 Maccabees, Tabernacles was (somehow) the template on which was patterned the Feast of Dedication –

---

[131] Lev 23:1–3; see Yee 1989:33.

[132] See now the treatment of Johannine Sabbaths along with feasts by Kerr (2002:255–66), in relation to the temple.

[133] Regarding the final Passover (at chapters 13–19), the association Yee makes between Jesus' blood and water pouring from his side (19:34) and the blood of the pascal sacrifice being poured out on the altar is overdone, since such pouring of blood would have characterized various kinds of sacrifices (cf. Lev 1:15; 4:7). Her point on this feast is not, thereby, undermined, however, since the other associations she notes are quite plausible: the 14 Nisan date of Jesus' crucifixion (18:28); the hyssop used to offer him vinegar (19:29); and the protection of his bones from fracture (19:36).

[134] Yee 1989:86–87.

[135] 1 Kgs 8:2, 65–66; Ezra 3:1–4.

to celebrate the re-consecration of the second temple by Judas Macca-bee.[136] The problem this creates for Yee's deduction at this juncture is brought into vivid relief by the fact that, in his criticism of animal vending in the temple, Jesus likely cites Zechariah 14:21, "Do not make my Fa-ther's house a house of merchandise" – a verse drawn from a passage which, as Yee notes elsewhere,[137] eschatologically associates Jerusalem (and its temple), not with Passover, but with Tabernacles (Zech 14:16–19).

As for the second Passover (at 6:4): the activity of Moses is not so ex-clusively tied to Passover in exodus typology that the connection Yee sees between Jesus and Moses in John 6 should, in itself, be considered festal. Her point may be arguable for Jesus' crossing of the Sea of Tiberias (6:16–21): if it is taken to allude to Moses' crossing of the Sea of Reeds (Ps 77:20–21), that episode of the exodus story perhaps lies close enough to the Passover celebration, itself, to merit festal connotations. Not so, how-ever, with the other parallels Yee notes. The ascent of a mountain; the mi-raculous provision of otherwise unavailable food; regard for Jesus as the prophet like Moses; a "murmuring" response from followers – all these belong to an exodus typology that is not, in itself, tantamount to Passover symbolism and that, in fact, runs (independently) throughout the Gospel of John, Passover context or no. Unless the allusion in question is some as-pect of (or near to) the observance of Passover (in Exodus 12–14), one cannot *ipso facto* equate a broader exodus typology with Passover symbol-ism.[138]

On Tabernacles – as with Passover symbolism and Moses typology in John 6, so with Tabernacles symbolism and messianic discourse in John 7 (specifically 7:25–31, 40–43): though the two overlap, the one cannot be exclusively equated with the other. Granted, the messianic deliberations at 7:40–43 could feasibly be tied to Tabernacles alone, since they respond to messianic claims drawn from the libation and eschatological/exodus themes expressed at 7:37–39 – the new temple and the rock in the wilder-ness motifs. It is more difficult to say the same, however, for 7:25–31.

Finally – and perhaps most problematic – the connection Yee alleges between the Feast of Dedication and Jesus' claim to be one with the Father (at 10:30–31) does not, in fact, function as a "replacement theology" but as the very opposite of such a theology. To be sure, it might be argued, as James C. VanderKam does, that the idolatry connoted by Jesus' self-

---

[136] 2 Macc 1:9; 10:6. See VanderKam 1987:32–34; 1992:2.124; Daise 2005:123–26. VanderKam is less inclined to see 2 Maccabees formally identifying the two feasts.

[137] Yee 1989:61, 73–74, 79–80.

[138] See the related critique of Aileen Guilding by Leon Morris (1964:53–59). This same criticism also applies to Williford, who ties 3:14–15 to the Passover at 2:13 on the (otherwise correct) grounds that its language of "lifting up" the Son of Man references the "lifting up" of the serpent in the wilderness at Num 21:8–9; 1981:41–43.

identification with the Father simply reflects the idolatry of Antiochus
Epiphanes that would have been "on the minds of Jesus and his audience
or on that of the author" during the Dedication.[139] But, in light of Yee's
peculiar contention, such an effect would not render Jesus a replacement to
what would have been commemorated by the feast, but a foil to it, wrongly
recalled in the perception of his interlocutors.

The second difficulty attending Yee's study concerns the specific way
she treats Sabbath texts alongside festal ones. Despite her innovative inclusion of the former along with the latter, her actual treatment of Sabbath
texts circumvents some important aspects of the way feasts are placed and
employed in the structure of the Fourth Gospel. Yee correctly notes the
parity Sabbaths enjoy with festivals in Leviticus,[140] even though they are
observed on a weekly, not annual, cycle. But, for chapter 5, she, in fact,
treats the Sabbath in lieu of (not along with) the feast mentioned at 5:1 –
she is rightly agnostic about what that feast's identity might be[141] but,
nonetheless, offers no (other) explanation for its presence in the narrative.
Moreover (and closely related to this first point), her exegesis of the Sabbath texts in both John 5 (5:1–47) and John 7 (7:14–24) fails to take into
account that, in those chapters, the Sabbaths do not appear independent of
feasts, as structuring contexts in their own right, but within feasts, being
subsumed under the more fundamental framing contexts of the unnamed
festival at 5:1 and Tabernacles at 7:2. Furthermore, if the Tabernacles context in John 7–8 extended to include John 9 (9:1–41), as many would as-
sert,[142] the same would apply to her discussion of the Sabbath in that chapter, as well.

Finally on Yee's study, her topical rather than sequential approach to
the feasts eclipses any significance that may attend the order in which they
appear in the narrative. If the meaning of those feasts is exclusively bound
up with the symbols they carry, a topical approach is as good a way as any
for deciphering that meaning. But, given the difficulties that emerge from
the attempts of Yee (as well as Mollat and Williford) to connect that symbolism to the narrative for every feast, such an assumption is improbable.
As such, one should proceed, rather, by giving as much attention to the order in which the feasts appear as to the ideas and events to which some
might allude.

---

[139] So VanderKam 1990:210–14; quotation p. 211.

[140] Lev 23:1–3; and one might add Num 28:9–10.

[141] Yee 1989:39.

[142] See the discussion in Chapter 2, under '2.3 The Feast of Tabernacles (John 7:2–52
[–10:21]).'

In sum, Yee's assessment of the symbolic significance of the feasts is insightful; and her inclusion of Sabbaths alongside those feasts is illuminating. Her symbolic connections, however, are often fragile; her treatment of Sabbath texts does not reckon with the more fundamental structuring role played by feasts (and is done at the expense of treating the feast at 5:1); and her topical approach eclipses the possibility that the significance of the feasts may (as much) lie in their sequence as in their symbolism.

3.2 Liturgical Theories

3.2.1 Reflexes to a Triennial Jewish Lectionary: Aileen Guilding

Aileen Guilding and Michael Goulder have taken a liturgical approach to feasts in the Fourth Gospel. A liturgical approach assumes that the feasts in John reflect a ritual referent outside the text; and, for Guilding and Goulder, those referents are the Jewish lectionary and the Quartodeciman Lenten calendar, respectively.

More precisely for Guilding, that referent was a triennial, Jewish lectionary cycle.[143] She maintained (following Adolf Büchler) that such a lectionary existed in first century Palestine; that through informed deduction from sundry sources,[144] its *sedarim* (readings from Torah), *haftaroth* (readings from the Prophets) and Psalter could be reconstructed; and that a comparison of its themes with those in the Johannine narrative shows the latter (the Johannine narrative) to have been patterned on the former (the lectionary readings). According to Guilding, the themes associated with each of the Jewish feasts were embedded in the lections assigned to (or near) them; and those same themes appear in (more or less) like sequence in the signs and discourses of the Fourth Gospel. Thus, through the medium of the Jewish lectionary, the Fourth Gospel was fashioned upon the Jewish liturgical year. More specifically, according to Guilding, the Fourth Gospel divides into three sections: chapters 1–4; chapters 5–12 (with chapters 5 and 6 inverted); and chapters 13–21. And the themes in each of these sections coincide *seriatim* with the lectionary readings slated for the three years of the triennial cycle.[145]

---

[143] For other reviews and critiques of Guilding, see Porter 1963:163–74; Heinemann 1968:41–48; Goulder 1978:20–21; Mlakuzhyil 1987:21–23; Devillers 2002:10–11; and, especially, Morris 1964 (entire).

[144] The Masoretic text, Rabbinic literature, Geniza lists, Karaite practice, scholarly suggestions.

[145] Guilding 1960:1–3, 6–57, 212–28.

An example is the dependence of John 7:1–8:59 (including 7:53–8:11) and John 15:1–16:24 on lections for the Feast of Tabernacles.[146] The Feast of Tabernacles was observed from 15–22 Tishri; and its themes, according to Guilding, were the pouring of water, illumination, tabernacles (which Guilding interprets as a metaphor for incarnation) and the grape harvest. With a lectionary starting from both Nisan and Tishri, the seasonal lections in which those themes were set are as follows[147]:

Table 10. Aileen Guilding: John 7:1–8:59; 15:1–16:24 & Lections for Tabernacles

Beginning of Year	First Year	Second Year	Third Year
Nisan-Cycle	2 Tishri/Gen 31:3	5 Tishri/Lev 6:12	1 Tishri/Deut 3:23
	9 Tishri/Gen 32:4	12 Tishri/Lev 8:1	8 Tishri/Deut 4:25 or 4:41
	16 Tishri/Gen 33:18	19 Tishri/Lev 10:8 or Lev 11:1	15 Tishri/Deut 6:4
	23 Tishri/Gen 35:9 (Isa 43:1)	26 Tishri/Lev 12:1 (Isa 66:1)	22 Tishri/Deut 7:12 (Isa 4:6 or Jer 9:22–24)
	30 Tishri/Gen 37:1 (Isa 32:18)	3 Cheshvan/ Lev 13:29 (2 Kg 5:1)	29 Tishri/Deut 9:1 (Jer 2:1)
	7 Cheshvan/ Gen 38:1 (2 Sam 11:2 or Hos 12:1)	10 Cheshvan/ Lev 14:1	6 Cheshvan/ Deut 10:1 (2 Kg 13:23 or 1 Kg 8:9)
Tishri-Cycle	(?)	Tishri/Num 5:1–31 ←(Hos 4:14)→	(?)

To the *haftaroth* in this chart, Guilding added Zechariah 14 and 1 Kings 8, both specifically prescribed to be read at Tabernacles in *Bavli Megillah* 31a.

According to Guilding, John 7:1–8:59 and John 15:1–16:24 contain the several Tabernacles themes mentioned above and do so by alluding to biblical passages (listed in Table 10) in which those same themes appear in

---

[146] Guilding 1960:92–118, 213–16.

[147] The following table combines all data available from Guilding's discussion and circumscribes the dates nearest Tabernacles (for broader chronological parameters [without *haftaroth*], see Guilding 1960:95, 234). *Sedarim* follow the forward slash after each date, *haftaroth* are in parentheses and the verse number for each chapter begins a lection that extends to the verse number listed for the next date's chapter. Guilding gives some *sedarim* and *haftaroth* alternates (to be treated below), leaves some *haftaroth* unidentified and (as also mentioned below) does not develop the Tishri-based sequence.

the Jewish lectionary. The Tabernacles theme of water at 7:37–40 draws upon similar motifs in Deuteronomy 8:11–15 (*seder* for 22 Tishri, third year), Isaiah 43:20 (*haftarah* for 23 Tishri, first year) and Jeremiah 2:13 (*haftarah* for 29 Tishri, third year). The clause "my time has not yet come" at 7:8 alludes to the idea of messianic incarnation found in the birth of Benjamin to Rachel at Genesis 35:16–21 (*seder* for 23 Tishri, first year) and the birth of the messianic progeny, Perez and Zerah, to Judah at Genesis 38:27–30 (*seder* for 7 Cheshvan, first year). And the idea of being persecuted "for the sake of Jesus' name" at 15:13–16:4 (especially 15:21) is catalyzed by readings on the persecution of Joseph by his brothers at Genesis 37 (*seder* for 30 Tishri, first year), as well as on the oracle declaring hatred of God's people by their kinsmen "for the sake of God's name" at Isaiah 66:5 (*haftarah* for 26 Tishri, second year).[148]

This example is a microcosm of what Guilding alleges to take place between the whole of the Fourth Gospel and other *loci* in the lectionary. An overview of the correspondences she makes between them is below. The chart follows a lectionary beginning at Nisan. Guilding contends the lectionary also (and simultaneously) began at Tishri but does not develop that dimension of it in sufficient detail to represent it:

---

[148] See, particularly, Guilding 1960:98–100, 104–106, 112–14.

Table 11. Aileen Guilding: The Triennial Jewish Lectionary &
the Structure of the Fourth Gospel

Calendar	Feasts	1st Division (John 1–4)	2nd Division (John 6,5, 7–12)	3rd Division (John 13–20)	Epilogue (John 21)
Nisan	Passover		John 6; 12	John 13; 19:28–20:30	
'Iyyar					
Sivan	Pentecost				John 21
Tammuz					
'Av					
'Elul					
Tishri	New Year Tabernacles	John 1	John 5 John 7–8	John 14 John 5:1–16:24	
Cheshvan			John 9		
Kislev	Dedication	John 2:1–11	John 10	John 16:25–17:26; 18:1–27	
Tebeth			John 11:1–46 ⎮		
Shebat		John 2:13–22 (–3:36) ⎮	⎮ John 11:1–46		
'Adar	Purim	⎮ John 2:13–22 (–3:36)	John 11:47–11:53	John 18:28–19:27	

Some of the connections Guilding makes between the Johannine and biblical (Old Testament) texts can be illuminating.[149] But her proposal, as a whole – as has often been noted – is fraught with difficulties. At the most fundamental level, her reconstructed lectionary is speculative and arbitrary.[150] *Seder* divisions are made by deduction, with no corroborating data.[151] And *haftaroth* are chosen eclectically, from an array of disparate sources that otherwise have little or no justification for their synthesis.[152] Among the *haftaroth* selected, two or more, drawn from different quarters, sometimes vie for the same *seder*. And, when they do, Guilding either entertains both as lections, entertains one over the other or neglects both, depending – it seems – on (the question-begging criterion of) whether or not they can be shown to have parallels in the Johannine text.

To use Guilding's treatment of the Feast of Tabernacles as an example,[153] the *haftaroth* she lists on or near Tabernacles are drawn from several disparate quarters: among those whose origins she indicates, Masoretic text divisions,[154] the Babylonian Talmud[155] and Bodleian MS 2727³,[156] as well as suggestions by Adolf Büchler[157] and Jacob Mann.[158] Among these *haftaroth* (see Table 10), two are sometimes listed for a single *seder*.[159] And, among these doublets, both are entertained for *seder* Genesis 38:1, one for *seder* Deuteronomy 10:1[160] and neither for *seder* Deuteronomy

---

[149] So VanderKam (1990:207–10), on a good deal of her work with the Feast of Dedication.

[150] On the dispute over a single, fixed first century lectionary, see Porter 1963:162–71; Morris 1964:11–34; Heinemann 1968:41–46; Mlakuzhyil 1987:23. For more specific opposition to the triennial (as opposed to annual) lectionary espoused by Guilding (and Adolf Büchler), see Goulder 1978:20–21. But, more forcefully – against all lectionary theories – see J.R. Perkin on Morris's critique of Guilding: "The critical axe, wielded more in sorrow than anger, has been laid at the root of the once-flourishing lectionary tree"; 1966:236–37, quotation p. 37.

[151] See Guilding 1960:10–20.

[152] As per above, cues in the Masoretic text, Rabbinic literature, Geniza lists, Karaite practice and scholarly suggestions; Guilding 1960:20 and *passim* throughout the work. On this point, see, also, the discussions by Morris 1964:20–29 and Heinemann 1968:46–48.

[153] For Guilding's treatment of Tabernacles on this point, see, particularly, 1960:94–97, 104–106, 111–13, 116–19.

[154] 2 Kgs 13:23; Jer 9:22–24.

[155] Zech 14 and 1 Kgs 8 from *b. Meg.* 31a.

[156] Isa 32:18; 43:1.

[157] 2 Sam 11:2; 2 Kgs 5:1; Isa 4:6 (drawing upon Karaite tradition); 66:1; Jer 2:1.

[158] Hos 12:1 and 1 Kgs 8:9.

[159] 2 Sam 11:2 and Hos 12:1 for Gen 38:1 (7 Cheshvan); Isa 4:6 and Jer 9:22–24 for Deut 7:12 (22 Tishri); and 2 Kgs 13:23 and 1 Kgs 8:9 for Deut 10:1 (6 Cheshvan), to which one must add Zech14 and 1 Kgs 8 from *b. Meg.* 31a.

[160] 1 Kgs 8:9 but not 2 Kgs 13:23.

7:12. Moreover, those which are treated are done so because Guilding perceives their themes to be present in the Fourth Gospel: 2 Samuel 11:2, because its description of David's sin and conviction forms the background, both to the Jews' claim that they were not born of fornication (John 8:41) and to Jesus' challenge that those without sin should cast the first stone (John 8:7); Hosea 12:1, because its mention of dew, the blossom of the vine and fruit creates a backdrop for Jesus' discourse on the true vine (15:1–11); and 1 Kings 8:9, because it shares with John 7:1–8:50 its Tabernacles context,[161] as well as its themes of incarnation,[162] water,[163] light[164] and efficacious prayer.[165]

But even if Guilding's lectionary is conceded, her notions on how it interplayed with the Gospel of John are, themselves, open to question.[166] For one, the thematic similarities she claims to discover between feasts, lections and gospel passages are often glib. Literary dependence is typically predicated on no more than a word, phrase or motif that occurs between two texts: in John 8:25, for example, Jesus' response that he is "that which I have told you from the beginning" is traced to LXX Isaiah 43:12–13, "I am the Lord God even from the beginning."[167] Moreover, little or no attempt is made to determine whether a better fit could be found among other sources: the theme of "witness" in John 8:17, for example, is traced to LXX Isaiah 43:9,[168] despite the fact that the verse is a formal citation of Deuteronomy 17:6 and/or Deuteronomy 19:15.

Further, Guilding does not make her case within the strictures she claims to have been in place. Her argument is that themes in any given passage of the Fourth Gospel correlate to (a) festal themes (b) in lections at or near the times of those feasts. Yet, in her discussions, both these parameters are transgressed. First, (a) the parallels she finds between gospel passages and lections often fall outside the themes she lists for their respective feasts. Again referencing her discussion of the Feast of Tabernacles, Guilding finds connections, not only with the four themes she lists for

---

[161] 1 Kgs 8:2, 65–66 with John 7:2.

[162] 1 Kgs 8:27 with John 7.

[163] 1 Kgs 8:35 with John 7:37–38.

[164] LXX 3 Kgdms 8:53 with John 8:12.

[165] 1 Kgs 8:22–53 with John 15:7,16; 16:23–24.

[166] Specifically on Guilding's application of the lectionary theory to the Fourth Gospel, see Morris 1964:41–52.

[167] The translation is that of Guilding. The Greek texts are John 8:25, τὴν ἀρχὴν ὅ τι καὶ λαλῶ ὑμῖν; LXX Isa 43:12–13, κύριος ὁ θεὸς ἔτι ἀπ' ἀρχῆς; Guilding 1960:108. In the Göttingen edition, Joseph Ziegler, in fact, punctuates κύριος ὁ θεός with the preceding clause (λέγει κύριος ὁ θεός.) and has ἔτι ἀπ' ἀρχῆς begin a new sentence; Ziegler 1939:282.

[168] Guilding 1960:108.

that festival – pouring water, illumination, tabernacles (as a metaphor for incarnation) and the grape harvest – but also with hatred and persecution,[169] circumcision,[170] the divine witness and the "I am" declaration,[171] adultery,[172] writing with the finger,[173] a woman's travail[174] and the efficacy of prayer.[175] Moreover, (b) the lectionary dates from which Guilding draws sometimes pre- or post-date the feasts in question by some remove. The chronological span she allows for passages related to the Feast of Tabernacles (see Table 10) extends from 19 Tishri (second year), the earliest, to 7 Cheshvan (first year), the latest – some two weeks after the feast would have ended.[176]

Finally, the matrices of Guilding's lectionary are so broad that they essentially render any corollaries between them and the Fourth Gospel meaningless. With Nisan-based lections augmented by Tishri-based ones – and this over periods that typically exceed festal seasons by some weeks (see Table 10) – it is difficult to imagine how thematic parallels between those lections and the Gospel of John could *not* be found somewhere within their number. One must conclude, therefore, that Guilding's hypothesis does not plausibly explain the role feasts play in the Gospel of John. Its basis is conjectured, its inferences are simplistic and its methodological execution is inconsistent.

3.2.2. Lections to the Quartodeciman Lenten Liturgy: Michael D. Goulder

With a different trajectory, Michael Goulder has proposed that the feasts in John correlate to the Sabbaths, Sundays and Pascal rites of the (proto-) Quartodeciman Lenten season.[177] According to Goulder, the Gospel of John, itself, was fashioned as a lectionary for Quartodeciman baptismal candidates undergoing instruction during Lent. The Quartodeciman Lenten season occurred over a six week period, culminating on the Sunday following 14 Nisan of the Jewish calendar year: it began the Sunday five weeks prior to the week in which 14 Nisan would fall in the Jewish calendar; and it climaxed on whichever days in the sixth week correlated to 10–14 Nisan in any given year. On the evening of the 13th the catechumens were bap-

---

[169] John 15:18–16:4 with Gen 37; Isa 66.

[170] John 7:22–24 with Lev 12 (through Col 2:11 and Eph 2:11); cf. also Gen 34; Deut 10:16; Jer 9:22–24.

[171] John 8:17–18, 58 with Isa 43.

[172] John 7:53–8:11 with Gen 38–39; 2 Sam 11:2.

[173] John 8:6–8 with Deut 9:1; Jer 2:1.

[174] John 16:21 with Isa 66.

[175] John 15:7, 16; 16:23–24; see Guilding 1960:102–103, 106–109, 111–17.

[176] Further on Guilding's arbitrary alignment of passages with feasts, see Porter (1963:165) and Mlakuzhyil (1987:23).

[177] On Goulder, see also the review by Mlakuzhyil 1987:23–25.

tized; from that evening till the evening of the 14th a fast and vigil were kept; on the evening of the 14th the fast was broken with an *agape* feast; and on the Sunday next Easter was celebrated. Though this pascal liturgy became characteristic of the church in Asia Minor during the late 1st and 2nd centuries C.E., it had its roots, according to Goulder, in the Palestinian church of the 30s and 40s C.E.; and, sometime during the interim, it became the template on which the Fourth Gospel was structured. The stated purpose of the Fourth Gospel, "that you might believe that Jesus is the Christ, the Son of God" (20:30–31), was pitched, argues Goulder, to these Lenten catechumens; and the Johannine narrative, itself, consisted in a sequence of lections to be read to them at different intervals during the several weeks of that season: John 1:1–11:54 through the five weeks of Lent; John 11:55–19:31 from 10–14 Nisan; John 20:1–25 on Easter Sunday; and John 20:26–31 on the Sunday following Easter.[178]

According to this hypothesis, the feasts in John and the sections they cover represent lections for special days in the pascal season – Sabbaths, Sundays and certain days just prior to and following 14 Nisan. The passages covered by the final Passover (11:55–19:42) were read from six days before Passover till 14 Nisan; those after the final Passover (20:1–23) were read on Easter Sunday and the Sunday next[179]:

---

[178] Goulder 1982:205–21. In a related proposal, Karel Hanhart argued that the temporal markers in 1:29–2:11 reflect an orthodox correction to rubrics originally aligned to the Quartodeciman Holy Week; 1977:335–46. See also C.T. Ruddick's suggestion (from his thesis that Gen 22 lay behind John 6) that the Fourth Gospel was fashioned on synagogue lections inherited by early Christians; 1967–68:341.

[179] For this schedule and the Sabbaths and Sundays listed below, see Goulder 1982:215–16 and his chart on pp. 220–21.

Table 12. Michael Goulder: The Final Passover in John & the Quartodeciman Passover Week

6 Days Before Passover	5 Days Before Passover	5th Day Before Passover till 13 Nisan	13 Nisan	14 Nisan	Easter
Bethany anointing: (11:11– 12:11) "Six days before Passover" (12:1)	Entry into Jerusalem: (12:12– 19) "The next day" (12:12)	Coming of the Greeks (12:20– 50) (between 5th day before Passover & 13 Nisan)	Footwashing (13:1–30) at sundown (13:30)	Betrayal, Arrest & Trial Before Annas (18:1–23) till 3am	Resurrection Appearance to Mary (20:1–18) morning
			Farewell Discourse (13:31– 14:31) till 9pm	Trial Before Caiaphas (18:24– 27) till 6am	Resurrection Appearance to Disciples (20:19– 23) evening
			Farewell Discourse (15:1– 17:26) till midnight	Trial Before Pilate (18:28– 40) till 9am	
				Trial Before Pilate (19:1–12) till noon	
				Crucifixion (19:13– 24) till 3pm	
				Crucifixion (19:25– 42) till sundown	

Passages covered by the remaining feasts in John, then, were recited during the Lenten Sabbaths and Sundays prior to 13–14 Nisan:

Table 13. Michael Goulder: Feasts in John & the Quartodeciman Lenten Season

1ˢᵗ Passover	John 2:13–22 on Sabbath, Lent I John 2:23–3:21 on Sunday, Lent II
Anonymous Feast	John 5:1–47 on Sabbath, Lent II
2ⁿᵈ Passover	John 6:1–21 on Sunday, Lent III John 6:41–71 on Sabbath, Lent III
Tabernacles	John 7:1–13 on Sunday, Lent IV John 7:37–10:21 on Sabbath, Lent IV
Dedication	John 10:22–39 on Sunday, Lent V

Goulder's broader hypothesis is vulnerable to several criticisms. Even if his reconstruction of the Quartodeciman Lenten season is conceded,[180] its alleged mid-first century origin, on which much of Goulder's thesis turns,[181] is open to some question. He makes his case by particularizing sources that generally describe early Christians retaining Jewish cultic,[182] calendrical[183] and initiatory[184] rites, then moving to Asia Minor.[185] But,

---

[180] Goulder concludes his piece admitting that the detail of his hypothesis "requires a large-scale justification," which he could not offer within the limits of an article; he rests his case largely on the internal consistency it yields: "It must suffice here that the picture I have given is a *coherent* one" (italics his); 1982:219. That accepted, one might question, nonetheless, the way Goulder does venture some detail in his discussion. Regarding one primary exemplar to which he appeals, for instance – the 9ᵗʰ century Greek Orthodox liturgical calendar – not only does it post-date the Quartodeciman controversy and Gospel of John by some eight centuries, but it is as readily abandoned as it was taken up when Goulder deems its reading of John between Easter and Pentecost to be incompatible with the internal logic of John, which he believes required a dénouement at Passover/Easter; 1982:217–18.

[181] Goulder does find more concrete support for aspects of his model existing from the second century onward (1982:211–13); the issue addressed here is its alleged apostolic beginnings.

[182] Luke 24:53; Acts 3:1.

[183] Acts 2:1; Gal 4:10; Col 3:16.

[184] Exod 12:48; Josh 5:2–9; *b. Pesaḥ.* 91b; *y. Pesaḥ.* 8.8. Goulder's point is that the Christian practice of baptizing at Passover emulated the early first century Jewish practice of doing the same with circumcision and immersion, as per the passages cited.

[185] So, Paul's opponents at Galatia and Colossae, as per Eusebius, *Hist. eccl.* 3.31.3–5; Goulder 1982:205–207, 209.

besides being sometimes misinterpreted,[186] these data are far too generic to yield such an elaborate Lenten schema as Goulder details. The lack of more specific sources between the crucifixion and Quartodecimanism renders it entirely possible that, even if the Quartodeciman Lenten liturgy is accepted, the flow of influence between it and the Gospel of John ran opposite to the direction Goulder suggests. It is not implausible that the Fourth Gospel came to its current form before the rise of Quartodecimanism (and outside its circles), then shaped the Quartodeciman catechism after it had later been adopted by the movement.

As for Goulder's criteria for seeing a lectionary structure in the Fourth Gospel, they are quite arbitrary. He assigns gospel passages to Lenten days on the questionable assumption that cues in the narrative either reflect liturgical practice or signal rubrics for lections. Jesus' summons, "Rise, let us go hence" (14:31), for instance, is considered a possible prompt for vigil participants to relocate from the baptistery to an assembly room. The timing of the foot washing episode at sundown on 13 Nisan (13:1–30) mirrors the time at which Lenten catechumens would be baptized. And the temporal references during Jesus' trial and crucifixion signal hours between 14 Nisan and Easter when each pericope was to be read: the cock crow after Peter's third denial (18:27) designates the reading of Jesus' trial before Annas/Caiaphas (18:15–27), to begin at 3am, 14 Nisan; the remark "and it was early" (18:28) puts the reading of Jesus' first appearance before Pilate (18:28–40) at 6am, 14 Nisan; the reference to "the sixth hour" (19:14) marks the reading of the trial on "the Pavement" (19:13–24) at noon, 14 Nisan; Jesus' appearance to Mary "early, while it was still dark" (20:1) schedules the reading of the first resurrection appearance (20:1–18) on Easter morning; and Jesus' later appearance to the disciples "when it

---

[186] Goulder's notion that Christian baptism at Passover followed an early first century Jewish practice of circumcising and immersing only at that feast (Exod 12:48; Josh 5:2–9; *b. Pesaḥ. 91b*; *y. Pesaḥ.* 8.8; 1982:205–207) is not supported by the sources to which he appeals. Exodus 12:48 and Joshua 5:2–10 do juxtapose circumcision and Passover but hardly prescribe their standard tandem observance: the first simply legislates that non-Israelites who wish to celebrate Passover must first (at some time prior to it) be circumcised; the second recounts the wilderness generation of Israelites becoming circumcised prior to Passover after crossing the Jordan. As for *b. Pesaḥ.* 91b and *y. Pesaḥ.* 8.8, both do treat of immersion just prior to Passover but in the context of contingent circumstances: the first centers on the debate between the Houses of Shammai and Hillel over whether a proselyte who happened to convert on the eve of Passover can partake of the feast immediately after immersion; the second, wherein *Yerushalmi* is, in fact, citing *t. Pesaḥ.* 7.14, concerns whether soldiers and guards who, having become defiled watching the gates at Passover, were, similarly, allowed to eat the Passover immediately after immersion.

was evening of that day" (20:19) puts the reading of that second resurrection appearance (20:19–23) on Easter evening.[187]

Finally on Goulder's broader thesis, the result of his reconstruction is inconsistent with the assumption on which it is built. If the Gospel of John was, in fact, fashioned as a lectionary for the Quartodeciman Lenten liturgy, one should expect that its text fills that season with readings. Yet, according to Goulder's outline, this is not the case. Even if one allows that no readings were assigned to Thursdays, as Goulder suggests,[188] one might still ask why it is that other days in certain Lenten weeks are sometimes absent lections[189] while their corollaries in other Lenten weeks are not. George Mlakuzhyil noted that some days in Goulder's schedule have no lections because the temporal markers for the next lections indicate a hiatus of some days[190]: no reading appears for the Wednesday in Lent II, for instance, because the lection for the following Friday begins with the words, "after two days" (4:43); nor do lections appear for the Monday, Tuesday or Friday of Lent IV, because the lections for that week mark the "middle" (7:14–36, Wednesday) and "last great day" (7:37–10:21, Saturday) of the Feast of Tabernacles. Yet this does not explain the absence of lections from the Tuesday, Wednesday and Friday of Lent III, when the next rubric for Saturday of that week has no such temporal marker (6:41–71). Similarly, if passages covered by feasts in the Gospel of John were to be read on the special Lenten days of Sabbaths and Sundays, why is the Bread of Life Discourse (6:22–40), which falls under the Passover at 6:4, read on Monday of Lent III? And why is a section falling within the Feast of Tabernacles (7:14–36) read on Wednesday of Lent IV? This last example is ostensibly justified, since 7:14 introduces a passage that recounts events "in the middle of the feast." But that a feast day in the Gospel of John (albeit an intermediate one) falls to a routine day in the Quartodeciman liturgy at all leads one to wonder how that liturgy and its principles were determinative for the shape of the Fourth Gospel.

More particularly for the issue at hand – Goulder's model hermeneutically divests the feasts in John's Gospel of their significance as feasts. That is to say, the import Goulder gives festivals in the Fourth Gospel has less to do with their identity as Jewish feasts (given them in the gospel) than it does with their correlation to Lenten holy days (given them in Goulder's reconstruction). This is less the case, of course, for the final Passover. In Goulder's scheme, the passages covered by that feast (11:55–

---

[187] Goulder 1982:215–216. On the tenuous idea that narrative time indicators are temporal rubrics, see also Mlakuzhyil 1987:25.

[188] Goulder 1982:218.

[189] For details of this discussion, see the chart in Goulder 1982:220–21.

[190] Mlakuzhyil 1987:25.

19:42) are deemed lections for the Quartodeciman pascal rites – from six days before Passover till 14 Nisan (see Table 12). Thus, the final Passover in the Fourth Gospel is calibrated to a liturgical event that more or less parallels the identity it is given in the text. But this is not the case for the remaining festivals. The passages they cover are considered lections, not for feasts parallel to those depicted in the narrative (as is the final Passover), but for Lenten Sabbaths and Sundays (see Table 13): the episodes covered by the first Passover are read on the Sabbath of Lent I (2:13–22) and the Sunday of Lent II (2:23–3:21); those covered by the anonymous feast (5:1–47), on the Sabbath of Lent II; the events and discourses falling under the second Passover, on the Sunday (6:1–21) and Sabbath (6:41–71) of Lent III; the pericopes subsumed under the Feast of Tabernacles, on the Sunday (7:1–13) and Sabbath (7:37–10:21) of Lent IV; and the discourse during the Feast of Dedication, on the Sunday of Lent V.[191] To be sure, in Goulder's schema these feasts do enjoy a certain elevated status over other lections (which would be read on weekdays during Lent). Nonetheless, the significance Goulder gives them is ultimately abstracted from the identity they are given in the text itself; and, as such, they become mere ciphers for a liturgical reality that has little or no correlation with them.

With the problems in Goulder's broader hypothesis, recounted above, this disconnect between festivals and their referents renders his overall explanation of the feasts in John problematic. His reconstruction of Quartodeciman Lenten liturgy is thinly founded and internally inconsistent; his early dating of it is overstated; his mechanism for relating it to the Fourth Gospel is tenuous; and the significance he gives most feasts in that gospel depreciates their identity as such.

---

[191] Exceptions here are the weekday lectionary dates for John 6:22–40 and John 7:14–36, noted above.

3.3 Anthropological Theory
'Tempo Sociale' to the *'Tempo Diverso'* of Jesus' 'Hour,'
Adriana Destro and Mauro Pesce

A third (and the most recent) way of broaching the feasts in John has been through the lens of the anthropology of religion, brought into the discussion by University of Bologna professors Adriana Destro and Mauro Pesce. Destro and Pesce make their case in several monographs and articles[192]; but, unlike Boismard and Mollat, who changed their views substantially over two or more publications, Destro and Pesce have more or less maintained their initial thesis throughout, elaborating more in some places than in others. Consequently, rather than addressing their work diachronically, as I did with Boismard and Mollat, I will treat their hypothesis synchronically, synthesizing all their data into a single, composite whole.

For Destro and Pesce, the feasts in John represent and facilitate part of an institutional matrix from which Johannine Christians were to trace their origins and clarify their identity. In their view, the Johannine redactor crafted the Fourth Gospel to show the members of his community how their new religious system had come about[193]; and to do this he created a dialectic in its narrative between the systems from which they came and the system into which they grew, allowing them to map their development out of the one and into the other as they read.[194] One side of this dialectic consisted in two sets of elements: (1) three divinely enacted rites that enveloped and were unique to Jesus and his movement – Jesus' baptism by John (1:32–34),[195] the "rite of the voice from on high" (12:23–36) and the breathing of the Spirit (20:19–23)[196]; and (2) an array of rituals practiced (or practiced differently) by the later Johannine community and imposed anachronistically onto the story of Jesus[197] – baptism in water *and Spirit* (1:33; 3:5); the (possible) abolition of handwashing before meals (2:7–10); worship apart from material space (4:23–24); activity on the Sabbath (5:17; 9:4); the Eucharist (6:48–58); the Christian initiation rite (9:35–39;

---

[192] Destro and Pesce 1995a (entire); 1995b:86–99; 1997:111–29; 2000:3–24, 118–22; Pesce 2001: 53–65. Destro and Pesce couch their theory in a much richer hypothesis of a gradual Johannine religious transformation, which they believe unfolds through the Fourth Gospel. Here I narrow the focus to the festal aspects of that theory.

[193] Destro and Pesce 1997:114–15; 2000:3–4; Pesce 2001:51. Destro and Pesce dub this system "giovannismo."

[194] Destro and Pesce 1995a:78; 1995b:101–102; 2000:3–6, 24; Pesce 2001:51–53.

[195] Though Jesus is not depicted as being baptized by John in the Fourth Gospel, Destro and Pesce understand it to be intimated; 1995b:89–90.

[196] Destro and Pesce 1995b:89–99 (the more elaborate discussion); 2000:6–7, 16–21.

[197] Here, like predecessors mentioned above, Destro and Pesce also follow the cue of J. Louis Martyn 1979.

11:26–27; 20:26–29); Christianized domestic hospitality rites (12:1–8); a Christianized (Sukkot-like) Passover (12:12–15); a mealtime rite of inversion, including the washing of feet and the giving of a morsel to Judas Iscariot (13:1–14:31); a liturgy consisting of homily and prayer (16:1–17:26); and two rites of institution that define functions within the group – familial/religious roles (19:25–27) and pastoral guide (21:15–19).[198] The other side of this dialectic, say Destro and Pesce, was an aggregate of three other sets of elements to be found in the narrative: rites and institutions from (a) the movement of John the Baptist – John's baptism with water only (1:33); (b) the Samaritans – the cult at Gerizim (4:20); and, most especially, (c) the Jews – pilgrimage, the Jerusalem cult, purification, Sabbath observance.[199]

The redactor used feasts, according to Destro and Pesce, both as part of and as a structuring agent to this last-listed group of rites, the rituals of the Jews. Besides being one of those rites, themselves, feasts require an array other rites to be performed for their proper observance – pilgrimage, purification, sacrifice at the cult and the like. Consequently, by structuring his narrative on those feasts, the redactor could, on the one hand, employ them as elements (in their own right) juxtaposed to the Jesus and Johannine movements, yet, on the other hand, use them as ritual magnets, so to speak, to draw other Jewish rituals into the story for similar juxtaposition. Supporting this view, for Destro and Pesce, is that the redactor did not organize the feasts into a sequenced, liturgical cycle.[200] That he placed them in the narrative with no apparent chronological design – and that he did so alongside other rituals equally associated with Jewish institutions – betrays that his aim was not merely to locate Jesus' activity within "a form of periodization" – though this, too, is in view. Rather, it was to set that activity over against "factors on which the (Jewish) culture is based or from which it draws its fundamental characteristics."[201] The dynamic of these interweaving factors is charted below in Table 14[202]:

---

[198] Destro and Pesce 1995a:83–98 (and the table on pp. 98–100); 2000:8–15, 21–24.

[199] Destro and Pesce 1995a:79–83; 2000:7–15, 24. By including (John the) Baptist and Samaritian rites alongside Jewish rituals, Destro and Pesce partially address Charles H. Talbert's question about whether the Fourth Gospel was evoked as much out of exclusion "from the Baptist movement and the Samaritan community" as it was from the Jewish synagogue; cf. Talbert 1993:355.

[200] Destro and Pesce 1995a:78, 81n9; 2000:6, 11–12.

[201] Destro and Pesce 2000:5–6, quotation p. 6; see also idem 1995a:77; Pesce 2001:59–65.

[202] See also the chart in Destro and Pesce 1995a:98–100.

Table 14. Adriana Destro & Mauro Pesce: Ritual Dialectic in the Fourth Gospel

Institutional Rites of the Jews	Institutional Rites of John the Baptist & Samaritans	Institutional Rites of Divine Manifestation	Contemporary Rites of Johannine Community
Wedding at Cana (2:1–11) • Purification (2:6)	• Baptism in water (1:33; cf. 3:25–26): John the Baptist	• Jesus' Baptism by John (1:32–34)	• Baptism in water & Spirit (3:5; cf. 1:33) • Turns purification water to wine (2:7–10)
Pesach (2:13–4:45) • Pilgrimage (2:13; 4:21) • Sacrificial cult (2:14) • Purification (3:25) • Worship at Jerusalem (4:20–24)	• Worship at Gerizim (4:20): Samaritans		• Expulsion of sacrificial animals (2:15) • Worship in Spirit & in truth (4:23–24)
Shavuot (5:1–47) • Pilgrimage (5:1) • Sabbath observance: rest (5:16)			• Sabbath observance: continued work (5:17)
Pesach (6:1–71) • Benediction for food (6:11) • Homily within synagogue liturgy (6:59)			• Eucharist (6:48–58)
Sukkot (7:1–10:21) • Pilgrimage (7:3–10) • Libation (7:37–38) • Sabbath observance (9:14)			• Discourse "on last great day of the feast" (7:37) • Sabbath observance: continued work (9:4) • Initiation rite (9:35–39)

Institutional Rites of the Jews	Institutional Rites of John the Baptist & Samaritans	Institutional Rites of Divine Manifestation	Contemporary Rites of Johannine Community
Hanukkah (10:22–11:54): • Centrality of temple/cult § Place where Jesus walks (10:23) § Place where priesthood & Sanhedrin make institutional petitions (11:46–53) § High priest given capacity to prophesy (11:51–52)			• Initiation rite (11:26–27)
Pesach (12:1–19:42) • Purification (11:55) • Anointing of Jesus' feet: domestic hospitality rite (12:1–8) • Entry into Jerusalem for feast (12:12–15)		• "Rite of the voice from on high" (12:23–36)	• Christianized hospitality rite (12:1–8) • Sukkot elements (palm branches) in entry to Jerusalem (12:12–15): Christianized Passover • Rites during retirement of the group § Meal: rite of inversion (13:1–14:31) § Liturgy: homily & prayer (15:1–17:26)

Institutional Rites of the Jews	Institutional Rites of John the Baptist & Samaritans	Institutional Rites of Divine Manifestation	Contemporary Rites of Johannine Community
Pesach (12:1–19:42) (continued) [Synagogue & temple as places of teaching (18:20): *not connected to Passover*] • Pascal lamb (19:28–30, 33–34) [Burial custom (19:39–42): *not connected to Passover*]			• Rite of institution: new familial & religious roles (19:25–27)
		• Breathing of the Spirit (20:19–23)	• Initiation rite (20:26–29) • Rite of institution: investiture of guiding leadership (21:15–19)

Further imposed on this dialectic is a forward temporal movement that, by the end of Jesus' public ministry, brings his disciples out from a Jewish periodization of time, measured by the feasts, into a new periodization of time, ushered in by Jesus' 'hour.' Destro and Pesce define Jesus' hour as "the decisive moment in which Jesus accepts his own destiny, suffers death and then experiences the resurrection and return to God."[203] That point formally begins in chapter 12. But it is so anticipated beforehand – and so worked out afterward – as to structure the whole narrative of the Fourth Gospel into four phases, three of them inaugurated by the three divinely manifested rites listed above: (1) Before the Hour (1:19–12:22), begun with Jesus' baptism by John (1:32–34); (2) the Advent of the Hour (12:23–17:26), begun by the "rite of the voice from on high" (12:23–36); (3) Within the Hour (18:1–19:42), not associated with a rite; and (4) After the

---

[203] Destro and Pesce 2000:6; see also p. 19.

Hour (20:1–21:25), begun with Jesus' breathing of the Spirit onto his disciples (20:19–23).[204]

From Jesus' baptism by John, when the coming of his 'hour' is first made imminent, the mode of time governing Jesus' public ministry differs from (and is in dialectic with) the rhythm of Jewish feasts otherwise permeating the narrative.[205] Pesce dubs it an "alternate time" (*tempo diverso*) over against the "social time" (*tempo sociale*) of the feasts.[206] At the "rite of the voice on high," however, when that 'hour' finally arrives, its peculiar mode of time transfers Jesus' disciples, themselves, out of the rhythm of the feasts into its own, alternate periodization – a periodization now severed from and, in fact, opposed to any Jewish (or other) calendrical rites:

> By placing an institutive rite (the "rite of the voice from on high")
> at the beginning of the decisive and dramatic phase of Jesus' life,
> the redactor imagines a new periodization, which does not coincide
> with any other calendar or which is removed from the more habitual
> and consecrated rites of the Jewish society. On the contrary, it seems
> to be opposed to them, since it occurs precisely during the period of *Pesach*.[207]

The broad categories of this fuller scheme are sketched in Table 15:

---

[204] Destro and Pesce 1995a:78–79; 1995b:86–99; 1997:112–26; 2000:6–7, 16–21, 118–20; versification for these four phases is mine, inferred from the discussions of Destro and Pesce. Note that, at 1995b:86n8, Destro and Pesce, in turn, subsume the first three of these phases under two larger categories, predicated on Jesus' vulnerability to hostile powers: (1) Before the Hour (1:19–12:22), when Jesus was protected from those powers; (2) the Coming of the Hour (12:23–19:42), when he was abandoned by God to them.

[205] Destro and Pesce 1995a:103–104; 2000: 5-7, 16–21, 118–20.

[206] Pesce 2001:55.

[207] Destro and Pesce 2000:20; italics theirs/parenthetical note mine; cf. Pesce 2001:55–56. In his 2001 article Pesce traces this development backward, to suggest that, in its earliest stages, the Johannine community, itself, had observed Jewish feasts and other rituals; 2001:55–67.

Table 15. Adriana Destro & Mauro Pesce: Feasts and Jesus' 'Hour'
in the Fourth Gospel

Periodization/Institutional Rites	The Dénoue-ment of Jesus' 'Hour'	Institutional Rites of Divine Manifestation	The Rhythm of Jewish Feasts
Old Periodization/Rites	• Before the Hour (1:19–12:22)	• Jesus' Bap-tism by John (1:32–34)	• Pesach (2:13–4:45) • Shavuot (so 5:1–47) • Pesach (6:1–71) • Sukkot (7:1–10:21) • Hanukkah (10:22–11:54)
New Periodization/Rites	• Advent of the Hour (12:23–17:26) • Within the Hour (18:1–19:42) • After the Hour (20:1–21:25)	• "Rite of voice from on high" (12:23–36) • Breathing of the Spirit (20:19–23)	• Pesach (12:1–19:42)

Questionable in this proposal by Destro and Pesce is their contention that the feasts in John serve to draw other rites into the narrative by requiring their presence for proper observance. It is correct that some rituals and ritual institutions do appear within the contexts of feasts – pilgrimages to Jerusalem (2:13; 5:1; 7:2–10; 10:22–23 [possibly]; 11:55/12:1); the Jerusalem temple and cult (2:14–22; 10:23; 11:46–53); the Sabbath, during the unnamed feast (5:9) and (possibly) Tabernacles (9:14)[208]; the manna homily (6:59) near the second Passover; the libation (7:37–38) during Tabernacles; the purification (11:55), entry into Jerusalem (12:12–15) and pascal lamb (19:32–36) during the final Passover. This is not the case, however, with other rites and institutions represented in the Fourth Gospel. Immedi-

---

[208] This, since "the last great day of the feast" may represent the eighth day Sabbath prescribed in Leviticus 23:39 and Numbers 29:35.

ately suspect are the rites referenced in 3:22–4:54 and 10:40–11:54. Like Mollat and Williford before them, Destro and Pesce extend the first Passover from 2:13 through 4:54, and the Feast of Dedication from 10:22 through 11:54. Consequently, they associate the mention of purification rites at 3:25 and of temple/cult at 4:20–24 with that first Passover at 2:13; and do the same with the mention of temple/cult at 11:46–53 and the Feast of Dedication at 10:22 – even though, in narrative time, those feasts had likely passed. Were those festal times restricted, however, to 2:13–3:21 and 10:22–39, respectively (as argued above), all three of those references to rites and institutions – the purification rites at 3:25, the temple/cult at 4:20–24 and the same at 11:46–53 – would appear in the narrative independent of any festal context.

But even if the broader festal contexts of the first Passover and Dedication were conceded, several other (alleged) rituals obtain in the narrative without being required by the feasts which precede them. Destro and Pesce admit as much for the allusion to temple and synagogue at 18:20, as well as the burial rite at 19:39–42.[209] But the same applies to at least four other rites occurring throughout chapters 2–19. (1) First, Jesus' travel to Galilee through Judea and Samaria (3:22–4:54). This is not the return journey of Jesus' pilgrimage for the Passover at 2:13, as Destro and Pesce seem to claim.[210] Rather, it is Jesus' Judean ministry cut short by Pharisaic pressure. Jesus went to Judea to begin baptizing (3:22); and he left, not to complete his pilgrimage back to Galilee, but because "the Pharisees heard that (he) was making and baptizing more disciples than John" (4:1–3).

(2) Second, the Sabbath broken by Jesus when he healed the lame man (5:16) is in no way facilitated by the unnamed feast at 5:1, as Destro and Pesce intimate. Destro and Pesce identify that feast as Pentecost and find a connection between it and the Sabbath based on the relation each one has to "weeks": Pentecost, as *Shavuot*, is "the Feast of Weeks"; Sabbath, as the seventh day, "scans the weekly ritual cycle" – that is, it more or less furnishes the numerical template on which feasts are framed.[211] But this correlation hardly makes the Sabbath a requirement for the feast. A case can be made for the Sabbath at 9:14 as a requirement for the Feast of Tabernacles (in which it appears), since, according to Leviticus 23:39 and Number 29:35, the last day of Tabernacles, on which this occurred (7:37), was legislated to be a festal Sabbath. But no such rubric obtains for the Feast of Pentecost: it was celebrated on a single day; and, if that day was calculated from the Waving of the 'Omer within a luni-solar calendar (as the Pharisees and Tannaim had it), it would have fallen on a different day of the

---

[209] Destro and Pesce 1995a:82.

[210] Destro and Pesce 1995a:79; 2000:8.

[211] Destro and Pesce 1995a:80, 104; 2000:8–9; quotation, 1995a:80.

week, year by year. If, in one year, that day fell upon a Sabbath, the congruence was only due to coincidence, not to some requirement inherent in Pentecost.

Finally, neither (3) the benediction over the meal near the second Passover (6:11) nor (4) the council of Pharisees, priests and high priest in the temple during the Dedication (11:46–53) were required by the feasts with which they are associated in the text (or any other feast for that matter). They were daily (benediction) or *ad hoc* (council) acts, of no consequence for the proper observance of Passover or the Dedication, respectively.[212]

Quite suggestive in the hypothesis of Destro and Pesce, however, is the interface they observe between the feasts and Jesus' 'hour,' particularly the period "before the hour" in chapters 2–12, when it is still imminent. Both motifs more or less span chapters 2–12; and both carry temporal connotations – the feasts, by marking months and seasons in the Jewish liturgical year; Jesus' 'hour,' by its ever intensifying imminence. At three junctures in the narrative events to occur or be effected at the arrival of that 'hour' are cast as being so near as to have already come: the change of worship venue from temple and cult to spirit and truth (4:21–23); the vivification of the dead by the voice of the Son of God (5:25); and the abandonment of Jesus by his disciples (16:31–32). Destro and Pesce see the rapport between these two motifs to be dialectical – in part, because the temporal momentum of Jesus' 'hour' does not seem matched by a chronological succession of feasts. Whereas Jesus' 'hour' is depicted as imminent and moving ever closer to its culmination, the feasts are not listed in liturgical order and, so, appear temporally stagnant by comparison.[213] To anticipate later discussion, however, were those feasts found to have once been listed in chronological order (rather than in the order in which they now appear), the temporal momentum they would then carry might yield different implications for their relationship to Jesus' 'hour.' Rather than being in dialectic against that 'hour,' as Destro and Pesce contend, they might better be cast as in harmony with (and in service to) it.

In sum, Destro and Pesce bring at least two new and important factors into the discussion of Johannine feasts: the rapport feasts enjoy with other rites in the narrative; and the interface those feasts have with the motif of Jesus' 'hour.' The first of these is somewhat overstated: some rites appear

---

[212] Further on this point: some of the rites in John that *are* required by the feasts with which they are associated are given such slight mention it is difficult to imagine the redactor would have intended them at all for some grand dialectic. Destro and Pesce note this for the reference to purification water during the wedding at Cana (2:6; Destro-Pesce 1995a:79; 2000:7–8); but similar obscurity would apply to the ritual purification debated at 3:25, the synagogal liturgy implied at 6:59 and the institution of the temple signified by Jesus' presence in Solomon's Portico at 10:23.

[213] Destro and Pesce 1995a:78, 82; 2000:6, 11–12.

in the Johannine narrative apart from any festal necessity. The second, however, is highly suggestive: feasts dovetail Jesus' 'hour' and seem to carry tandem temporal connotations alongside it.

3.4 Summary

Scholars who have broached the question of feasts in John have treated them on three sets of assumptions: that they are literary devices, structuring or informing the narrative (Boismard and Lamouille, Mollat, Williford, Yee); that they are cues to Johannine liturgical practice (Guilding, Goulder); or that they are emblems and facilitators of institutional Judaism (Destro and Pesce). Several theories generated by these approaches labor under significant difficulties: the numerological significance ascribed to the feasts by Boismard and Lamouille strains to find textual, structural and logical support; the commemorative/christological import credited to the feasts by Mollat (followed by Williford and Yee) is plausible for some but stretched (if not untenable) for others; the liturgical functions alleged for the feasts by Guilding and Goulder enjoy little external corroboration and require exegetical inconsistency; and the role of institutional facilitator assigned to the feasts by Destro and Pesce does not apply to all rituals and institutions appearing in the narrative. A number of insights, however, endure scrutiny and provide contributions on which further reflection can build: particularly, the view of Mollat that *some* feasts furnish commemorative imagery for Johannine christology and that such imagery can function as a facilitator rather than a foil to that christology; the observation by Yee that, from a *halakhic*/calendrical point of view, Johannine festal episodes and Sabbath controversies are of a piece; and the perception by Destro and Pesce that the Johannine feasts carry a tandem form of periodization to the imminence of Jesus' 'hour.'

On this last insight I will now construct my own hypothesis for the way feasts were ordered and the purpose they served in the Fourth Gospel. I present it, not as a replacement to the observations gleaned here (though not all of its features will harmonize to the same degree with each), but rather as a complement to them – an idea on how else the feasts functioned (or could have functioned) while also serving as salvific symbols, sacred times or institutional facilitators. The premise on which that hypothesis turns is the way we read the Passover at 6:4; and it is to that issue that I now turn.

Chapter 4

John 6:4 as 'Second Passover'

4.1 Temporal Tension: 'Barley Loaves' and the Law of Ḥadaš

4.1.1 John 6:9, 'Five Barley Loaves and Two Fish'

My point of departure for this premise is a temporal tension that surfaces in John 6 when 6:4 is read as a regular Passover. Its cue is that the loaves used to feed the five thousand at 6:1–15 are specifically described as "barley loaves." While Jesus is testing Philip on how he and his disciples were to secure bread for the multitude (6:5–7), Andrew interrupts, noticing a youth carrying five loaves and two fish. Significant in Andrew's remarks is that, unlike other gospel accounts of miraculous feedings,[1] he specifically describes those loaves as ἄρτοι κρίθινοι – loaves made from barley:

> Then Jesus, lifting up (his) eyes and seeing that a great multitude
> was coming to him, said to Philip, "Where might we buy bread
> that these may eat?" (This he was saying to test him, for he knew
> what he was about to do.) Philip answered him, "Two hundred denarii
> worth of bread are not sufficient that each might receive a little."
> One of his disciples, Andrew, the brother of Simon Peter, said to him,
> "There is a youth here who has five barley loaves (πέντε ἄρτους κριθίνους)
> and two fish. But what are these for so many?"[2]

4.1.2 The Law of Ḥadaš (Leviticus 23:9–14)

Exegetes have made various deductions from this mention of barley: that it betrays historicity, since John's purpose for inserting it is otherwise indiscernible[3]; that it echoes (though not necessarily derives from) the pagan notion of barley as a divinely given bringer of luck; that the reputation of barley as bread for the poor reflects the socio-economic stratum of both the characters in the story and the community behind them.[4]

---

[1] Matt 14:13–21; 15:32–39; Mark 6:32–44; 8:1–9; Luke 9:10–17.

[2] John 6:5–9.

[3] Johnston 1961–62:52–53.

[4] These last two are offered by Michael Labahn in his recent, detailed treatment of the term; 2000:20–23, 173–76. Labahn draws the pagan idea from Artemidorus' *De somniorum interpretatione* and, in it, sees a christological parallel for John 6: "The barley

Yet unnoticed, however, is the significance barley had in the Jewish festal year. It has already been noted that barley would have come to harvest at the beginning of that year. It was sown from mid-Tishri to mid-Kislev; ripened some four to six months later; and, though affected by sundry climatic, technological, calendrical and methodological factors, would typically yield its crop between Nisan and Sivan. At issue, however, is that, according to the law of *ḥadaš* ("new produce"), this newly harvested barley could not be consumed for non-cultic purposes until its first fruits had been offered at the Waving of the 'Omer. This is legislated, along with the Waving of the 'Omer, in Leviticus 23:

> And the Lord spoke to Moses, saying, "Speak to the sons of Israel and say to them,
> 'When you come to the land which I am giving you and reap its harvest,
> you shall bring the 'omer (אֶת־עֹמֶר), the first of your harvest, to the priest.
> And he shall wave the 'omer (וְהֵנִיף אֶת־הָעֹמֶר) before the Lord
> for your favor; on the day after the Sabbath the priest shall wave it...
> And neither bread nor parched grain nor fresh shall you eat until this very day
> (עַד־עֶצֶם הַיּוֹם הַזֶּה), until you bring the offering of your God.
> (It is) an eternal statute for your generations in all your dwellings.'"[5]

4.1.2.1 Barley and the Waving of the 'Omer

Barley is not named explicitly in the passage: the kind of 'omer (or "sheaf"[6]) to be waved is not identified; and the words "bread" (לֶחֶם), "parched grain" (קָלִי) and "fresh grain" (כַּרְמֶל) are generic, just as apt to designate wheat, oats or spelt. Nor can help be solicited from the sister passage Deuteronomy 16:9–10, which, as mentioned above, depicts the same day as the time "from the beginning of the sickle upon the standing grain." The term translated "standing grain" is קָמָה, again a generic word, denoting a genus of grain covering several species.[7]

That barley is in view, however, is clear on two other grounds. It was the only cereal that would have ripened at the time specified. And, more concretely, it is stated plainly to be such in Second Temple and early Rabbinic traditions. With regard to Second Temple sources, Philo states out-

---

bread given to the crowd by Jesus is an expression of the gift of life, which, by God, Jesus is for humanity (cf. 6:34)" (p. 174).

[5] Lev 23:9–11, 14.

[6] An "'omer" could designate either of two items (Borowski 1987:60–61, 60n7), perhaps both at different times in cultic life (see Thackeray 1957:438n*a*): the yet unbound bundle of stalks left on the ground immediately after reaping (δράγμα in Philo *Spec.* 2.175; text for Philo [here and throughout]: L. Cohn and P. Wendland as per Colson and Whitaker 1927–1962); or the measure of one-tenth an *ephah* (*m. Menaḥ.* 6:6; 10:4; *t. 'Ed.* 1.1 [cf. Exod 16:36]; *t. Menaḥ.* 8.14).

[7] See Zohary 1982:74. According to Borowski (1987:57–58), "standing grain" was the stage at which (all) cereals were ripe and ready for reaping. Further on the generic nature of biblical rubrics for the Waving of the 'Omer, see Yadin 1977/1983:1.102–103; cf. 2.76–78.

right that "the sheaf of the first fruits is barley" (κρίθινον) and, on the grounds of barley's more mundane status among the grains, he reasons that this is why "the law decreed to offer barley (κριθήν) as the first fruits."[8] Josephus, likewise: "On the second day of unleavened bread, that is, also, the sixteenth...they bring him the first fruits of barley (τὰς ἀπαρχὰς αὐτῷ τῆς κριθῆς)..."[9] And, assuming a sectarian date for the Waving of the 'Omer, Qumran documents *4QCalendrical Document/Mišmarot D* (4Q325) and *4QCalendrical Document C* (4Q326) similarly designate the twenty-sixth day of the first month as מועד שעורים, the "Feast of Barley."[10]

In Tannaitic tradition, *Mishnah Soṭah* mentions in passing that, "the offering of the 'omer (מנחת העומר) comes "from barley" (מן־השעורים).[11] *Tosefta Sukkah* and *Roš Haššanah* recount R. Aqiba specifically calling the 'omer "the 'omer of barley" (עומר שעורין) and saying, further, that the 'omer consists of this grain because the time at which it is to be offered (Passover) is "the season of barley" (פרק שעורין).[12] The *Ruth Targum* dates the return of Naomi and Ruth from Moab precisely on Passover, adding that, "on that day the sons of Israel began to harvest the 'omer of the wave offering, which was of barley" (ית עומרא דארמותא דהוה מן שעורין).[13] And *Targum Jonathan* on Hosea, interpreting Hosea's "fifteen shekels of silver and *ḥomer* of barley" (וחמר שערים) in light of the exodus event on 15 Nisan, elaborates on the 'omer to be waved at that time by similarly identifying it with barley:

> And I delivered them by my word on the fifteenth day of the month Nisan;
> and I gave the currency of shekels as atonement for their life.
> And I commanded that they offer before me
> the 'omer of the wave offering from the barley harvest
> (עומר ארמותא מעללת סערין).[14]

---

[8] *Spec.* 2.175. Philo numbered the Waving of the 'Omer fifth of Israel's ten feasts, though he treats it as sixth; *Spec.* 2.41, 162–175.

[9] *Ant.* 3.250; text (here and below): Thackeray 1957.

[10] 4Q325 1 3; 4Q326 4 [partially reconstructed]; text (here and throughout): Talmon with Ben-Dov 2001d–e. Yadin argued that the Waving of the 'Omer in the fragmented 11Q19 xvii 1–10 was also a First Fruits Feast of Barley; 1977/1983:1.102–103; 2.76–78.

[11] *M. Soṭah.* 2:1; text of *Mishnah* (here and below): Blackman 1951–1956.

[12] *T. Sukkah* 3.18; *t. Roš Haš.* 1.12. Texts for *Tosefta* (here and below): for *Zeraim-Neziqin*, Lieberman 1955–88; for *Qodoshim-Tohorot*, Zuckermandel with Lieberman 1937.

[13] *Tg. Ket.* Ruth 1:22; text: Sperber 1968. D.R.G. Beattie (1994:22n27) notes that this targum follows *m. Menaḥ.* 10:3, which allows reaping to begin the first day of Passover.

[14] *Tg. Neb.* Hos 3:2; text: Sperber 1962. See Cathcart and Gordon 1989:35n2; and, further on the 'omer as barley in general, Vogelstein 1894:57.

4.1.2.2 Non-Cultic Consumption of New Produce

The law of *ḥadaš* for barley mandated that, until this 'omer of barley had been offered at the Waving of the 'Omer, no barley (or any new produce) could be consumed for secular (non-cultic) purposes. This is the import of Leviticus 23:9–14, quoted above: "And neither bread nor parched grain nor fresh shall you eat until this very day (עַד־עֶצֶם הַיּוֹם הַזֶּה), until you bring the offering of your God."[15] And, like the identification of that 'omer as barley, it, too, is amply attested in Second Temple and Tannaitic sources.

4.1.2.2.1 Second Temple Sources

Philo suggests it when he reasons that the 'omer of barley was offered, in part, because it would not be pure "to enjoy and partake of any of the (grains) as food without having given thanks for it, as is fitting and right."[16] Josephus is more explicit:

> On the second day of unleavened bread – that is, also, the sixteenth – they partake of the fruit which they have reaped, for they did not touch it earlier. And regarding it to be right to honor God first, from whom they came upon the abundant supply of these things, they bring him the first fruits of barley in such a manner...[17]

Further, a Qumran fragment, *4QHalakha A* (4Q251) 9 (*olim* 5), seems to have assumed as much, if it had not actually stated it in a now lost portion. No specific proscription of barley appears; but, following the reconstruction and commentary of Joseph Baumgarten,[18] one might plausibly be inferred, at two *loci*. First, at lines 1–2, within a partially reconstructed command not to consume "grain, wi]ne or oil unless [the priest has waved] their chief portions, the first fruits."[19] The term glossed (and reconstructed) as "grain" is the generic דָּגָן but may readily have included barley, especially since barley was the first produce annually to be waved by the priest. Second, at lines 5–6, from a prohibition against consuming "new wheat" before Pentecost. Whereas Leviticus does not restrict the secular use of wheat before Pentecost (as it does barley before the Waving of the 'Omer),[20] *4QHalakha A* does: "Let no pe[rs]on eat of the new wheat

---

[15] Lev 23:14. Further on the law of *ḥadaš*, see Segal 1957:266, 302n1 and Baumgarten 1976: 36–40, 45.

[16] Philo *Spec.* 2.175.

[17] *Ant.* 3.250–251.

[18] See Baumgarten 1976:36–46.

[19] 4Q251 9 1–2; the text used here has been published since Baumgarten's initial discussion; Larson, Lehmann and Schiffman 1999.

[20] So, also, the Tannaim, who allowed wheat to be consumed with barley immediately after the Waving of the 'Omer; *Sifre Num.* §148 (on Num 28:1–29:40). See also Baumgarten 1976:38, 38n8.

(חטים חדשים[21]) [...] until the day comes for the bread of first fruits."[22] It
can be deduced *a maiori ad minus* that, if this fragment intensifies Levitical legislation so as to proscribe wheat consumption before Pentecost, it
likely ruled the same for barley consumption before the Waving of the
'Omer.[23]

4.1.2.2.2 Tannaitic Tradition

Mishnah and *Tosefta* list a number of concessions to (or liberties taken on)
the law of *ḥadaš*[24] but, on the whole, show the Levitical legislation to have
been sustained. For new produce, "the 'omer was authorizing (מתיר) for
the country."[25] Barley, along with wheat, spelt, oats and rye, was "prohibited by *ḥadaš* (ואסורים בחדש) before Passover and from reaping before
the 'omer" (ומל קצור מלפני העומר).[26] And, as for the Israelite who did
eat it before Passover (קודם לפסח), "behold, this one is punished with
forty (lashes)."[27] When the second temple stood, the precise time barley
became permissible differed relative to proximity to the cult: for those in
Jerusalem, immediately (מיד) after the Waving of the 'Omer; for those
farther away, midday (מחצות היום). After the temple was destroyed, the
wait was extended through the entire day of the Waving of the 'Omer
(יום הנף כולו) by one of Joḥanan ben Zakkai's *takkanot*.[28] The economic
pressure created by this law moved vendors to set the new produce on the
market at the very moment the 'omer was being waved in the temple.[29]
And, if one of the reasons for intercalating an extra month was "an early

---

[21] In his *editio princeps*, Józef T. Milik restored the end of line 5 so as to make barley
consumption contingent upon Pentecost instead of the Waving of the 'Omer: "Let no o[n]e
partake of the new wheat [or barley (או שעורים)] until the day of the first fruits of bread
comes" (4Q251 9 5–6); Baillet, Milik & de Vaux with Baker 1962:300. Baumgarten has
(rightly) disputed this, however, on the grounds that such a rubric would be unworkable for
the much earlier barley harvest; 1976:37–38.

[22] 4Q251 9 5–6. Baumgarten finds a parallel to this intensification in Philo's comment at
Spec 2.175, cited above; 1976:38–39.

[23] Or, further, that, if *4QHalakha A* did not state such a prohibition in any portion
now lost, it at least represents a *halakhic* position that would have. This is certainly assumed in Baumgarten's discussion; cf. 1976:37–39.

[24] Under various conditions, barley, before the Waving of the 'Omer, could be (or was,
regardless) reaped, stacked, used for healing, fodder, dog food and food for Gentiles; cf. *m.
Pesaḥ.* 4:8; *m. Menaḥ.* 10:8–9; *t. Menaḥ.* 10.28–29; cf. *t. Pesaḥ.* 3.19.

[25] *M. Menaḥ.* 10:6. *T. Menaḥ.* 10.27 reads somewhat differently but carries the same
point: "With respect to the 'omer, it (fresh produce) becomes permitted in the province"
(העומר היה מותר במדינה).

[26] *M. Menaḥ.* 10:7; *m. Ḥal.* 1:1.

[27] *T. Menaḥ.* 10.30.

[28] *M. Menaḥ.* 10:5; cf. *t. Menaḥ.* 10.26.

[29] *M. Menaḥ.* 10:5; cf. *t. Menaḥ.* 10.25.

stage of ripening" (אביב), the people "would rejoice" (היו שמחים)[30]: the rationale is that, though the added intercalary month would push the Waving of the 'Omer back thirty days, the delayed consumption of barley that ensued would have lasted no longer than the state of the grain would have allowed anyway.[31]

Sifra and *Sipre on Numbers* rehearse some of the pertinent *halakhoth* found in *Mishnah-Tosefta*.[32] Pressing further, *Sifra* explains how *Mishnah Menaḥot* applies the law of *ḥadaš* to "barley (שעורים), spelt, oats and rye"[33] and, also, declares that law to be as applicable in the Diaspora as it is in the land of Israel – "The *ḥadaš* is forbidden by Torah in every place" (R. Simeon).[34] Moreover, in *Sipre on Deuteronomy*, R. Simeon uses the law of *ḥadaš* to resolve the *halakhic* discrepancy over how many days of unleavened bread are prescribed for Azyma. In Deuteronomy 16:8, it is six; in Exodus 12:15, seven; and, by drawing upon the law of *ḥadaš*, R. Simeon argues that the first refers to new barley from the new harvest, while the added seventh day of the last refers to old barley from the previous year's crop:

> "Six days shall you eat unleavened bread" (Deut 16:8):
> R. Simeon says, "One passage (Deut 16:8) says,
> 'Six days shall you eat unleavened bread';
> one passage says, 'Seven days unleavened bread shall you eat' (Exod 12:15).
> Unleavened bread is eaten all seven (days):
> it is consumed six (days) from the new (crop);
> but on the seventh, from the old" (ובשביעי מן הישן).[35]

As Reuven Hammer has noted on this passage,[36] the seventh day, in which old barley is to be eaten, is the first day of Azyma (15 Nisan); and the six days, in which new barley is to be eaten, are the second through seventh days of Azyma (16–21 Nisan). The same type of allocation is expressed more clearly in *Targum Pseudo-Jonathan* on Deuteronomy 16:8:

---

[30] *T. Sanh.* 2.2.

[31] Further on the *Tosefta Sanhedrin* passages, particularly in relation to the chronology of Jesus' crucifixion, see Beckwith 1996:282–86.

[32] On the immediate availability of new produce at the Waving of the 'Omer (*Sifra* on Lev 23:9–14 [*Emor* §231/Parashah 10]); on the more specific times that produce became permissible during the day of the Waving of the 'Omer, including Joḥanan ben Zakkai's ruling on it (*Sifra* on Lev 23:9–14 [*Emor* §231/Parashah 10]; *Sifra* on Lev 23:39–44 [*Emor* §238/Pereq 16]); and, more generally, on the 'omer rendering consumption of the new harvest permissible (*Sipre Num* §148 [on Num 28:1–29:40]).

[33] *Sifra* on Lev 23:9–14 (*Emor* §231/Parashah 10); cf. *m. Menaḥ* 10:7. Text for *Sifra* (here and below): Weiss 1946.

[34] *Sifra* on Lev 23:9–14 (*Emor* §231/Parashah 10).

[35] *Sipre Deut.* §134 (on Deut 16:7); text (here and throughout): Finkelstein 1969.

[36] Hammer 1986:446n5 to *Pisqa* 134.

On the first day (after 15 Nisan) you shall offer the 'omer (יח עומרא)
and shall eat unleavened bread from the old harvest;
but for the six days that remain (ושיתא יומין דאשתיירו),
you shall begin to eat unleavened (bread) from the new harvest.[37]

And further in the targums, *Targum Jonathan* on Jeremiah 2:3 draws an analogy from the guilt incurred by those who break the law of *ḥadaš* to accentuate the guilt of those who plunder Jerusalem:

Holy is the house of Israel before the Lord concerning those who plunder them;
like the fruit of the wave offering of the harvest (כדימע ארמות עללא),
concerning which anyone who consumes it is liable unto death.
And, as are the first fruits of the harvest,
the 'omer of the wave offering (עומר ארמותא), (which, as long as the priests,
the sons of Aaron, have not made an offering from it upon the altar, all who consume
it are guilty), so, also, are all who plunder from the house of Israel guilty.
Shame shall be upon them, says the Lord.[38]

A final Tannaitic witness, with peculiar relevance to John 6, is R. Meir's treatment of the *halakha* "They do not intercalate the year because of a famine," in *Tosefta Sanhedrin*. This ruling is, itself, bound up with the law of *ḥadaš*: since new barley could not be consumed until the 'omer had been waved – and, since inserting an intercalary month at the end of the year would push that event back by one month[39] – such intercalation was prohibited during a famine year, due to the added hardship it would create. R. Meir perceives this ruling to be supported in 2 Kings 4:42–44, the story in which Elisha feeds one hundred sons of the prophets with twenty loaves of fresh barley. And, in his attempt to demonstrate his point, he uses the law of new produce as an exegetical criterion. I quote the episode (from the MT) in full:

---

[37] *Tg. Ps.-J.* on Deut 16:8.

[38] *Tg. Neb.* Jer 2:3; text: Sperber 1962. Further, according to Daniel J. Harrington and Anthony J. Saldarini (1987:24n10), the change in *Tg. Neb.* Josh 5:10–11 from the MT "from the morrow after Passover" (ממחרת הפסח) to simply "after Passover" (מבתר פסחא; text: Sperber 1959b) also "reflects the *halakhic* argument over when the sheaf is offered." The biblical reading has Israel eating the new produce of the land the day after Passover, 15 Nisan; the targumic reading accommodates the Waving of the 'Omer by allowing that day to be 16 Nisan or later. This contra Baumgarten (1977:111–12), who sees the Masoretic texts of both Josh 5:10–11 and Lev 23:11, 15 (ממחרת השבת) as "synonymous expressions"; see the question on Baumgarten's reading raised by VanderKam 1979:396n22. Further on the law of *ḥadaš* in Rabbinic literature, see Feliks 1963:189–91.

[39] As noted above, the addition of a "second 'Adar" would delay the beginning of Nisan by some thirty days; see Chapter 2, under '2.2 The Unnamed Feast and a Second Passover (John 5:1–6:71).'

> A man came from Baʿal Shalisha and he brought for the man of God
> bread of the first fruits (לחם בכורים), twenty loaves of bread, barley and fresh grain
> (עשרים־לחם שערים וכרמל) in his sack. And (Elisha) said,
> "Give (it) to the people that they may eat." But his servant said,
> "How will I give this before a hundred men?" And (Elisha) replied,
> "Give to the people, that they may eat. For thus says the Lord,
> '(They will) eat and (they will) have (something) left over.'"
> And he gave to them; they ate and they had (something) left over.[40]

From several features in this passage, R. Meir deduces a twofold premise; namely, that its episode at once predated harvest and postdated the Waving of the ʿOmer. For the first half of that premise – that the episode predated harvest – R. Meir draws upon Baʿal Shalisha's reputation for fecundity: since Baʿal Shalisha typically yielded an array of produce early in the year – yet Elisha's servant arrived from there only with barley (the first grain to ripen) – the incident in question had to have occurred at the beginning of (if not before) harvest proper:

> Behold, is it not the case that there exists no place in the land of Israel
> in which (grain) ripens before Baʿal Shalisha?
> Nevertheless, did not (the servant) produce first fruits
> only from that kind of produce (barley) (אלא מאותו המין)
> which he brought to the man of God?[41]

But, if this (pre-harvest) time period might suggest that the episode also predated the Waving of the ʿOmer, R. Meir continues – with the second half of his premise – that, by the law of *ḥadaš*, the incident equally had to have occurred after that rite had taken place. That Elisha uses this freshly harvested barley to feed the prophets, he reasons, indicates that barley had already been permitted for non-cultic consumption; and this, in turn, implies a date after its first sheaf had been offered:

> Can it be that he (the servant) brought it before the ʿomer? (קודם לעומר)
> Scripture says, "(Elisha) said, 'Give to the people that they may eat'" (2 Kgs 4:43),
> teaching that he (the servant) did not bring it except after the ʿomer
> (שלא הביאו אלא אחר העומר).

From these two factors – a pre-harvest date that also postdated the Waving of the ʿOmer – R. Meir concludes that, in this episode, the liturgical calendar was running ahead of the agricultural year and, thus, warranted intercalation: "So, behold, was it not the case that the year was fit for intercalating?" The reason it had not been intercalated, he finds, is that, according to 2 Kings 4:38, there was a famine that year: "And why did they not intercalate it (at the time of) Elisha? Because it was a year of famine (2 Kings 4:38) and all the people ran to the threshing floors." Thus is confirmed for

---

[40] For a comparative analysis of both Hebrew and LXX texts, see Labahn 2000:166–67.
[41] *T. Sanh.* 2.9.

R. Meir the *halakha*, "They do not intercalate the year because of a famine"[42]; and integral to the exegesis by which he came to that conclusion is
the law of *ḥadaš* for barley.

4.1.3 A Chronological Problem in John 6

Applied to John 6, this law of *ḥadaš* exposes a chronological problem
when the Passover at 6:4 is taken as a regular Passover, observed on 14
Nisan. As recounted above, the Waving of the 'Omer, on which the consumption of new barley depended, was prescribed to occur "on the day after the Sabbath" following Passover.[43] Debate ensued over which Sabbath
(and, therefore, which day for the 'omer offering) was in view: the first
day of Azyma; the first weekly Sabbath after Passover; the last day of
Azyma; or the first weekly Sabbath after Azyma.[44] But, in each scenario,
the Waving of the 'Omer, which followed that Sabbath, would have necessarily post-dated (not preceded) Passover itself. Regarding John 6: on the
one hand, the Passover introduced at 6:4 has not arrived but is only "near"
– "And the Passover, the feast of the Jews, was near." Yet, on the other
hand, the loaves possessed by the youth at 6:9 are described as having already been baked from barley – "There is a youth here, who has five barley
loaves (πέντε ἄρτους κριθίνους) and two fish." If read in light of the law
of *ḥadaš* for barley, these two statements ought not coincide: barley could
not have been used this way until Passover had passed; yet, according to
6:4, that Passover had not yet come.

---

[42] In relation to the *Bavli* version of this discussion (*b. Sanh.* 11b–12a), Jacob
Shachter suggests that the point here turns on the fact that Elisha fed a group rather than
an individual and that, accordingly, "When alone the new crop is permitted" (Shachter
and Freedman 1935:51n9). This inference, however, may be explicitly contradicted by
Josephus in *Ant.* 3.250–251. After describing how the 'omer was prepared and offered on
that day, Josephus concludes, "And then from that time on it is publicly allowed to all
and to each (πᾶσι καὶ ἰδίᾳ) to harvest." That Josephus identifies both the whole of the
people and each individual among them as being allowed to harvest after the 'omer was
offered suggests that neither were so permitted beforehand.

[43] Lev 23:11, 15.

[44] See Chapter 2, under '2.6.2 The Waving of the 'Omer.'

4.2 A Resolution: John 6:4 at 14 'Iyyar

4.2.1 Possible Solutions

4.2.1.1 'Near' (ἐγγύς) as 'Recently Passed'

Assuming the characters in John follow (rather than demur from) Jewish custom,[45] two solutions immediately present themselves. First, that the "nearness" (ἐγγύς) of the Passover at 6:4 refers backward in time, not forward; that is, that "And the feast of the Jews, the Passover, was *near*" means "And the feast of the Jews, the Passover, *had just passed*." Irenaeus may have read 6:4 as such.[46] Doing so identifies the Passover introduced at 6:4 with the unnamed feast at 5:1, which presumably had just occurred; and this, in turn, allows the Waving of the 'Omer to have been performed prior to John 6, solving the chronological tension otherwise caused by the barley at 6:9. Problematic for this proposal, however, is that, while such a reading of ἐγγύς does have precedent outside the Fourth Gospel,[47] it runs directly against convention within it. At every other juncture in John where ἐγγύς describes a feast, that feast occurs in the imminent future[48]:

Table 16. 'Near' (ἐγγύς) in Johannine Festal Introductions[49]

Feast	Festal Introduction	Narrative Parameters of Feast Introduced
1st Passover	"And the Passover of the Jews was near" (ἐγγύς)... (2:13)	John 2:13–3:21
Tabernacles	"And the feast of the Jews, Tabernacles, was near" (ἐγγύς)... (7:2)	John 7:2–52(–10:21)
Last Passover	"And the Passover of the Jews was near" (ἐγγύς)... (11:55)	John 11:55–19:42

---

[45] Luc Devillers, for instance, suggests John 6 was a later insertion into the narrative and that its omission of any pilgrimage for Jesus reflects a growing Christian indifference to Jewish ritual; Devillers 1999:202–205; cf. idem 2002:273–280.

[46] *Adv. Haer.* 2.22.3; see the discussion by Friedrich Kirmis 1940:16–20.

[47] Edmund Sutcliffe (1938:31n1), though not following this reading himself, showed it nonetheless to have extra-biblical support in the superlatives ἐγγύτατος and ἔγγιστος, in Xenophon (*Anabasis* 2.2.11) and *1 Clement* (*1 Clem.* 5:1), respectively. Cf. also Kirmis 1940:18–19.

[48] So, also, the conclusion of Kirmis (1940:20). George Ogg further argues against this retrospective reading of 6:4 on the grounds that the phrase "after these things" (μετὰ ταῦτα) at 6:1 connotes too lengthy a duration between John 5 and 6; 1962:729.

[49] The term "near" (ἐγγύς) does not appear in the introductions to the unnamed feast at 5:1 or the Feast of Dedication (10:22–23).

4.2.1.2 Old Barley

A second possible solution is that the barley of 6:9 was not new barley from the current harvest, but old barley from the previous year's harvest – thereby, permissible by the law of *ḥadaš*. Barley was not completely consumed immediately after harvest, but stored and eaten all year long.[50] As much was assumed in Rabbinic discussion. It was mentioned above that, in *Sipre on Deuteronomy*, R. Simeon resolved the discrepancy between the six days of unleavened bread in Deuteronomy 16:8 and the seven days in Exodus 12:15 by ruling that Deuteronomy spoke of unleavened bread from the new harvest, while Exodus spoke of unleavened bread from the old harvest:

> "Six days shall you eat unleavened bread" (Deut 16:8):
> R. Simeon says, "One passage (Deut 16:8) says,
> 'Six days shall you eat unleavened bread';
> one passage says, 'Seven days unleavened bread shall you eat' (Exod 12:15).
> Unleavened bread is eaten all seven (days):
> it is consumed six (days) from the new (crop);
> but on the seventh, from the old" (ובשביעי מן הישן).[51]

While this *pisqa* primarily shows how the law of *ḥadaš* was used to solve midrashic problems, it also reveals that, in the mind of the Sages, old barley from the previous year's crop could be (and, in fact, was being) consumed up until the new barley was harvested from the next year's crop. The same is attested, in slightly different ways, in *Mekilta* and (albeit less explicitly) in *Sifra*:

> "Seven days shall you eat unleavened bread" (Exod 13:6).
> Another word (of interpretation):
> One passage says, "Six days" (Deut 16:8)
> and one passage says "seven days" (Exod 13:6)
> How are the two readings maintained?
> They are (as follows): the six (days) are from the new (harvest)
> and the seven (days) from the old.[52]

> R. Simeon ben Eleazar says,
> "One passage says, 'Six days shall you eat unleavened bread' (Deut 16:8);
> and one passage says, 'Seven days unleavened bread shall you eat' (Exod 12:15).
> How can the two passages be maintained?
> They are (as follows): it is unleavened bread, which you cannot eat all seven (days);
> but (you can) consume six (days) from the new (harvest)."[53]

---

[50] Borowski 1987:71–83; cf. Wright 1955:54.

[51] *Sipre Deut.* §134 (on Deut 16:7).

[52] *Mek.* on Exod 13:6 (*Pisha* 17.50–52); text (here and below): Lauterbach 1961.

[53] *Sifra* on Lev 23:15–16 (*Emor* §232/Pereq 12).

Reading the barley at John 6:9 as old barley from the previous year's harvest would render the law of *ḥadaš* moot for John 6, thus, solving the chronological difficulty.

Challenging this solution, however, are one, possibly two, biblical allusions in John's miraculous feeding episode (6:1–15) that connote its barley to be, not old, but newly harvested. Possibly Ruth 2:14:

> And, at the time for food, Boaz said to her (Ruth),
> "Come here, eat from the bread and dip your morsel in the vinegar."
> And she sat beside the reapers and he passed her parched grain.
> And she ate and was filled and had (some) left over.

David Daube notes two major parallels that suggest this passage lay back of John 6:1–15. As the multitude in John ate "as much as they wished" (6:11), so Ruth, likewise, eats "until filled"; and, as, in John, twelve baskets "were left by those who had eaten" (6:13), so, too, Ruth, when she had finished eating, "had (some) left over."[54]

Second (and more salient) is 2 Kings 4:42–44, the story of Elisha's miraculous feeding of the prophets, cited earlier in relation to *Tosefta* and the law of *ḥadaš*. I quote it again in full:

> A man came from Ba'al Shalisha and he brought for the man of God
> bread of the first fruits (לחם בכורים), twenty loaves of bread, barley and fresh grain
> (עשרים-לחם שערים וכרמל) in his sack. And (Elisha) said,
> "Give (it) to the people that they may eat." But his servant said,
> "How will I give this before a hundred men?" And (Elisha) replied,
> "Give to the people, that they may eat. For thus says the Lord,
> '(They will) eat and (they will) have (something) left over.'"
> And he gave to them; they ate and they had (something) left over.

Like Ruth 2:14, this passage echoes the Fourth Gospel's description of the abundance of food provided: as the multitude in John 6 ate "as much as they wished" and left enough fragments to fill twelve baskets (6:11–13), so Elisha "gave" to his prophets, they "ate" and, similarly, they "had (something) left over" (2 Kings 4:43–44). But more so: the youth with "five barley loaves and two fish" at John 6:9 recalls Elisha's servant bringing "twenty loaves of bread, barley and fresh grain" (2 Kings 4:42)[55]; Philip's doubts to Jesus about buying sufficient bread to feed the multitude (6:7)

---

[54] Daube 1956:47–51. Daube has noticed two further points: that the LXX term for "gleaning" (συλλέγειν; Ruth 2:3, 7–8, 15–19, 23) interchanges at Ruth 2:7 with "gathering" (συνάγειν; cf. also Ruth 2:2), used in John 6:12; and, also, that the "work" (ἐργασία) Boaz ascribes to Ruth at Ruth 2:12 is tantamount to an act of trust, as is the "work" (ἔργον; ἐργάζεσθαι) Jesus prescribes for the multitude at John 6:27–29.

[55] LXX 4 Kgdms 4:42 uses the same adjective, κρίθινος, for "barley" – one of only five times it is used in the LXX, the others being LXX Num 5:15; Judg 5:8; 7:13; Ezek 4:12. Further on the common reference to "barley bread" in these passages, see Heising 1964:91, 91n39.

bring to mind the servant's question to Elisha about the sufficiency of his loaves to feed so many prophets (2 Kgs 4:43); and the use of παιδάριον to identify the "youth" who furnished the barley loaves and fish at 6:9 is matched by the LXX use of the same term to describe Elisha's servant earlier, at LXX 4 Kingdoms 4:38.[56]

Alkuin Heising would add several minor parallels: that, as the man comes to the prophet at 2 Kings 4:42, so a multitude comes to Jesus at John 6:2; that, as Elisha's disciples are already present at 2 Kings 4:42, so Jesus' disciples are the same at 6:3; that, as Elisha issued (and then renewed) a command to give the people something to eat at 2 Kings 4:42–43, so Jesus issued a command to have the multitude lie down at 6:10; and that, as the execution of that command is described at 2 Kings 4:44, the same is done for the execution of Jesus' command at 6:10–11.[57] Further, despite some qualifying factors,[58] Michael Labahn has suggested certain formal characteristics shared by both episodes: besides their overall structure,[59] (1) that the miracle worker (Elisha/Jesus), his assistant (Elisha's servant/Philip, Andrew [?]) and those in need (prophets/multitude) are identified; (2) that the miracle worker takes initiative for the feeding (2 Kings 4:42c/John 6:5c); (3) that the insufficiency of available bread is stated (2 Kings 4:43a/6:8–9); and, (4) similar to the first major point listed above, that the miracle is confirmed two-fold, by statements that the people ate and that some was left over (2 Kings 4:44/6:12–13b).[60]

---

[56] See Brown 1966/1970:1.246; Mayer 1987–88:172; and, more recently, Öhler 1997:246, 246n667.

[57] Besides those just listed, see the larger catalogue of correspondences listed by Heising; 1964:92n40. In Heising's view, the Fourth Evangelist drew upon one of two circulating Elisha traditions (Tradition B); this, over against the Synoptics, which assimilated both (1964:91–93).

[58] Their common narrative structure and "feeding" genre; their different situational contexts; the possibility that ostensible parallels in the Fourth Gospel could be traced to Johannine *Tendenz* and/or other elements of the author's milieu; Labahn 2000:172–73.

[59] *Exposition*: the identification of the place and people involved (2 Kgs 4:38/John 6:1a, 5a); *Preparation*: the articulation of the intention to feed (2 Kgs 4:42–43/John 6:5b, 8–9); *Implementation*: the description of the distribution of bread (2 Kgs 4:43–44/John 6:10–11); *Demonstration*: the two-fold confirmation of the miracle – that is, statements that the people ate and that some food remained (2 Kgs 4:44/John 6:12–13b); *Reaction*: the stated or described response to the miracle (2 Kgs 4:44/John 6:15).

[60] Labahn 2000:169–73. J.M. Léonard notes the (likely) similar dates of 2 Kgs 4:42–44 and John 6:1–15 – near Passover; 1980:269. Less convincing, however, are several other parallels he alleges: the superlative connotation of Elisha's anonymity (2 Kgs 4:42–44) with the Mosaic connotation of Jesus' miraculous feeding (John 6:14); the false gods Ba'al (of Ba'al Shalisha) and Tiberius (from the "Sea of Tiberias"; John 6:1); the dried fruit (παλάθη) in LXX 4 Kgdms 4:42 with the fish in John 6:9; 1980:268–70. Also problematic is the suggestion by Bernard P. Robinson that the "men" (מֵאָה אִישׁ/ἑκατὸν ἀνδρῶν) Elisha feeds in 2 Kgs/4 Kgdms 4:43 explains the exclusive reference to the same in John 6:10; 1965:107–108.

In both these passages to which John 6 likely alludes – Ruth 2:14 and 2 Kings 4:42–44 – the food in question is freshly harvested barley. Ruth 2:14 is set during the barley harvest[61]; thus, the "parched grain" (קָלִי) of which it speaks is newly reaped barley. And 2 Kings 4:42 tells us that the man coming from Ba'al Shalisha "brought for the man of God bread of the first fruits (לֶחֶם בִּכּוּרִים), twenty loaves of bread, barley and fresh grain (עֶשְׂרִים־לֶחֶם שְׂעֹרִים וְכַרְמֶל) in his sack." It will be recalled that, in *Tosefta Sanhedrin* 2.9, R. Meir appealed to this very feature of the passage to confirm the *halakha* against intercalation during famine: he dated the incident after the Waving of the 'Omer on the grounds that, had it been before, Elisha would not have fed the prophets with recently harvested barley:

> Behold, is it not the case that there exists no place in the land of Israel
> in which (grain) ripens before Ba'al Shalisha?
> Nevertheless, did not (the servant) produce first fruits
> only from that kind of produce (barley) (אֶלָּא מֵאוֹתוֹ הַמִּין)
> which he brought to the man of God?
> Can it be that he (the servant) brought it before the 'omer? (קוֹדֶם לָעוֹמֶר)
> Scripture says, "(Elisha) said, 'Give to the people that they may eat'" (2 Kgs 4:43),
> teaching that he (the servant) did not bring it except after the 'omer
> (שֶׁלֹּא הֱבִיאוּ אֶלָּא אַחַר הָעוֹמֶר).[62]

From this aspect of these verses one might infer that, if such is the case for the passage(s) to which John 6:9 alludes, the same may be meant for John 6:9, itself. That is to say, if the "parched grain" of Ruth 2:14 and the "barley and fresh grain" of 2 Kings 4:42–44 are new barley, not old, perhaps the "five barley loaves" of John 6:9 are the same – freshly harvested barley, from the recent harvest, not stored barley, from the previous year's harvest.[63] To be sure, the inference is not necessary: a clear allusion to

---

Elisha, himself, references these individuals as "people" (עַם/λαός) at 2 Kgs/4 Kgdms 4:42. Moreover, John 6:10 likely speaks of both men and women, on the one hand, and men alone, on the other, since it uses both ἄνθρωπος and ἀνήρ: ἄνθρωπος for Jesus' command to sit ("Jesus said, "Make the people [τοὺς ἀνθρώπους] sit"); ἀνήρ for the count of those who did ("Therefore, the men [οἱ ἄνδρες] sat, in number around five thousand"; οἱ is absent in P^{66} [original scribe] P^{75} D L N W Ψ *Family 1* 33 565 579 892 1010 1241).

[61] Ruth 1:22; 2:17; 3:2, 15, 17, though Ruth's gleaning in the book extends into wheat harvest (Ruth 2:23).

[62] *T. Sanh.* 2.9.

[63] On a more theological plane, Daube and Bertil Gärtner perceive both these allusions to give the Johannine feeding of the five thousand a messianic, eschatological hue. Regarding Ruth 2:14, Daube sees it through the lens of *Ruth Rab.* 5.6 (on Ruth 2:14), which casts either Ruth's eating or Boaz's serving as types of messianic action (Daube 1956:47–48); Gärtner interprets it through *b. Šabb.* 113b, which allegorizes Ruth's "being filled" to mean "the days of the Messiah" and her subsequent departure – "when she rose to glean" (Ruth 2:15a) – as "the Age to Come" (Gärtner 1959:20–25). As for 2 Kgs 4:42–44, it is understood to cast Jesus as a new Elisha, miraculously using meager resource to care for the faithful. Further on an

some details in a biblical passage does not require other details to be carried over with it.[64] But, perhaps, were a further solution available – one that was sensitive to this aspect of Ruth 2 and 2 Kings 4 and that, also, allowed for the future sense of ἐγγύς at 6:4 – that reading might be preferable.

4.2.2 A Third Solution: John 6:4 as 'Second Passover' (Numbers 9:9–14)

For such a reading I propose taking the Passover at 6:4, not as a regular Passover, celebrated on 14 Nisan (the first month), but as the so-called 'Second' (פסח שני) or 'Lesser' (פסחא זעירא/פסח קטן) Passover, observed on 14 'Iyyar (the second month). This Passover is biblically prescribed amidst an episode of ritual uncleanness at Numbers 9:1–14. When some Israelites find themselves ineligible to observe the Passover on 14 Nisan due to corpse impurity (Numbers 9:1–8), God (through Moses) grants them to do so on 14 'Iyyar, one month later. As the legislation has it, all who were pure and present for the first Passover were still bound to observe the feast at its proper time, on pain of death (Numbers 9:13). But, should anyone be defiled through corpse impurity at that time – or, it is added, should anyone at that time be traveling at some distance from the cult – s/he was to keep Passover, instead, on the fourteenth of the following month:

> And the Lord spoke to Moses, saying, "Speak to the sons of Israel, saying,
> 'Each person among you or your generations,
> if he becomes unclean through a deceased person or on a distant journey,
> shall (nonetheless) observe the Passover to the Lord.
> In the second month, on the fourteenth day, between the evenings
> they shall observe it; and they shall eat it with unleavened bread and bitter herbs.
> They shall leave none of it till morning nor shall they break (any) bone in it,
> according to the entire statute of Passover shall they observe it.'"[65]

4.2.2.1 Second Passover in Second Temple Sources

As a minor and (as will be seen) conditional festival, the Passover on 14 'Iyyar tends to be eclipsed by the Passover on 14 Nisan; as such, it can easily be overlooked as an option for the Passover at 6:4. In fact, however, the Passover in 'Iyyar enjoyed great currency in Second Temple and Tan-

---

"Elisha christology" and the issues attending its possibility in this passage, see Heising 1964:91–93; Öhler 1997:246, 246n667; and Labahn 2000:175–76. For Öhler, the feeding of the five thousand at 6:1–15 "is a precise surpassing of the Old Testament miracle (2 Kgs 4:42–44) through the Kyrios Jesus" (p. 246).

[64] For this observation I am indebted to Professor Christophe Rico, University of Strasbourg and École Biblique et Archéologique Française de Jerusalem, who noted it in a personal communication, 10 October, 2005.

[65] Num 9:9–12.

naitic discussion and, thus, could have readily fallen within the purview of the Fourth Evangelist. Treatments are to be found in Philo, Qumran literature, *Mishnah, Tosefta, Mekilta, Sipre on Numbers, Sipre on Deuteronomy, Seder 'Olam Rabbah, Megillat Ta'anit* and the *Chronicles Targum*. Therefore, before I argue the specific point I wish to make regarding this Passover, I will first offer a synopsis of those treatments, so as to give a sense of its pervasiveness and, as such, its viability as an option for 6:4. I will review its Second Temple and Tannaitic attestations, in turn, giving particular attention to the issues it raised for each respective tradent.

A note on terminology. Qumran and Rabbinic sources (as noted above) reference the Passover on 14 'Iyyar as the 'Second Passover' or the 'Lesser Passover'; and, to distinguish that 'Second Passover,' Rabbinic sources often reference the Passover on 14 Nisan as the 'First Passover.' For the sake of clarity in subsequent discussion (given the complicating factor that there are 'three' Passovers in the Gospel of John, usually referenced in ordinal numbers), I will reference the Passover on 14 'Iyyar as the 'Second Passover' (in capital letters), the regular Passover on 14 Nisan as the 'First Passover' (in capital letters) and the three Passovers in John as the 'first' (2:13), 'second' (6:4) and 'final' (11:55) Passovers (in lower case letters).

4.2.2.1.1 Philo Judaeus

Philo treats the Second Passover in *On the Life of Moses II*. For him it is an example of the way Moses exercised his prophetic office through question and answer.

Philo's broad aim in this work is to show Moses apt for royal, legislative, sacerdotal and prophetic office.[66] The last of these offices, Philo claims, manifested itself in three ways – proclamation for, consultation with and inspiration by God[67]; and Moses' judgment on the Second Passover (at Numbers 9), he contends, furnishes the third of four incidents exemplifying the second of these three – that is, consultation with God.[68]

In the account of Numbers 9 which Philo offers, the Israelites who are unclean for the First Passover have become so from mourning recently deceased kin. They find themselves experiencing the dual grief of having lost loved ones, on the one hand, and being banned from the feast, on the other:

---

[66] *Mos.* 2.1.2–3.
[67] *Mos.* 2.35.187–190.
[68] *Mos.* 2.41.221–42.232. The other three being his judgments on blasphemy, Sabbath-breaking and inheritance; *Mos.* 2.36.193–40.220; 2.43.233–44.245.

On the one hand, then, all the other people were rejoicing and exuberant
(each deeming themselves to have been honored with the priesthood),
while others, on the other hand, were spending (the time) weeping and lamenting,
because kin of theirs had recently deceased,
whom, by mourning, (these others) possessed grief twice over,
receiving in addition to the (grief) over kin who had died, that grief
(which came) from being deprived of the pleasure and honor of the sacred observance
(of Passover). (For) it was not permitted them to be purified or sprinkled that day,
inasmuch as the period of their mourning, which exceeded a single day,
did not yet lay behind (them).[69]

This twofold grief, according to Philo, puts Moses on the horns of a dilemma. "Mercy and justice" bade leniency for the grief-stricken; but "the law of the Passover sacrifice" required that Passover be observed in the first month of the year, since, beginning as it does with the vernal equinox, it aligns with the period in which nature begins to yield grain, humankind's most necessary food.[70] Wavering between the two, Moses consults God, who, in response, establishes a perpetual Passover on the fourteenth of the second month, both for anyone who "would ever again experience the same circumstances" and for "those who are hindered from performing the rite with the entire nation, not by mourning, but because of a distant journey"[71]:

(God) said, "Mourning as kin is a necessary grief for those of (the same) blood
and is not inscribed among offenses. Therefore, while (the period of mourning) lies
before (such persons), let it be driven out from the sacred enclosures,
which are to be pure from all pollution...But when it lies behind (those persons),
let them not be deprived an equal share in the sacred observances, lest those who live
might be an extension of those who have deceased. And let them go as second
(observers) in the second month (ἅτε δεύτεροι δευτέρῳ μηνί),
again on the fourteenth day (πάλιν τεσσαρεσκαιδεκάτῃ ἡμέρᾳ),
and let them sacrifice in the same manner as the first (observers),
and let them employ a similar rule and custom for the sacrifices as did those
(first observers). And let the same things be permitted, also,
for those who are hindered from performing the rite with the entire nation,
not by mourning, but because of a distant journey."[72]

---

[69] *Mos.* 2.41.225; cf. 2.41.226–227.
[70] *Mos.* 2.41.222–224, 228.
[71] *Mos.* 2.42.229, 232.
[72] *Mos.* 2.42.230–232.

4.2.2.1.2 Qumran Literature

4.2.2.1.2.1 Calendrical/Mišmarot Texts

Second Passover also appears in three Calendrical/*Mišmarot* documents from Qumran: *4QOtot* (4Q319), *4QCalendrical Document/Mišmarot A* (4Q320) and *4QCalendrical Document/Mišmarot C* (4Q321).[73] Calendrical/*Mišmarot* documents calibrate a repertoire of astronomic and cultic events[74] relative to one another within the medium of a 364-day solar ephemeris over cycles of varying length – three, six and seven years. Among these events are feasts; and, in these three documents, one of the feasts listed is the 'Second Passover' of the second month, specifically titled פסח שני. In *4QOtot* (4Q319), perhaps part and parcel with the *Serekh Ha-Yaḥad* documents,[75] it is reckoned (with other feasts) relative to the numbered days of the priestly courses in which it falls, over a period of six years[76]:

- [On the fifth, in Se'orim, the Second Passover (הפסח השני)][77]
- [On the fifth, in Yeḥezq'el] the Second [Passover] (הפסח [השני)[78]
- [On the fifth, in Ma]'oziah, the [Second] Passover ([הפסח] השני)[79]

In *4QCalendrical Document/Mišmarot A* (4Q320), 'Second Passover' is plotted (with other festivals) relative to the numbered days of the priestly courses in which it would fall over a six-year cycle:

---

[73] A complete list of the Calendrical/*Mišmarot* documents, with detailed categorization, can be found in Tov 2002:133–36.

[74] Particularly, days, lunar months, solar months, quarter years, full years, courses of priestly temple service (*mišmarot*), Sabbaths, first days of months, first and last days of quarters, jubilee years, as well as the enigmatic unnamed occurrence labeled "X" and the *duqo/ah* of 4Q320–321a.

[75] *4QOtot* (4Q319) was written on the same scroll as the *Serekh Ha-Yaḥad* fragment *4QSerekh Ha-Yaḥad[e]* (4Q259) and debate has ensued over whether the two are discrete works or of a piece. The two sides are currently expressed by the editors of the respective *editiones principes*: on the two as a single work, see Philip Alexander and Geza Vermes (1998a:11; 1998b:134), the editors of 4Q259; on the two as separate works, see Jonathan Ben-Dov (2001:196), the editor of 4Q319. For further history of the debate, see Ben-Dov (as listed).

[76] In the Qumran fragments treated in this section, brackets represent reconstructions of lost text; parentheses around English words are inferences based on context. The presence of 'Second Passover' in certain lines within these documents is sometimes entirely deduced and reconstructed. But, given the formulaic, repetitive and even arithmetic character of these texts, those reconstructions are well grounded.

[77] 4Q319 12 1; text (here and below): Ben-Dov 2001.

[78] 4Q319 13 1.

[79] 4Q319 13 4.

- on the fifth, in Se'orim, the [Second] Passover (הפסח[השני])[80]
- [on the fifth, in] 'Abiah, [the Second Passover] (הפסח[השני])[81]
- on the fifth, in Yaq[i]m, the [Second] Passover (הפסח ה[ש]ני)[82]
- on the fif[th, in 'I]mmer, the Second Passover (הפסח השני)[83]
- [on the] fifth, in Yeḥezq'el, the Second Passover (הפסח השני)[84]
- [on the fif]th, in Ma'oziah, the [Second] Passover (הפסח ה[ש]ני)[85]

And, similarly, in *4QCalendrical Document/Mišmarot C* (4Q321), 'Second Passover' is calculated relative to priestly courses in which it would fall over a six-year cycle. Unlike 4Q320, however, the numbered days within each course are not specified; and those courses, themselves, are calibrated to the numbered months in which they occur:

- [The second (month arrives) in Yeda'iah; in] Se'orim [comes the Second Passover] (הפסח השני])[86]
- The second (month arrives) in Mi[yamin; in 'Abiah] comes the Second Passover (הפסח השני)[87]
- The sec[ond] (month arrives) in Šekaniah; in Yaqim comes the [Sec]ond Passover (הפסח [הש]נ[י)[88]
- [The second (month arrives)] in Yeš[eb'a]b; in ['Immer comes the Second Passover] (הפסח השני])[89]
- The se[cond (month arrives) in Happiṣṣeṣ]; in Yeḥezq'el comes [the] Second Passover (הפסח [ה]ש[ני)[90]
- [The second (month arrives) in Gamul; in Ma'oziah comes the Second Passover] (הפסח השני]).[91]

4.2.2.1.2.2 *Excursus: Second Passover in the* Temple Scroll*?*

Yigael Yadin suggested that a Second Passover had also been listed in two *lacunae* in *11QTemple Scroll[a]*: at 11Q19 xi 11, within a digest of appointed times at which rites of exchange were to be offered (11Q19 xi 9–13); and at 11Q19 xviii, within a series of rubrics on how those rites were to be performed (11Q19 xiii 8–xxx [1]). At the beginning of 11Q19 xi 11, according to Yadin, the designation 'the Second Passover' (הפסח השני) would have come immediately after the phrase "on the day of the Waving of the 'Omer" (וביום הנף העומר) at the end of 11Q19 xi 10. The same

---

[80] 4Q320 4 iii 4; text (here and below): Talmon with Ben-Dov 2001b.
[81] 4Q320 4 iii 14.
[82] 4Q320 4 iv 9.
[83] 4Q320 4 v 3.
[84] 4Q320 4 v 12.
[85] 4Q320 4 vi 8.
[86] 4Q321 iv 9 (frg 4.); text (here and below): Talmon with Ben-Dov 2001c.
[87] 4Q321 v 4–5 (frg. 4).
[88] 4Q321 v 9 (frg. 4).
[89] 4Q321 vi 3–4 (frgs. 4–5).
[90] 4Q321 vi 7–8 (frgs. 4–5).
[91] 4Q321 vii 2 (frg. 5).

sequence, he noted, occurs several times in *4QCalendrical Docu-
ment/Mišmarot A–B* (4Q320–321), partly represented above:[92]

1) *4QCalendrical Document/Mišmaro*t A (4Q320)

- On the first, [in] Yeda'[iah], the Waving of the ['Omer] (הנף ה[עמר]);
  on the fifth, in Se'orim, the [Second] Passover (הפסח [השני])[93]

- [On the first], in Miya[mi]n, the Waving of the ['Omer] (הנף ה[עמר])
  [on the fifth, in] 'Abiah, [the Second Passover] ([הפסח השני])[94]

- On the first, in Šekaniah, the Waving of the 'Omer (הנף העמר);
  on the fifth, in Yaq[i]m, the [Second] Passover ([הפסח ה[שני])[95]

- On the first, [in Yeše]b'ab, the Waving of the 'Omer (הנף העמר);
  on the fif[th, in 'I]mmer, the Second Passover (הפסח השני)[96]

- [On the] first, in Happiṣṣeṣ, the Waving of the 'Omer (הנף העמר);
  [on the] fifth, in Yeḥezq'el, the Second Passover (הפסח השני)[97]

- On the first, in Gamul, the Waving of the 'Omer (הנף העמר);
  [on the fif]th, in Ma'oziah, the [Second] Passover ([הפסח ה[שני])[98]

2) *4QCalendrical Document/Mišmaro*t B (4Q321)

- [The fi]rst [year. The fir]st (month arrives) in Ga[mul;
  on the thi]rd (day), in Ma['oziah] comes
  [the Passover; in Yeda'iah comes the Waving of the 'Omer (הנף העומר).
  [The second (month arrives) in Yeda'iah; in] Se'orim [comes
  the Second Passover] (הפסח השני)[99]

- The second (year). The first (month arrives) in Yeda'i[ah]; in Se'orim comes
  the Passover; i[n] [Mi]yamin [co]mes the Waving of the 'Omer (הנף העומר).
  The second (month arrives) in Mi[yamin; in 'Abiah] comes
  the Second Passover (הפסח השני)[100]

---

[92] Yadin 1977/1983:2.45. At the time Yadin wrote, only a sampling of these were published, in a preliminary report by J.T. Milik (1957:25). Here they are given in full, as per their
editiones principes. Lacunae are as represented.

[93] 4Q320 4 iii 3–4.

[94] 4Q320 4 iii 13–14.

[95] 4Q320 4 iv 8–9.

[96] 4Q320 4 v 2–3.

[97] 4Q320 4 v 11–12.

[98] 4Q320 4 vi 7–8.

[99] 4Q321 iv 8–9 (frg. 4).

[100] 4Q321 v 4–5 (frg. 4).

- [The] third (year). The fir[s]t (month arrives) in [Miyami]n; in 'Abiah comes
  the Passover; in Šekan[ia]h comes the Waving of the 'Omer (הנף העומר).
  The sec[ond] (month arrives) in Šekaniah; in Yaqim comes
  the [Sec]ond Passover (הפסח [הש]נ'י)[101]

- [The fourth (year). The first month (arrives) in Šekaniah; in Yaqim comes
  the] Pa[ssover; in Yešeb'ab comes the Waving of the 'Omer (הנף העומר);
  the second (month arrives)] in Yeš[eb'a]b; in ['Immer comes
  the Second Passover] (הפסח השני['])[102]

- The fifth (year). The fi[rst] (month arrives) in [Yešab'ab; in 'Immer] comes
  the Passover; in Happ[isses com]es the Waving of the 'Omer (הנף העומר);
  the se[cond (month arrives) in Happisses]; in Yeḥezq'el comes
  [the] Second Passover (הפסח [ה]ש[נ'י)[103]

- [The sixth (year). The first (month arrives) in Happisses; in Yeḥezq'el comes
  the Passover; in Gamul comes the Waving of the 'Omer (הנף העומר);
  the second (month arrives) in Gamul; in Ma'oziah comes
  the Second Passover] (הפסח השני['])[104]

As for 11Q19 xviii, Yadin alleged that a brief rubric for Second Passover
could have obtained in the six lines now missing at the top of the column.
The extant portion of the column (11Q19 xviii 2–10a) consists in final directives for the Waving of the 'Omer. The lost portion at the top, according
to Yadin, would contain the first part of those directives, preceded by "a
short command about 'Second Passover.'"[105]

Yadin is correct that a brief prescription for Second Passover could have
fit atop 11Q19 xviii. I can confirm this judgment by reckoning his figures
on the available lines and ruled column width of 11Q19 xviii with measurements I have taken on lettered line lengths in 11Q19 xvii and xviii.[106]

I proceed in two major steps, each divided into several sub-steps. First, I
calculate the amount of letter space taken up by the rubric for First Passover at 11Q19 xvii 6–9. I do this by (a) measuring the lengths of the currently visible lettered portions of its lines (that is, excluding Yadin's reconstructions, as well as several letters at the beginning or end of some
lines that were discernible to him but are no longer visible); (b) calculating

---

[101] 4Q321 v 8–9 (frg. 4).

[102] 4Q321 vi 3–4 (frgs. 4–5).

[103] 4Q321 vi 7–8 (frgs. 4–5).

[104] 4Q321 vii 1–2 (frg. 5). Cf. also now the same sequence at 4Q319 12 1; 13 3–4 (and
implicitly 13 1), partly recounted above.

[105] Yadin 1977/1983:2.76; cf. also 1.99–100.

[106] This courtesy of the Israel Antiquities Authority, which allowed me access to
11Q19 and several other fragments on 10 and 14 July, 2003. My thanks also to the College of William & Mary, for a Faculty Summer Research Grant in 2003 that funded my
research.

the average ratio of line length to letter in columns xvii and xviii; (c) applying that ratio to the portions of Yadin's text excluded from (a) – that is, to his reconstructions and to the letters that were discernible to him but are no longer visible; and then (d) adding the results to the length determined in (a).

With Yadin's reconstructions, the passage treating the First Passover at column xvii reads thus:

11Q19 xvii 6–9[107]

וֹעשׁ]וּ [בארב]עה עשׂר בחודש הראישׁון [בין הערבים]
[פסח ליהוה] וזבחו לפני מנחת הערב וזבחון במועדו(?)]
מבן עשׂרי[ם] שׁנה ומעלה יעשׂו אותו ואכלוהו בליל ה
בחצרות [ה]ק[וֹ]>ל<דש והשׁכימו והלכו אישׁ לאוהלו [ ][108]

[And they shall obs]erve [on the fou]rteenth, in the first month, [between the evenings] [a Passover to the Lord.] And they shall sacrifice before the evening offering.

And they shall sacrifice [at its appointed time.]

From twent[y] years old and upward they shall observe it; and they shall eat it at night in the courts of [the] holy place. And they shall rise early and each go to his tent [ ].

(a) The currently visible lettered portions of these lines span as follows:

· xvii 6, עשׂר בחודש הראישׁון, 4.45 cm
· xvii 7, וזבחו לפני מנחת הערב וזבחו, 5.2 cm
· xvii 8, עשׂרי[ם] שׁנה ומעלה יעשׂו אותו ואכלוה, 6.7 cm[109]
· xvii 9, בחצרות [ה]ק[וֹ]>ל<דש והשׁכימו והלכו אישׁ לאוהל, 8.1 cm[110]

(b) The average ratio of line length to letter in 11Q19 xvii and xviii is .22 cm/letter. This is calculated by measuring the full length of the lettered portions of each line and setting that number against the amount of letters (and single letter spaces between words) in that line.[111] The details are charted below: lettered lines broken by substantive lacunae within any part of the lettered portion are omitted from the count:

---

[107] Text: Yadin 1977/1983.

[108] Supralinear.

[109] Included in the count is the lacuna in which Yadin reconstructs [ם], measuring 3 mm.

[110] Included in the count is the lacuna in which Yadin reconstructs [ה], measuring 6 mm. from the ה before it; >ל< is written as a supralinear between קֹ.

[111] Both columns are likely written by the same scribe (Yadin 1983:1.11–12) and, so, represent the same hand.

Table 17. Space to Letters in 11Q19 Column XVII

Line	First/Last (Portions of) Words Measured[112]	Length	Length/ Letters
1	הנים – עט	2.4 cm	2.4 cm/13
2	מחו – עליהם	3.2 cm	3.2 cm/17
3	יה – להמה	3.5 cm	3.5 cm/16
4	מושבותמה – ויש	4.2 cm	4.2 cm/19
5	Lacuna		
6	עשר – הראישון	4.45 cm	4.45 cm/17
7	וזבחו – וזבחו	5.2 cm	5.2 cm/26
8	Lacuna[113]		
9	Lacuna		
10	ובחמשה – ק	6.4 cm	6.4 cm/27
11	כול – ימי	9.5 cm	9.5 cm/44
12	ליהוה – הא	9.5 cm	9.5 cm/43
13	עולה – שבע	9.4 cm	9.4 cm/43[114]
14	תמימים – ונסכמה	10 cm	10 cm/42
15	Lacuna		
16	Lacuna		
Total		67.75 cm	67.75 cm/307

---

[112] The letters visible for these measurements did not always match the span represented in Yadin's transcriptions.

[113] Though the full spans of xvii 8–9 could be (and were) measured to determine the full visible line lengths under step (a), lacunae within them preclude their use for counting the more precise length-to-letter ratios within those lines.

[114] Not counted is a sublinear ו, placed between two ה's having no space between them.

Table 18. Space to Letters in 11Q19 Column XVIII

Line	First/Last (Portions of Words) Measured	Length	Length/ Letters
1	ה – א	.7 cm	.7 cm/3
2	לאיל – הזה	1.65 cm	1.65 cm/8
3	היום – ו	2.15 cm	2.15 cm/11
4	עזים – לחטאת[115]∘	2.7 cm	2.7 cm/11
5	סכו – סולת	4.2 cm	4.2 cm/20
6	יין – ההין	4.4 cm	4.4 cm/20
7	ל – אשמת	4.35 cm	4.35 cm/19
8	קות – להמ	4.4 cm	4.4 cm/20
9	ואחר – פע	5.5 cm	5.5 cm/24
10	Lacuna		
11	שבע – העומר	7.9 cm	7.9 cm/38
12	פורו – תספורו	8 cm	8 cm/34
13	יום – ממושבותיכמה	9.3 cm	9.3 cm/41
14	Lacuna		
15	Lacuna		
16	Lacuna		
Total		55.25 cm	55.25 cm/249

The resulting ratio is as follows:

Total lettered space measured   123 cm
Total letters counted   556
Average space per letter   .22 cm/letter

---

[115] Measured to the letter space left of לחטאת and just right of a visible dot representing the right side of a letter.

(c) When this ratio is applied to the portions of texts reconstructed by Yadin (or discernible to him but no longer visible), it yields the following: line 6 could be extended by 5.06 cm; line 7, by 3.74 cm; line 8 by 2.42 cm; line 9 by .22 cm.

	Reconstruction	Letter Number (including spaces)	Calculated Length (letter number × .22 cm)
Line 6	וְעַשׂ]וּ [בָּארב]עה[116]	12	2.64 cm
	[וְ]בין הערבים][117]	11	2.42 cm
		Total 23	5.06 cm
Line 7	[פסח ליהוה][118]	10	2.20 cm
	[במועדו(?)[119]	7	1.54 cm
		Total 17	3.74 cm
Line 8	מבן[120]	4	.88 cm
	וּ בלילה[121]	7	1.54 cm
		Total 11	2.42 cm
Line 9	וּ[122]	1	.22 cm
		Total 1	.22 cm

(d) When these figures from (c) are added to the lettered line lengths measured in (a), they render the treatment of First Passover at 11Q19 xvii 6–9 to span some 35.89 centimeters (allowing for about 163 letters or single letter spaces):

Line 6   9.51 cm (4.45 cm + 5.06 cm)
Line 7   8.94 cm (5.2 cm + 3.74 cm)
Line 8   9.12 cm (6.7 cm + 2.42 cm)
Line 9   8.32 cm (8.1 cm + .22 cm)
          Total 35.89 cm

For the second major step in confirming Yadin's speculation, I weigh the total from the first major step against the available space at the top of column xviii. I do this by (a) multiplying the number of lines lost in column xviii by the width of its ruled column; (b) measuring the result against 35.89 cm, the amount of space calculated to be taken up by the rubric for

---

[116] Including one space between עשר and עַ] (before it).

[117] Including one space between בין and הראישון (before it).

[118] Including one space between וזבחו and ליהיה (before it).

[119] Including one space between במועדו and וזבחו (before it), and only counting to the end of במועדו.

[120] Including one space between עשרי[ם] and מבן (before it).

[121] The ו concludes the previous ואכלוהן[

[122] Concluding the currently visible לאוהל.

the First Passover at 11Q19 xvii 6–9; and (c) making accommodation for the beginning of the rubric for the Waving of the 'Omer in 11Q19 xviii – as mentioned above, it spans lines 2–10 in the extant portion of the column, but began prior to line 2.

(a) According to Yadin, the lost portion of column xviii would have covered six lines; and the width of the ruled column is +/- 10.5 cm[123]: multiplying the one by the other puts the amount of available space at the top of column xviii at 63 cm (6 cols. × 10.5 cm).[124]

(b) Since the rubric for First Passover would have taken up 35.89 cm, the amount of space available at the top of column xviii exceeds what would be required by some three quarters of that rubric's size, extending beyond it by 27.11 cm.

(c) Thus, even allowing for the beginning of the command for the Waving of the 'Omer (spanning 11Q19 xviii 2–10a) – and supposing that a command for Second Passover might be shorter than the one for the First Passover – there seems to be arithmetic justification for Yadin's suggestion that a rubric for Second Passover might have appeared atop 11Q19 xviii.

These numbers notwithstanding, Yadin's inferences about the Second Passover, in both places mentioned, are highly improbable. A command for a Second Passover at the top of column xviii would violate the chronological order that otherwise governs the list in 11Q19 xiv 9 – xxix 1. All other fixed times in that list are catalogued sequentially, following the temporal order by which they would have unfolded through the liturgical year[125]: the first day of the first month; the Ordination of Priests (eight days between 1/1–13[126]); Passover (1/14); Azyma (1/15–21 or 22[127]); the

---

[123] Yadin 1977/1983:1.12–13.

[124] Dividing this available space by the length of space per letter calculated above renders the number of possible letters for the top of column xviii at some 286 (63 cm ÷ .22 cm/letter).

[125] On this *Temple Scroll* festal list, see Yadin 1977/1983:1.40–41, 49–54, 89–142; 2.56–127; Wise 1990: 129–30.

[126] Yadin suggested these days start on the first day of the first month. Based on the *Damascus Document* prohibition against offering anything but the Sabbath sacrifice on Sabbath (at CD xi 17–18), he extended their duration (and the duration of other periods of six to eight days) by one day, to account for a skipped Sabbath within them; 1977/1983:1.130–31. By contrast, Shemaryahu Talmon and Jonathan Ben-Dov have observed that the Psalms Scroll (11Q5 xxvii 4–7) implies festal days did, in fact, overlap the Sabbath, since the three hundred and sixty-four songs David is alleged to have written for daily offerings are supplemented with (not reduced by) the fifty-two he wrote for Sabbath offerings; 2001e:137.

[127] The final day would depend on whether or not the Sabbath coming within the festal week was skipped, as per Yadin in the previous note.

Waving of the 'Omer (between 1/16–23 or 1/26[128]); the First Fruits of Wheat (fifty days from the Waving of the 'Omer); the First Fruits of Wine (fifty days from the First Fruits of Wheat); the First Fruits of Oil (fifty days from the First Fruits of Wine); the Festival of the Wood Offering (six consecutive days between the First Fruits of Oil and the first of the seventh month[129]); the first day of the seventh month; the Day of Atonement (7/10); and the Feast of Tabernacles (7:15–22/23). A command to observe the Second Passover at the top of 11Q19 xviii, however, would place the Second Passover prior to the command for the Waving of the 'Omer, which is treated in the first nine lines of extant text later in that column (11Q19 xviii 2–10a); and this, in turn, would have inverted their temporal order, since the Second Passover was to be observed on the fourteenth of the second month, while the Waving of the 'Omer came sometime, either between the sixteenth and twenty-third of the first month or on the twenty-sixth of that first month. Such an inversion would reflect a significant departure from the consecutive presentation that typifies the rest of the list; and, on that basis, it is unlikely a Second Passover rubric would have obtained at that juncture.

As for הפסח השני at 11Q19 xi 11, the Calendrical Document/*Mišmarot* fragments to which Yadin appealed for his reconstruction are not true parallels to the *Temple Scroll* festal year. The full cycle of feasts listed in those fragments consists in Passover, the Waving of the 'Omer, Second Passover, the Feast of Weeks, the Day of Remembrance, the Day of Atonement and the Feast of Tabernacles.[130] All of these (bracketing the Second Passover) do appear in the *Temple Scroll*; but the *Temple Scroll* departs from this particular Calendrical/*Mišmarot* cycle by listing more: the first day of the first month, the Ordination of Priests, Azyma

---

[128] On the grounds that the *Temple Scroll* assumes a 364-day solar ephemeris, Yadin (and many following him) have dated the Waving of the 'Omer specifically to the twenty-sixth of the first month, the First Fruits of Wheat to the fifteenth of the third month, the First Fruits of Wine to the third of the fifth month and the First Fruits of Oil to the twenty-second of the sixth month; Yadin 1977/1983:1.116–19 (referencing Milik's report [1957:25; cf. 1959:109–10] on the Calendrical/*Mišmarot* documents that attest to this last date listed, the First Fruits of Oil on 6/22 [see now 4Q325 2 6–7; 4Q394 1–2 v 3–6]). Here those feasts are dated, more generically, relative to one another: allowing for the other possibilities treated above (see Chapter 2, under '2.6.2 The Waving of the 'Omer'), the Waving of the 'Omer might lie either on the twenty-sixth of the first month (the sectarian date) or anywhere between the sixteenth to the twenty-third of that month (the three other options, allowing for a skipped Sabbath). On the debate over the type of calendar implied in the *Temple Scroll*, see Wise 1990:10–11.

[129] Yadin, allowing for the Sabbath, dates the observance from the twenty-third to the twenty-ninth of the sixth month; 1977/1983:1.128–31.

[130] 4Q319 12 1–3; 13 1–5; 4Q320 4 iii 1–14; 4 iv 1–14; 4 v 1–14; 4 vi 1–12; 4Q321 iv 8–9 (frg. 4); v 1–9 (frg. 4); vi 1–9 (frgs. 4-5); vii 1–6 (frg. 5).

(maybe as part of Passover), the First Fruits of Wine, the First Fruits of Oil and the Festival of the Wood Offering. Other Calendrical/*Mišmarot* texts – *4QCalendrical Document/Mišmarot D* (4Q325), *4QCalendrical Document C* (4Q326) and *4QCalendrical Document D* (4Q394 1–2) – do attest some of these extra feasts: the First Fruits of Wine; the First Fruits of Oil; the Festival of Wood[131]; and the Ordination of the Priests.[132] But these lists are separate and distinct from those listed above (in 4Q319–321), in which the Second Passover appears; and, in them, no Second Passover obtains, whatsoever. This is particularly clear in the relevant portion of *4QCalendrical Document/Mišmarot D* (4Q325): in it, Sabbaths and feasts are calculated relative to the numbered days of the first and second months, with no mention of a Second Passover between the ninth and sixteenth, where it would have been slated if part of the list:

> [The Passover ,the thi]rd (day); on the eighteenth (is) the Sabbath up[on (which enters) Yoiarib] in the evening; on the twenty fifth, the Sabbath upon (which enters) Yeda'iah; and they go up[...the Fea]st of Barley, on the twenty sixth, after the Sabbath. The beginning of the [second] month,
> [on the sixth, on the Sabbath] upon (which) enters Yeda'iah; on the second, the Sabbath of Ḥarim; on the ninth, the Sabbath, [Se'orim];
> on the sixteenth, the Sabbath, Malkiah; on the twenty thir[d, the Sabbath, Miya]min; on the thirtieth, the Sabbath, Haqqoṣ.[133]

It is arguable, in fact, that at least two discrete festal sequences obtain in the Calendrical/*Mišmarot* texts: one at 4Q319–321, which includes a Second Passover but not the additional *Temple Scroll* feasts represented in 4Q325–326 and 4Q394 1–2; and one at 4Q325–326 and 4Q394 1–2, which incorporates those unique *Temple Scroll* feasts but omits any Second Passover, such as one finds in 4Q319–321.[134] It is possible, as Shemaryahu

---

[131] 4Q325 2 1–7 and 4Q394 1–2 i–v.

[132] 4Q326 1–5. So the reconstruction by Talmon with Ben-Dov (2001e:134–37), on the basis of 11Q19 xiv 9–xv 14.

[133] 4Q325 1 1–6. For the reconstruction by Talmon and Ben-Dov, see Talmon with Ben-Dov 2001d:126–28. This same point is also strongly suggested in the reconstruction Talmon and Ben-Dov offer for 4Q326 1–5: "In the first (month), on the fourt[h, a Sabbath; on the eighth, the Feast of (the Priest's) Ordination]; on the eleventh, a Sabba[th; on the fourteenth, the Passover, the third day; on the fifteenth,] the Feast of Unleavened Bread, the fourt[h day; on the eighteenth, a Sabbath; on the twenty-fifth, a Sabbath; on the twenty sixth, the Feast of B[arley, after the Sabbath: the first month (consists) [in] thirty (days). On the second (day of the second month) comes [a Sabbath; *on the ninth (day) comes a Sabbath; on the sixteenth*]" (italics mine); 2001e:134–35.

[134] Anomalous to both, in fact, is 4Q325 1 1–6 (represented above). Like the second sequence and unlike the first, it lists the Waving of the 'Omer under the title "Feast of Barley" (שעורים מ[וע]ד); unlike the second sequence, however, and like the first, it registers no Azyma between Passover and the Feast of Barley (though possibly implying it in its reference to Passover; see Talmon with Ben-Dov 2001d:127).

Talmon has argued, that, in sectarian practice, these two festal sequences (along with others) were conflated into a single, liturgical year.[135] Not so, however, in the schematic calendars of *11QTemple Scroll*[a] and the Calendrical/*Mišmarot* documents, for which and on which (respectively) Yadin made his case. When these false parallels are considered alongside the chronological problem that occurs when a Second Passover is inferred atop 11Q19 xviii, that case falls altogether. If a Second Passover is attested in 4Q319–321, it is not so in 4Q325–326, 4Q394 1–2 and, by extension, the *Temple Scroll.*

4.2.2.2 Second Passover in Tannaitic Tradition

4.2.2.2.1 Mishnah

Second Passover pervades Tannaitic sources. In *Mishnah*, the criteria regulating its observance are expanded and refined: Second Passover must further be observed if a person "erred or was constrained" (שגג או נאנס) in (or from) observing the First Passover[136]; and, for a variety of specified circumstances, its requirement is either maintained or waived, depending on which contingencies ensue.[137] Debate is waged over the distance one must be from the temple during the First Passover to be bound (or permitted) to observe the Second[138]; and an inventory is taken of the differences, as well as similarities, existing between the two.[139] A vignette is recounted about Joseph the Priest, who would bring his sons and household "to observe the Lesser Passover in Jerusalem"(לעשות פסח קטן בירושלים).[140] And we are told that, while the temple still stood, messengers went forth to proclaim the new moon "also on 'Iyyar, because of the Lesser Passover" (אף על אייר מפני פסח קטן).[141]

4.2.2.2.2 Tosefta

In *Tosefta*, those who must "prepare the Second (Passover)" (אילו עושין את השני) are further itemized[142]; the contingencies for which observance of a Second Passover is required or waived are elaborated[143] or in-

---

[135] Talmon 2001:207–215; cf. Talmon with Ben-Dov 2001a:15 ('Appendix 1').

[136] *M. Pesaḥ.* 9:1.

[137] *M. Pesaḥ.* 7:6; 8:2, 6; 9:9.

[138] *M. Pesaḥ.* 9:2; the distance from Jerusalem to Modiith (R. Aqiba); "from the threshold of the temple Court" (R. Eliezer, supported by R. Yosé).

[139] *M. Pesaḥ.* 9:3; *m. 'Arak.* 2:3.

[140] *M. Ḥal.* 4:11.

[141] *M. Roš. Haš.* 1:3.

[142] *T. Pesaḥ.* 8.1.

[143] *T. Pesaḥ.* 7.5.

creased[144]; the distance one must be from the temple during the First Passover to be liable (or allowed) to observe the Second is further defined[145];
the question of whether a proselyte who converted between the two Passovers must "observe the Second Passover" (שריך לעשות פסח שני) is
debated[146]; the differences (דברים שביך),[147] as well as similarities
(דברים ששויי),[148] "between the First and Second" (הראשון לשיני)
Passovers are expanded still more; and discussion occurs over whether a
single woman, at either the First or Second Passover, is to have her own
Passover sacrifice or to be included with the sacrifice of others.[149]

4.2.2.2.3 Midrashic Literature

As for midrashic works, in *Mekilta*, debate continues over whether a proselyte who converted "between the two Passovers" (בין שני פסחים) should
observe the Second Passover.[150] In *Sipre on Deuteronomy*, R. Judah considers whether "the Lord...may require" an overnight stay in Jerusalem for
the Lesser Passover (פסח קטן).[151] *Seder 'Olam Rabbah* summarizes
Numbers 9:6–11, reading, "on fourteen 'Iyyar, those unclean due to a
corpse slew the Second Passover" (פסח שני).[152] And *Megillat Ta'anit* lists
the 'Lesser Passover' (פסחא זעירא) on fourteen 'Iyyar among the days
"in which (one) is not to fast or, in some cases, not to mourn."[153]

In *Sipre on Numbers*, as one might expect, an array of issues are considered. Two were found in Tannaitic sources listed above: (1) the distance
one must be from the temple during the First Passover to be liable (or allowed) to observe the Second[154]; (2) and the question of whether a proselyte who converted between the two Passovers must keep the Second.[155]
But further treated are (3) how Second Passover observance ranks against
Sabbath-keeping and impurity – that is, Second Passover "confirms (a ruling) that suspends the Sabbath" (פסח שני יוכיח שדוחה את השבת),
though not one that suspends impurity (ואינו דוחה את הטומאה)[156];

---

[144] *T. Pesaḥ.* 7.6, 11–13; 8.4; *t. Naz.* 6.2.

[145] *T. Pesaḥ.* 8.1–3.

[146] *T. Pesaḥ.* 8.4.

[147] *T. Pesaḥ.* 8.7.

[148] *T. Pesaḥ.* 8.8.

[149] *T. Pesaḥ.* 8.10; cf. *m. Pesaḥ* 8:7.

[150] *Mek.* on Exod 12:48 (*Pisha* 15.108–112); cf. *t. Pesaḥ.* 8.4.

[151] *Sipre Deut.* §134 (on Deut 16:7).

[152] *S. 'Olam Rab.* viii (text: Guggenheimer 1998:88–89).

[153] *Meg. Ta'an.* 5–6; text: Lichtenstein 1931–32. On this reference in relation to the Qumran Calendrical/*Mišmarot* documents, see also Milik 1959:108–109.

[154] *Sipre Num.* §69 (on Num 9:1–14).

[155] *Sipre Num.* §71 (on Num 9:1–14).

[156] *Sipre Num.* §65 (on Num 9:1–14). At *Sipre Num.* §70 (on Num 9:1–14), the reading
"for he did not bring the Lord's offering at its appointed time" (כי קרבן יהוה לא הקריב)

(4) the scope of Second Passover observance relative to that of First Passover – that is, whether the scriptural rubrics assigned to Second Passover are "within" (במצות שבגופו) or "beyond" (במצות שעל גופו) those of the First Passover[157]; (5) the possible personal and communal aspects of Second Passover – whether Second Passover observance can be "both for the individual and for the congregation" (אחד יחיד ואחד צבור)[158]; and (6) the import of the mandate for "cutting off" at Numbers 9:13 – whether it applies "rather to the Second Passover" (אלא על פסח שני) than to the First (על פסח ראשון).[159]

4.2.2.2.4 Hezekiah's 'Second Passover,' 2 Chronicles 30:1–27

A particularly fertile *locus* for Tannaitic reflection on Second Passover was Hezekiah's delayed Passover in 2 Chronicles 30. In that chapter, Hezekiah decrees a Passover to be observed on the second month of the calendar year. His reforms began in the first month of that year, which was also the first month of his reign; but, since that gave little time for enough priests to purify themselves (or enough people to make pilgrimage), the Passover of his reforms was pushed back one month from its prescribed date:

> And the king, his officials and the entire assembly in Jerusalem took counsel
> to observe Passover in the second month. For they could not observe it
> at (that) time, because the priests had not sanctified themselves in sufficient measure
> and the people had not gathered in Jerusalem.[160]

After Hezekiah sent a proclamation "throughout all Israel" (v.5), lambs were sacrificed on the fourteenth day of the second month, Azyma was observed for the next seven days and, by common consent, those first seven days were extended into another seven, presumably ending on the twenty eighth day of the second month.[161]

In the biblical account, this Passover seems *ad hoc*. But, in certain Tannaitic views, it was, in fact, deemed a Second Passover. In *Tosefta Pesaḥim* and *Sanhedrin*, this judgment emerges amidst *halakhic* debates between R. Judah and R. Simeon, which are either synthesized (*Pesaḥim*) or supplemented (*Sanhedrin*) by R. Simeon b. Judah in the name of R. Simeon. In both instances, appeal is made to 2 Chronicles 30:18, where it

---

במועדו at Num 9:13 "teaches concerning the Second Passover that it suspends the Sabbath" (ולימד על פסח שני <שדוחה את השבת); text for *Sipre on Numbers* (here and below): Horovitz 1966.

[157] *Sipre Num.* §69 (on Num 9:1–14).
[158] *Sipre Num.* §70 (on Num 9:1–14).
[159] *Sipre Num.* §70 (on Num 9:1–14).
[160] 2 Chr 30:2–3.
[161] 2 Chr 30:15–23.

is said that many from Ephraim, Manasseh, Issachar and Zebulun came to
the feast and partook of it defiled:

> For a great number of people, many from Ephraim and Manasseh,
> Issachar and Zebulun, had not purified themselves;
> thus they ate the Passover in a state not as prescribed.[162]

In the first of these, *Tosefta Pesaḥim*, the issue under debate is whether a
Second Passover celebration should be individual or communal if the third
temple is built between the First and Second Passovers. R. Judah argues it
should be communal on the grounds that 2 Chronicles 30:18 shows Hezekiah to have compelled the whole congregation to observe a Second Passover; R. Simeon dissents, arguing that Hezekiah, rather, intercalated the
month of Nisan instead of a "second 'Adar"[163]; and, in response, R.
Simeon b. Judah seems to merge the two by rehearsing the view of R.
Judah (that Hezekiah decreed a communal Second Passover) in the name
of R. Simeon:

> If he grants Israel to build the temple (between the First and Second Passovers),
> an individual observes Second Passover (פֶסַח שֵני) but the congregation does not
> observe Second Passover (פֶסַח שֵני). R. Judah says, "The congregation also
> observes Second Passover" (אַף הַצבור עושה פסח שני).
> R. Judah says, M'SH B: "Hezekiah, king of Judah, made the congregation
> observe Second Passover (שהעשה את הצבור לעשות פסח שני).
> For it is said, 'For a great number of people, many from Ephraim and Manasseh,
> from Issachar and Zebulun, had not purified themselves...'" (2 Chr 30:18).
> R. Simeon says, "It was not because he made the congregation observe
> Second Passover (לא מפני שהעשי את הצבור לעשות פסח שני)
> but because he intercalated a Nisan (שעיבר ניסן); they only intercalate 'Adar."
> R. Simeon b. Judah says, in the name of R. Simeon,
> "Also, because he made the congregation observe Second Passover"
> (אַף מפני שהעשי את הצבור לעשות פסח שני).[164]

In *Tosefta Sanhedrin*, the debate between R. Judah and R. Simeon concerns whether a First Passover should be postponed through intercalation
because of impurity. The text (and R. Judah following it) argues it should,
again on the grounds that 2 Chronicles 30:18 shows Hezekiah to have done
so; R. Simeon counters that, though this might have been done by intercalating a "second 'Adar," Hezekiah, in fact, intercalated a second Nisan;
and, in response, R. Simeon b. Judah, again in the name of R. Simeon,
adds that Hezekiah rather had compelled communal observance of Second
Passover:

---

[162] 2 Chr 30:18a–b.

[163] On "second 'Adar" and intercalation, see Chapter 2, under '2.2 The Unnamed
Feast and a Second Passover (John 5:1–6:71).'

[164] *T. Pesaḥ* 8.4–5.

They do not intercalate the year because of impurity.
M'SH B: Hezekiah the king intercalated the year because of impurity.
For it is said, "For a great number of people, many from Ephraim and Manasseh,
from Issachar and Zebulun, had not purified themselves; thus, they ate the Passover
in a state not as prescribed" (2 Chr 30:18); for Hezekiah prayed for them, saying,
"May the good Lord atone on (their) behalf" (2 Chr 30:18).
R. Judah says, "They intercalate the year because of impurity."
R. Simeon says, "If (it is a matter of) intercalating it because of impurity,
it is already intercalated. He (Hezekiah) intercalated Nisan;
but they only intercalate 'Adar."
R. Simeon b. Judah says, in the name of R. Simeon,
"Also, because he made the congregation observe a Second Passover"
(אף מפני שהיעשו את הציבור לעשות פסח שיני).[165]

The merger of these two views seems to have been written into the text of
the *Chronicles Targum* on 2 Chronicles 30. Its rendering of 2 Chronicles
30:2 reads that the Passover Hezekiah decreed for the second month of
'Iyyar was simultaneously an intercalated Nisan:

> The king, his officers, all Israel and the entire assembly in Jerusalem took counsel
> to displace the month of Nisan[166] and to observe Passover in the month of 'Iyyar;
> that is, the second month.[167]

Yet its rendering of 2 Chronicles 30:18 reads that this same Passover was,
in fact, a Second Passover. Specifically, the Passover which those from
Ephraim, Manasseh, Issachar and Zebulun had eaten while defiled is not
considered Hezekiah's Passover (as the biblical text has it) but a prior First
Passover. Hezekiah's Passover, by contrast, is the Second Passover that
followed it:

> Indeed, a multitude of the people, from the house of Ephraim,
> from the house of Manasseh, from the house of Issachar
> and from the house of Zebulun had not purified themselves.
> For they had eaten the First Passover (ית פסחה קדמאה), not as it is prescribed;
> and then they returned to observe the Second Passover (פסח תנייאנ),
> as it is prescribed.[168]

In sum, the Passover in 'Iyyar enjoyed great currency in Second Temple
and Tannaitic thought. Philo deemed it an example of Moses' prophetic
legislation; the Qumran sect listed it among its significant calendrical moments; and the Tannaim refined its criteria and implications into an exqui-
site part of its *halakhic* system. Such a Passover could easily have been
known to (and used by) the Fourth Evangelist in the writing of his gospel;
and to the implications of that possibility I now turn.

---

[165] *T. Sanh.* 2.10–11.
[166] On the textual basis for reading "displace" or "intercalate," see McIvor 1994:219n2.
[167] *Tg. Ket.* 2 Chr 30:2; text (here and below): Sperber 1968.
[168] *Tg. Ket.* 2 Chr 30:18.

4.2.2.3 Second Passover and the Chronological Tension in John 6

It should first be noted that the feast at 6:4 need not be titled 'Second Passover' or 'Lesser Passover' for it to be such. Such titles are used to designate the Passover in 'Iyyar in Qumran and Rabbinic sources, but not so in the *locus classicus* of the feast, Numbers 9:11–14, nor in Philo. In Numbers 9, it is simply called 'the Passover' and only distinguished from the First Passover by the month in which it is to be observed:

> Each person among you or your generations,
> if he becomes unclean through a deceased person or on a distant journey,
> shall (nonetheless) observe the Passover to the Lord.
> In the second month, on the fourteenth day, between the evenings
> they shall observe it; and they shall eat it with unleavened bread and bitter herbs.
> They shall leave none of it till morning nor shall they break (any) bone in it,
> according to the entire statute of Passover shall they observe it.[169]

Similarly, in *On the Life of Moses II*, Philo has it simply as a second month emulation of the first month Passover, to accommodate those mourning kin or traveling during the first:

> And let them (those mourning kin) go as second (observers)
> in the second month (ἅτε δεύτεροι δευτέρῳ μηνί),
> again on the fourteenth day (πάλιν τεσσαρεσκαιδεκάτῃ ἡμέρᾳ),
> and let them sacrifice in the same manner as the first (observers),
> and let them employ a similar rule and custom for the sacrifices as did those
> (first observers). And let the same things be permitted, also,
> for those who are hindered from performing the rite with the entire nation,
> not by mourning, but because of a distant journey.[170]

As such, it is altogether possible that a feast introduced as "the Passover, the feast of the Jews," as is the case at 6:4, could designate Passover in 'Iyyar rather than Passover in Nisan. Whether it actually does would depend on the extent to which other factors in the context suggest so.

One such factor is that reading 6:4 as Passover in 'Iyyar resolves the temporal tension that otherwise surfaces in John 6 if it is read as Passover in Nisan – and this, without forcing a marginal rendering on the term "near" (ἐγγύς) in that verse and without discounting certain biblical allusions that may resonate in the "barley" at 6:9. Doing so dates the Passover that is "near" to mid-'Iyyar and puts the feeding of the five thousand in early to mid-'Iyyar, about half to three quarters of a month after the Waving of the 'Omer. Since the law of *ḥadaš* would have already been satisfied at this Waving of the 'Omer some weeks earlier, the "five barley loaves" at 6:9 could connote new barley rather than old, as allusions to Ruth 2:14 and 2 Kings 4:42–44 seem to suggest. Yet, since the Passover in 'Iyyar post-

[169] Num 9:9–12.
[170] *Mos.* 2.42.231–232.

dated the Waving of the 'Omer by nearly a month, its "nearness" at 6:4 can still be taken to mean "imminent" rather than "recent," following Johannine convention at 2:13; 7:2 and 11:55.

But the resolution of this chronological problem is not the only factor suggesting 6:4 might have the Passover in 'Iyyar in view. Further support can be found along three other lines: the date of the manna episode in the Exodus/Priestly tradition; the contingent character of the Passover in 'Iyyar; and – considering the possible inversion of John 5 and 6 – the festal scheme that results in chapters 2–12.

4.3 Corroborating Factors

4.3.1 The Date of the Exodus Manna Story

First, reading 6:4 thus would explain the association of Passover with manna in John 6. That John 6 turns on manna tradition is beyond question. Jesus launches his Bread of Life discourse when his interlocutors cite it[171]; the early part of that discourse assimilates that citation as a metaphor for its christology[172]; and, in response, the Jews and Jesus' disciples "murmur" (γογγύζειν),[173] after the manner the Israelites did when they first provoked God to give them quails and manna[174] and when they later tired of that manna in favor of meat.[175]

To be sure, exegetes have alleged further ties between John 6 and the manna story. Generally, the miraculous aspect of the feeding of the five thousand (6:1–15), its Passover setting[176] and several summaries of the manna experience scattered throughout the chapter (6:31a, 49, 58). More specifically, however, the initial lack of bread (6:5), Jesus' question on how to feed so many,[177] the two fish (as meat),[178] the multitude's eating till

---

[171] "Our fathers ate manna in the wilderness, as it is written, 'He gave them bread from heaven to eat'" (6:31).

[172] John 6:32–33, 35, 48–51, 58. Peder Borgen defines 6:32–58 as a midrashic paraphrase on the quotation at 6:31; see 1963:232–40.

[173] John 6:41–44, 60–61.

[174] Compare 6:41–44, 60–61 with Exodus 16:2, 6–9, 11–12.

[175] Num 11:4–6. The word used for the Israelites' complaint in LXX Num 11 is not "murmur" (γογγύζειν or a cognate), as in John 6, but "weep" (κλαίειν); Num 11:4, 10, 13, 18–20. The two are so juxtaposed at Num 14:1–2, however, that some interchangeability between them can be assumed: "And, having taken up, the whole congregation gave voice, and the people were weeping (ἔκλαιεν) all that night. And all the sons of Israel were murmuring (διεγόγγυζον) against Moses and Aaron, and the whole congregation said to them, 'Would that we died in the land of Egypt! Or that we had died in this wilderness!'"

[176] John 6:4 in relation to manna and the Sabbath at Exod 16:25–30.

[177] John 6:5 with Moses' similar question to God at Num 11:13.

[178] John 6:9 with Moses' question to God at Num 11:13.

satisfied,[179] the collection of leftover fragments,[180] the christophany on the water,[181] the greater interest in eating than in believing or obeying,[182] the demand for more food,[183] manna as bread[184] and as bread from heaven,[185] the Father as giver of that manna,[186] eating flesh,[187] eating Jesus' flesh instead of manna[188] and Jesus as the manna and word that proceeds from the mouth of God.[189]

Moreover, opinions differ as to the sources from which these allusions were drawn: some trace them to Exodus 16 alone[190]; others to Psalm 78 alone[191]; still others to a combination of matrices, including other biblical *loci* on the manna story.[192] And complicating those options has been debate over the provenance of the quotation at 6:31b. Four primary candidates vie for it: Psalm 78:24b; Exodus 16:4b; Exodus 16:15d; Nehemiah 9:15a (with

---

[179] John 6:12, 26, 48 with Ps 78:18, 25, 29.

[180] John 6:12–13 with the collection of manna according to (daily) need (and twice as much before Sabbath) at Exod 16:16–26.

[181] John 6:19–20 with the theophany through quails and manna at Exod 16:6–12.

[182] John 6:25–26, 36, 64.

[183] John 6:26, 31–35 with Ps 78:18.

[184] John 6:7, 23.

[185] John 6:31–35, 41–42, 48, 50–51, 58.

[186] John 6:32; cf. 6:48, 50 with the Lord as the same giver of manna at Exod 16:15.

[187] John 6:51–56 with Ps 78:27 (or Num 11:13).

[188] John 6:51–58 with the giving of meat for manna in Numbers 11:4–35.

[189] John 6:32–58 with Deut 8:3. This list gleaned from Sahlin 1950:22–25; Enz 1957:213; Hunt 1958:59–60; Croatto 1975:11–13, 15–19; Geiger 1984:460; Hanson 1991:238; Valletta 1991:132–41; Cothenet 1993:249–52; Theobald 1997:330–31, 330n19, 339n59, 342–45; and Kerr 2002:214–15 (verses are represented either as referenced by or [if not referenced] as inferred from the exegetes cited). Further, in his forced hypothesis that John 6 follows the motifs of Exodus 12–17 "in the same order," Herman Ludin Jansen, who otherwise links the feeding of the five thousand (6:1–15) with the celebration of the Passover in Exod 12–13, nonetheless concedes an affinity between the gathering of fragments at 6:12–13 and the quails and manna episode of Exodus 16; 1985:131–32. More problematic, however, is Robert Houston Smith's hypothesis that John 2:1–11:44 is fashioned on the template of Exodus 2:23–12:51, precluding Exodus 16 (or any manna) typology from John 6 altogether: for him, the feeding of the five thousand alludes to the plague of locusts (Exod 10:1–20) and the stilling of the storm (as Smith labels it) to the plague of hail (Exod 9:13–35); 1962:333–38.

[190] Sahlin 1950:22–25; Enz 1957:213; Jansen 1985:131–32.

[191] Porporato 1929:79–86; and, with more precision, Geiger 1984:459–61.

[192] Some examples, Exod 16–17; Num 11; 16–17; Deut 8 (Feuillet 1960:807–11 and, similarly, Croatto 1975:11–12, 16–19; Valletta 1991:133); Exod 15–17; Num 11; 14 (Cothenet 1993:251); (a targum to) Joshua 5 (le Déaut 1970:80–83, following Malina 1968:77–84, 102–104). Michael Theobald (1997:328–31, 339n59, 342–47) sees LXX Ps 77:24b as the reference of John 6:31 with Exodus 16 as the "Bezugstext" informing John 6:31a, 41, 48, 49, 51, 58. Further, according to Malina, LXX Ps 77:24b, itself, reflects influence from Exodus 16 – the manna "raining down" motif is what he dubs the "Moses and they" tradition (Exod 16:4abα, 5, 16a, 17b, 18–20, 22–27, 28–30, 35b); 1968:2–10, 33–35.

their LXX counterparts). And the imprecise correlation between each of those candidates and the text cited has led some to speculate that, if the modifications were not rendered by the Evangelist himself,[193] they reflect either a polyvalent reference (between two or more of the primary candidates and/or other biblical verses[194]) or the brokerage of a contemporary targumic, [195] haggadic[196] or peer Christian[197] tradition.

Such differences and complexity notwithstanding, all are agreed that John 6, in some way, depends heavily on manna tradition. In that chapter, as J. Severino Croatto has put it, "Gesù si identifica con il 'pane del cielo'...ed è il 'segno' della presenza di Dio, che 'opera' in Lui": "Jesus is identified with the 'bread from heaven'...and is the 'sign' of the presence of God, who 'works' in him."[198]

While many exegetes see the Passover reference at 6:4 to be conducive to this manna tradition,[199] some have voiced concern. Over a century ago, Johannes van Bebber and Johannes Belser noted that the theme of manna is better identified with Israel's wilderness sojourn than with Israel's (First) Passover observance.[200] And, more recently, Bruce Malina has questioned why manna should be mentioned at all at this juncture of the Fourth Gospel:

> The manna figures prominently in the homiletic midrash in Jn 6, 31–58, commonly known as the Bread of Life discourse.
> The problem is why the mention of the manna at all; why does John (or Jesus) make reference to the manna at this point in the gospel?[201]

---

[193] So Menken 1988:41–45.

[194] For instance, Ps 78:24b with Exod 16:4 (Franke 1885:283); LXX Ps 77:24b with 2 Esdr 19:15 (Feuillet 1960:808; idem 1962:113; and see Braun 1964:10); Exodus 16:4, 15 (Borgen 1965:40–42, 41n5); Ps 78:24b with Exod 16:4, 15, considering Neh 9:15 (Hengel 1989:267); Exod 16:13–15 with Ps 78:24 (Hanson 1991:84). Other potential complementary verses are Num 11:7–9; 21:5; Deut 8:3, 16; Josh 5:12; Neh 9:20; Ps 105:40; Wis 16:20 (and their LXX counterparts). Jean-Noël Aletti goes so far as to contend that 6:31 reflects the feeding in the wilderness "_in its globality_" (italics his) and, therefore, summons "all the other readings of the event in question"; 1974:190–91, 196.

[195] For example, a speculated targum on Exod 16:4, 15 (Boismard and Lamouille 1987:196–97); _Tg. Neb._ Josh 5 (Ms 607 [ENA 2576]; Malina 1968:77–84); _Tg. Neof._ Exod 16:15 (Vermes 1969:262–63).

[196] Borgen 1965:20–25, 38–43; Richter 1972:208–31, 245–50; Finkel 1974:158–59.

[197] Braun 1964:26–29. A thorough review of debate on the quotation, with critique, can be found in Georg Richter (1972:196–208, 231–45), with valuable updates by M.J.J. Menken (1988:41–46) and A.T. Hanson (1991:83–87).

[198] Croatto 1975:19.

[199] See, for instance, the recent discussion by Kerr 2002:219–26.

[200] Van Bebber 1898:163; cf. Belser 1904:169–70 and, also, Bultmann 1971:212n2.

[201] Malina 1968:102; final question mark supplied.

Van Bebber and Belser addressed the question by (untenably) excising the reference to τὸ πάσχα at 6:4, reading the verse, instead, to anticipate Tabernacles at 7:2.[202] And Malina suggested a (First) Passover tradition mediated through a Targum to Joshua 5 similar to MS 607 (ENA 2576), wherein the Passover and manna motifs are juxtaposed to and joined by other themes found in John 6 – the death of the desert generation (6:49, 58); murmuring (6:41, 43); the hunger and thirst, death and raised serpent of Numbers 21:6–9 (6:35–40); and the status of Torah relative to the Prophets and Jesus (6:45, citing Isaiah 54:13).[203]

In this light, however, it becomes significant that, according to the Priestly tradition of Exodus 16, the feast implicitly associated with the first giving of manna is, in fact, the Second Passover. Exodus 16:1 dates the episode to the fifteenth day of the second month from the exodus:

> They set out from Elim and all the congregation of the sons of Israel
> came to the wilderness of Sin, which is between Elim and Sinai;
> on the fifteenth day of the second month from their going out from the land of Egypt.

Since Exodus considers "the beginning of months" to be the one in which the First Passover was observed (Exodus 12:1–2), the second month "from their going out from the land of Egypt" would have also been the second month of the year. This is made explicit in *Targum Pseudo-Jonathan*, which identifies that month outright as 'Iyyar: "They moved from Elim...on the fifteenth day of the month of 'Iyyar, that is, the second month from their going forth from the land of Egypt."[204] Heising and Malina have ascribed this temporal note to the Priestly redactor, whose chronological concern, according to Malina, is also evident in the chapter's priority interest in Sabbath observance (Exodus 16:22–30).[205] Though

---

[202] Van Bebber 1898:33–35, 154–72 (Appendix II); cf. Belser 1904:169–70. This hypothesis will be treated in further detail in Chapter 5, under '5.1 Implications for the *Praedicatio Domini*.'

[203] Malina 1968:103–106; on MS 607 (ENA 2576), see pp. 77–81.

[204] *Tg. Ps.-J.* Exod 16:1; text: Clarke 1984. The association appears more obliquely in *Targum Rishon* to Esther: in an extension on Haman's casting of lots to determine the month in which he would exterminate Jews from Persia (Esther 3:5–11), the lot is said not to have come up for 'Iyyar because, in that month, the manna had descended; *Tg. Ket.* Esth I 3:7.

[205] Heising 1964:82n6; Malina 1968:10, 10n2, 18–19. Malina unnecessarily bases his inference on Patrick Skehan's application of Annie Jaubert's calendrical thesis to Exodus 16 (Skehan 1958:194–95; cf. Jaubert 1965:32–38, as well as the earlier works on which her discussion there is based, cited by VanderKam 1979:390n1). On the grounds that the Priestly redactor followed a 364-day calendar, Skehan reasons that the fifteenth of the second month (Exod 16:1) fell on a Friday before Sabbath, that the quail arrived (Exodus 16:13) on Saturday evening after Sabbath, that the manna began (Exodus 16:13) the following Sunday morning and that the "morning by morning" till the sixth and seventh days (Exodus 16:21–22, 27) extended one full week. The extension of Jaubert's hypothesis to the calendars of late Priestly works, however, is open to question: though it has found supporters (Vogt 1955:405–407;

'Second Passover' is dated to the fourteenth day of the second month at Numbers 9:11, its observance was to span, like the First Passover, "between the evenings" (בֵּין הָעַרְבַּיִם; Numbers 9:11); that is, into the next morning,[206] the fifteenth day of the second month. Inasmuch, then, as Exodus 16:1 dates its manna episode, also, to "the fifteenth day of the second month," it places the first giving of manna squarely on the date of the Second Passover, a coincidence not lost on Gale Yee.[207]

If the Passover at 6:4 is read as a Second Passover, its relation to manna in John 6 is thus explained – and explained in a more direct way than does the textual emendation proposed by van Bebber and Belser or the targumic mediation suggested by Malina. On such a reading, the reference at 6:4 occurs in John 6 because, in the exodus story, Second Passover is the feast peculiarly associated with the manna tradition, on which that chapter turns. Put the other way round, a Second Passover is introduced at 6:4 because Second Passover functions symbolically toward John 6 in the same way that the regular Passover introduced at 11:55 does to John 12–19 and the Tabernacles introduced at 7:2 does to John 7:1–10:21. As 11:55 furnishes commemorative First Passover symbolism for the lamb christology of the Johannine Passion, and as 7:2 does the same with Tabernacles symbolism for the "water" and "light" christology of "the last great day of the feast" (7:37; 8:12; 9:4–5), so 6:4 furnishes commemorative Second Passover symbolism for the manna christology of Jesus' Bread of Life discourse. Thus, reading 6:4 as a Second Passover (rather than First) not only resolves the temporal problem created by barley consumption at 6:9, it also explains the thematic connection obtaining between Passover and manna in John 6.

Milik 1959:110; Cazelles 1962:204–209), it has also had its critics (Segal 1957:251; Kutsch 1961: 41–45; Baumgarten 1977:103–112 [esp. 109–110]; and, for fuller reviews of the discussion with [partial] defense, Cazelles 1962:202–203 and VanderKam 1979:391–99; 1998:58). Moreover, though *Mekilta* and *Seder 'Olam Rabbah* date the fifteenth of the second month in Exod 16:1 to a Sabbath (*Mek.* on Exod 16:1 [*Vayassa'* 2.13–17]; *S. 'Olam Rab.* v [Guggenheimer 1998:67–68]), nothing in Exodus 16, itself, requires it; nor does anything in that chapter require the sixth and seventh days of the week at Exod 16:22, 27 to be the sixth and seventh days from the time manna first appeared. Similar to this last point is the critique of Baumgarten that "Skehan was constrained to extend the murmuring of the people for two days, a premise which has no basis in the text"; 1977:110–11.

[206] See van Goudoever 1961:8–9, 13.

[207] Yee infers it from *Mek.* on Exod 16:1 (*Vayassa'* 2.25–32), which is concerned with how long the "cake" from Egypt sustained the Israelites before manna began to fall (1989:55–56). The passage, itself, does not make an explicit connection with Second Passover.

4.3.2 The Contingent Observance of Second Passover

A further factor supporting 6:4 as a Second Passover is that it accounts for the absence of pilgrimage in John 6. As noted above, the Passover at 6:4 is the only one of the six feasts in John for which Jesus is not portrayed as making pilgrimage to (or already in) Jerusalem. He miraculously feeds five thousand (6:1–15), walks on the Sea of Tiberias (6:16–21), proclaims himself the "Bread of Life" (6:22–59) and suffers a schism among his disciples (6:60–71); but at no point is he described as "going up" to Jerusalem to observe this festival. Sundry proposals have been made to account for or treat this (some of them already reviewed): that a pilgrimage is to be inferred; that Jesus celebrated this Passover in Galilee[208]; that the "nearness" of 6:4 looks back to Jesus' attendance at the feast at 5:1[209]; that, with John 5 and 6 reversed, the "nearness" of 6:4 anticipates Jesus' (future) attendance at the feast at 5:1[210]; that 6:4 originally anticipated Jesus' pilgrimage for the Passover at 2:13[211]; or that Jesus is simply presented as ignoring (or defying) Jewish ritual.[212] By contrast to these suggestions, reading 6:4 as a Second Passover addresses the issue by suggesting such a pilgrimage would, in fact, have been unnecessary, if not prohibited.

The Second Passover was a contingent festival. It was allowed (or required) for anyone who could not observe Passover in Nisan due to uncleanness or travel[213]; but, for those who could observe Passover at that time, it was moot – Passover was to be kept on 14 Nisan, on pain of death. So Numbers 9, directly after its prescription of the Second Passover:

> But the person who is clean and is not on a journey and refrains
> from observing the Passover, this life shall be cut off from its people,
> for s/he did not bring the offering of the Lord at its appointed time.
> This person shall bear his/her sin.[214]

The Pharisees and Tannaim expanded and elaborated on the Second Passover (as sketched above); but, in so doing, they did not remove its conditional nature. This is partly betrayed in the debates that occurred over whether proselytes who convert between 14 Nisan and 14 'Iyyar should observe Second Passover:

---

[208] Gärtner 1959:38–39.
[209] Ireneaus, *Adv. Haer.* 2.22.3.
[210] Cassel and Norris 1871:109–12; Menoud 1947:13.
[211] Klug 1906:152–63, especially pp. 157–59.
[212] See, for instance, Devillers 1999:202–205.
[213] Num 9:10–11; Philo *Mos.* 2.42.231–232.
[214] Num 9:13.

"A proselyte who converts between the two Passovers must observe
the Second Passover," the words of Rabbi. R. Nathan says,
"It is not necessary (for him) to observe the Second Passover,
for he was not obligated at the First (Passover)."[215]

R. Simeon ben Eleazar says, "Behold, regarding one who converts between
the two Passovers – I understand that he observes the Second Passover.
The teaching, '(He shall be) like a native' (Exod 12:48),
what does 'native' (mean)? (That) the (native) who does not observe
the First (Passover) observes the Second (Passover); thus, any proselyte
who does not observe the First (Passover) observes the Second (Passover).[216]

R. Simeon b. Eleazar says, "Behold, the one who converts between the two Passovers,
I understand that he observes the Second Passover"
The teaching (means he observes) as the native:
inasmuch as the native who does not observe the First (Passover)
observes the Second (Passover), so also (the proselyte),
who does not observe the First (Passover), observes the Second (Passover)." [217]

Some of these interlocutors saw Second Passover, in this instance, as
obligatory; others, as optional. But the very dispute, itself, could not have
arisen had they all not commonly assumed that, under normal circumstances, observing Passover in 'Iyyar was contingent upon having legiti-
mately missed Passover in Nisan.

More pointedly, in the anecdote about Joseph the Priest (mentioned
briefly above), it is told that, when he attempted to bring his household to
the temple for Second Passover, he was rebuffed by the cult, lest doing so
set a precedent that Passover in 'Iyyar was obligatory in its own right:

Joseph the priest brought the first fruits of wine and oil;
but they did not accept it from him.
He also brought up his sons and the sons of his household
to observe the Lesser Passover in Jerusalem;
but they turned him back, that the matter (his unnecessary observance
of the Lesser Passover) not be established as an obligation.[218]

Applied to John 6, this conditional character of the Second Passover explains Jesus' lack of pilgrimage by rendering such an act unnecessary,
even discouraged. That is, Jesus does not make pilgrimage for the Second
Passover at 6:4 because he had already done so for a regular Passover that
had preceded it. In the current text, that regular Passover can either be the
feast at 5:1 or an inferred festival coming sometime between 5:1 and 6:4.

---

[215] *T. Pesaḥ.* 8.4.

[216] *Mek.* on Exod 12:48 (*Pisḥa* 15.108–112).

[217] *Sipre Num.* §71 (on Num 9:1–14).

[218] *M. Ḥal.* 4:11. Though, in *t. Pesaḥ.* 8.10, Joseph retorts that the real reason for his dis-
missal was the ruling (ascribed to R. Eleazar b. R. Simeon) that "they do not slaughter the
Second Passover for a woman in her presence."

But, if it be considered that, in an earlier phase of the Fourth Gospel's composition history, chapters 5 and 6 were inverted, that regular Passover would have been the first Passover to appear in the narrative – the Passover at 2:13. Chapter 6 would have followed immediately on chapter 4, making 6:4 play the Second Passover to the regular Passover at 2:13.

Buttressing such a reconstruction is the cogent narrative it yields. It will be recalled that 4:35 – if it has any chronological bearing on the story – can date the Samaritan episode in either of two time frames, depending upon which half of the verse is read as a temporal marker. If 4:35a, "Do you not say, 'There are (still) four months and the harvest comes?',", the scene occurs around Kislev, some nine months after the Passover at 2:13; if 4:35b, "Behold, I say to you, lift up your eyes and look at the fields, that they are (already) white unto harvest," it occurs between Nisan and Sivan, immediately following the Passover at 2:13. Supporting the first is (1) that the proverbial nature of 4:35a (on which the second reading depends) is open to question; (2) that, similarly, no proverbial counterpart to 4:35 has been found; and (3) that Rabbinic literature measures the interval between sowing and harvest at six months, not four. Supporting the second is (1) that 4:35a is, in fact, arguably proverbial; (2) that several other ways in which the Jewish year was divided allow for a (proverbial) four month interval; and (3) that a spring date fits nicely with 4:43–45, where, two days later (4:40), Galileans receive Jesus well, due to their impressed experience of him, presumably "in Jerusalem during the feast" at 2:23.[219]

Neither view enjoys such compelling evidence over the other that it can be used as an irrefutable premise for further argument. It can be noted, however, that, if 6:4 is read as a Second Passover immediately following John 4, the narrative from 2:13–6:71 coheres chronologically, thematically and theologically under the second of the two; that is, with 4:35b as the temporal marker to narrative time. The feeding of the five thousand (6:1–15) occurs one month after the initial Passover at 2:13; and, within the barley harvest that takes place between the two events, Jesus engages in the Judean ministry (3:22–36), pauses two days in Sychar *en route* back to Galilee (4:41–42; cf. 4:40), is received in Galilee by pilgrims who had just seen his signs during the Passover at 2:13 (4:45; cf. 2:23) and then heals the son of an official at Capernaum (4:46–54). In such a scenario, the harvest to which Jesus directs his disciples at 4:35b is the very barley harvest from which the "five barley loaves" at 6:9 will have been baked. And this creates a subtle, but detectable, thematic and theological continuity between chapters 4 and 6: the barley which Jesus bids his disciples to "lift up (their) eyes and see" is the same barley used for the sign (6:1–15) on

---

[219] See the discussion in Chapter 2, under '2.2 The Unnamed Feast and a Second Passover (John 5:1–6:71).'

which he then predicates his Bread of Life discourse (6:25–65). Further weaving the two chapters together is the Hebraism "lifting up the eyes" (ἐπαίρειν τοὺς ὀφθαλμούς), used with θεᾶσθαι in the New Testament only at 4:35b and 6:5a[220]: at 4:35b, Jesus bids his disciples "lift up your eyes" (ἐπάρατε τοὺς ὀφθαλμοὺς ὑμῶν), that they might notice, not only the literal barley harvest, but the spiritual harvest of the Samaritans coming from Sychar (4:30); at 6:5a, Jesus, himself, "having lifted up his eyes" (ἐπάρας οὖν τοὺς ὀφθαλμούς), beholds the multitude whom he would now miraculously nourish from the very same barley harvest he referenced at 4:35a.[221]

In all, the contingent character of the Second Passover lends further support to reading the Passover at 6:4 as such. The Passover in 'Iyyar was only to be observed if, for various reasons, the Passover in Nisan had not been; and, when applied to John 6, this accounts for the absence of any such observance in the narrative. Jesus did not make pilgrimage for this Second Passover because he had already done so for a regular Passover preceding it. John 6 can be plausibly read this way in the text as it stands. But it would have harmonized with the narrative all the more tautly if, in an earlier recension, John 5 and 6 were reversed: as such, 6:4 plays the Second Passover to the First Passover at 2:13; and the narrative of 2:13–6:71 coheres chronologically, thematically and theologically.

In such a scenario, one might well ask why a Second Passover is mentioned at all in 6:4. That is, why would the Evangelist write, "And the Passover, the feast of the Jews, was near," if Jesus, in fact, did not (and did not need to) celebrate that feast? Part of the answer doubtless lies with the concurrence between the date of Second Passover (14/15 'Iyyar) and the date of the Exodus manna story (15 'Iyyar), on which John 6 largely turns. As stated above, manna is commemorative symbolism for Second Passover in the same way the pascal lamb is commemorative symbolism for First Passover.

More fundamentally, however, it derives from a further purpose, which the feasts in John once served (and which I will elaborate more fully in the next chapter). Simply put, 6:4 mentions a (Second) Passover in order to mark time. As I will develop further below, the Fourth Gospel peculiarly casts Jesus' public ministry as being driven by a temporal current, culminating in a moment called his 'hour.' From the instant Jesus manifests his

---

[220] Vallauri 1985:164–65; on the clause as a Hebraism, see particularly p. 164.

[221] A theological link also appears with the Johannine resurrection. Since Jesus' self-proclamation as Bread of Life in John 6 is drawn from a sign performed from freshly harvested barley – and, since Jesus' resurrection occurs on the day of the Waving of the 'Omer, when new barley was allowed to be consumed – one might say that, with Jesus' resurrection in John, the "eating of his flesh" and "drinking of his blood," of which he speaks in 6:51–58 is "authorized" (מֻתָּרִין); *m. Menaḥ.* 10:6.

first sign (2:11) till the day he arrives in Jerusalem for his final Passover (12:27), he moves toward an 'hour,' which, on the one hand, has not yet come, but which, on the other, is drawing ever nearer (4:21–23; 5:25; 16:31–32). Besides functioning as rituals in their own right, feasts could also serve as indicators of passing time. Their intermittent placement within the calendar year rendered them ready-made gauges of time as it elapsed; and, in relation to Jesus' 'hour' in John, it was this task, I will argue, for which they were most fundamentally designed. As Jesus' 'hour' grew so near as to have essentially already "come," the feasts in John measured that increasing imminence by marking the months and seasons from its introduction (2:4) till its arrival (12:27). Serving such a purpose, a 'Second Passover' could purposefully be mentioned at 6:4, even if Jesus did not make pilgrimage for it. Since Second Passover came in mid-'Iyyar, the reference would demonstrate that, from the beginning of Jesus' ministry during the Passover at 2:13, time had passed one month nearer to his 'hour.'

This leads to the final factor supporting 6:4 as a Second Passover.

4.3.3 Liturgical Design

When 6:4 is so read, and when John 5 and 6 are inverted, the feasts in John sequence themselves into a design that implies intent. The arrangement, as so far discussed, is thus:

Table 19. The Penultimate Sequence of Feasts

John 2:13	John 6:4	John 5:1	John 7:2	John 10:22	John 11:55
14 Nisan	14 'Iyyar	???	15–22 Tishri	25 Kislev	14 Nisan
Feast of Passover	Second Passover	Unnamed Feast	Feast of Tabernacles	Feast of Dedication	Feast of Passover

The feasts appear more or less chronologically and, in so doing, span a single year, from the Passover at 2:13 to the Passover at 11:55.

The question that arises is whether the unnamed feast at 5:1 accommodates such a chronological scheme or undermines it. As noted above, the identity of that feast has been subject to a wide range of proposals: Passover, Pentecost, Remembrance, Tabernacles, Purim.[222] Were it one of the feasts lying between Second Passover and Tabernacles – Pentecost (5–7

---

[222] See the discussion in Chapter 2, under '2.2 The Unnamed Feast and a Second Passover (John 5:1–6:71).'

Sivan/3rd month[223]), Remembrance (1 Tishri/7th month) or, I might add, the Day of Atonement (10 Tishri/7th month) – it would align chronologically with the other feasts, rendering their full series a single annum. Were it any feast other than those three, however, it would break that sequence, removing any sense of liturgical design and requiring the festivals to extend (as has traditionally been thought) at least two years.

To address this question I will not engage the debate over the identity of that feast as it has been waged. With others, I am inclined to see that identity as hermeneutically irrelevant to John 5 and, accordingly, beyond finding out in and of itself. Rather, building on the sequence of other feasts reconstructed in this schema, I will apply a(n aforementioned) dynamic governing the relationship of John 5 to John 7 (which are now juxtaposed) and, by it, suggest that the feast at 5:1 can at least be circumscribed to the several month period that would pass if the Tabernacles at 7:2 followed the Second Passover at 6:4 in the same year.[224] Thus, it would support, not undercut, the suggested chronological order in the schema.

The dynamic in question is the temporal immediacy required between John 5 and 7.[225] As noted above, one of the reasons some have proposed an earlier juxtaposition of these two chapters is that several of their features suggest the hostility Jesus was shown during the feast at 5:1 (5:16–18) still obtained during Tabernacles at 7:2: (1) Jesus expects such hostility before he attends Tabernacles (7:6–7); (2) before his arrival for Tabernacles, some Jews are already seeking him with malicious intent (7:13); (3) when he does appear and begins speaking with the crowd, he immediately raises the Sabbath controversy of chapter 5 as an issue, asking them why they (still) sought to kill him and comparing his healing at that time to Moses' circumcision (7:19–23); and, (4) when he is identified by other Jews later during the feast, they state outright that some among them were seeking to kill him (7:25–26).[226] For narrative time, this carry over implies that the

---

[223] In a luni-solar calendar with the Waving of the 'Omer placed on 16 Nisan (as it likely came to be), Pentecost would have fallen near the beginning of the third month, Sivan. It was slated to be observed fifty days after the Waving of the 'Omer (Lev 23:15–21), which, given the fluctuation of month lengths due to the varying perceptibility of new moons, would typically fall between 5–7 Sivan. See, also, on this VanderKam 1979:398.

[224] And, so, I do not contravene my criticism of Yee for neglecting the feast at 5:1 completely in favor of the Sabbath; see Chapter 3, under '1.4 Johannine *'Takkanot,'* Gale A. Yee.'

[225] See Chapter 2, under '2.2 The Unnamed Feast and a Second Passover (John 5:1–6:71).'

[226] If, in this earlier recension, 7:14–24 was of a piece with 5:1–47 (as some have surmised), factor (3) would not suggest temporal proximity between two different feasts (one at 5:1 and one at 7:2), since Jesus' words in 7:19–23 about the Sabbath controversy

feast at 5:1 would not have occurred long before Tabernacles at 7:2. That the controversy of chapter 5 remains fresh on the minds of Jesus and his interlocutors in chapter 7 suggests that, in the passage of time within the story, the two would likely have occurred near one another. Since, in the schema reconstructed here, the feast at 5:1 is preceded by a Second Passover, which, in the Jewish liturgical year, is scheduled some five months prior to Tabernacles (so 7:2), it becomes more likely than not that the feast at 5:1 falls within such a five month period, spanning 6:4 to 7:2. That is to say, the proximity required between the feast at 5:1 and Tabernacles at 7:2, coupled with the placement of chapter 5 between that Tabernacles and the prior Second Passover at 6:4, suggests the feast at 5:1 would probably represent one of the festivals dating between the two – Pentecost (5–7 Sivan), Remembrance (1 Tishri) or the Day of Atonement (10 Tishri) – and this within the same year.

As such, the chronological order and one year duration of the schema would be maintained. The feasts would align more or less sequentially; and together they would span a single, liturgical annum. The reconstruction could be modified to the following:

Table 20. The Penultimate Sequence of Feasts:
The Feast at John 5:1 Between Sivan and Tishri

John 2:13	John 6:4	John 5:1	John 7:2	John 10:22	John 11:55
14 Nisan	14 'Iyyar	Sivan-Tishri	15–22 Tishri	25 Kislev	14 Nisan
Feast of Passover	Second Passover	Pentecost? Remembrance? Day of Atonement?	Feast of Tabernacles	Feast of Dedication	Feast of Passover

For 6:4 as a Passover in 'Iyyar, this schema lends further corroborative support by facilitating a design that, in turn, suggests intent. Reading 6:4 as such, with John 5 and 6 reversed, assembles the Johannine feasts into a liturgical pattern that is more likely to have come from strategy than from happenstance. The feasts align into a chronological sequence spanning a single year's time; and the prospect that this reflects acumen rather than chance lends some weight to the reading. Taken with the three factors outlined above, it forms part of an increasingly more plausible case for reading 6:4 as a Second Passover.

---

in chapter 5 would have occurred within the feast at 5:1. This would not void the larger point, however, since factors (1), (2) and (4) would still suggest such proximity.

4.3.4 Excursus: The Feast at John 5:1, Pentecost by Elimination?

At the risk of contradicting the agnosticism I just expressed about the feast at 5:1, I note that, on this reconstructed schema, the three options for it listed above – Pentecost, Remembrance and the Day of Atonement – can be reduced further. This, through an argument made (but rejected) by Aileen Guilding against the notion that the feast at 5:1 was Remembrance (which she referenced as the Feast of the New Year).

Its gist is that, if the feast at 5:1 immediately preceded Tabernacles at 7:2 – and, if that feast was considered to be a festival later than Pentecost (Remembrance or the Day of Atonement) – Jesus' pilgrimage for Tabernacles at 7:2 would be chronologically impractical, if not altogether impossible. To do the numbers more specifically than Guilding had – the interval between the beginning of Tabernacles (15 Tishri) and the prior feast of Remembrance (1 Tishri) is fifteen days; that between Tabernacles and the prior Day of Atonement (10 Tishri) is five days. Since pilgrimage from Galilee would have required about three days each way for each feast, that interval would be reduced by some six days for each pair: this would give Jesus nine days back in Galilee, if 5:1 was Remembrance; and it would make 5:1 as the Day of Atonement impossible. Even given that Jesus went up "in the middle" of Tabernacles (7:10, 14) – for instance, leaving on 16 Tishri to arrive on 18 Tishri – the span from Remembrance to Tabernacles would be some twelve days (4–15 Tishri) and that between the Day of Atonement and Tabernacles, some three days (13–15 Tishri). This does not seem long enough to account for 7:1, where it is said that, in the interim between those feasts, Jesus engaged in a Galilean itinerary:

> And after these things Jesus was walking about in Galilee;
> for he did not wish to walk about in Judea,
> because the Jews were seeking to kill him.

"But the words περιεπάτει ὁ Ἰησοῦς ἐν τῇ Γαλιλαίᾳ," writes Guilding on this point, "seem to indicate a more prolonged stay."[227]

Guilding concluded that the festival at 5:1 was the Feast of Remembrance, in spite of her observations to the contrary – largely on corollaries she perceived between John 5 and her speculated lectionary.[228] A more apt inference, however, would be that the feast at 5:1 must date earlier than Tishri; and, on the premises established here, this would mean a Pentecost lying between the Second Passover at 6:4 and Tabernacles at 7:2. That is to say, since the immediacy between John 5 and John 7 requires the feast at

---

[227] Guilding 1960:69–70; quotation p. 69.
[228] Guilding 1960:69–86. On Guilding, see Chapter 3, under '3.2.1 Reflexes to a Triennial Jewish Lectionary, Aileen Guilding.' For a specific critique of her conclusion for this feast, see Kerr 2002:206–207.

5:1 to have occurred close to Tabernacles at 7:2 – and, since the feast at 5:1 cannot be one of the two feasts that date before Tabernacles in Tishri (Remembrance or the Day of Atonement) – the only festal option remaining for the feast at 5:1 is a Pentecost situated between that Tabernacles and the prior Second Passover at 6:4. Such greater specificity is not necessary for the feast at 5:1 to fit the scenario being proposed here: all that is required is that it occur sometime between Second Passover and Tabernacles. But, given the popularity its identification with Pentecost has had among some exegetes (on other grounds), it is suggestive.

4.4 Summary

My own proposal for the feasts in John turns on the premise that the Passover at 6:4 be read, not as the Passover prescribed for 14 Nisan, but as the Passover of Numbers 9, prescribed for 14 'Iyyar. It follows as a resolution to the calendrical conflict that otherwise occurs in John 6 when 6:4 is read as a regular Passover and set over against the "five barley loaves" of 6:9. On the one hand, that Passover has not yet arrived but is only "near"; on the other hand, the law of *ḥadaš* would have forbidden new barley to be baked or eaten until at least two days after that Passover had passed. Leviticus 23:9–14 legislates that new produce could not be used for non-cultic consumption until its first fruits had been offered on the day following the Sabbath after Passover. And that same rubric is attested generously (and with more specificity) throughout Second Temple and Rabbinic traditions.

Though the tension could be resolved by reading the "nearness" of 6:4 to refer to the recent past (and, thus, to the feast at 5:1) or by taking the barley at 6:9 to be old barley rather than new, the first option runs against Johannine usage elsewhere and the second overlooks elements of biblical passages about new barley on which 6:1–15 depends. Reading 6:4 as the Passover in 'Iyyar equally solves the problem, but does so in a way that is both compatible with the Johannine import of ἐγγύς and sensitive to the timbre of Ruth 2:14 and 2 Kings 4:42–44. Passover in 'Iyyar was a minor but much discussed feast, enjoying generous attention from Philo, the Qumran sectarians and, especially, the Pharisees and Tannaim. Regarding it as the referent of 6:4 allows its occurrence to remain "imminent," while permitting the "five barley loaves" at 6:9 to be new: the Waving of the 'Omer would have been performed – and, thus, the law of *ḥadaš* satisfied – some two to three weeks prior to the feeding of the five thousand.

Besides this ability to resolve the calendrical difficulty in John 6, Passover in 'Iyyar enjoys three other features that commend it as the referent to 6:4: its dating to the fourteenth of 'Iyyar coincides with the Exodus manna account, on which John 6 largely turns; its contingent character explains Jesus' peculiar absence from Jerusalem in chapter 6; and, with John 5 and 6 inverted, its placement soon after Passover in Nisan fashions the whole of John's feasts into a liturgical sequence that implies intent. The Johannine festivals span a single year, from Passover to Passover, in more or less chronological order: Passover (14 Nisan), Second Passover (14 'Iyyar), Pentecost?/Remembrance?/Day of Atonement? (Sivan – early Tishri), Tabernacles (15–22 Tishri), Dedication (25 Kislev), Passover (14 Nisan).

Chapter 5

Feasts and Jesus' 'Hour'

5.1 Implications for the *Praedicatio Domini*

Before I apply this schema to the purpose of feasts in John, I pause to note its implications for an issue teasing studies in Christian Origins: the duration of Jesus' public ministry. Namely, it offers a more textually sound way than has been done for bringing the Johannine chronology of Jesus' public ministry into conformity with the chronology implied in the Synoptic gospels and espoused by early patristic (and Gnostic) writers.

Primarily at issue is the discrepancy between the minimum length of Jesus' ministry required in the Gospel of John and the likely length of that ministry intimated in the Synoptics. With its three Passovers, John demands Jesus' ministry to span at least two years. By contrast, the Synoptics suggest – and most of the earliest fathers argued – that it lasted little more than one. The Synoptics do this by setting Jesus' final Passover over against indications of a springtime (that is, Nisan/Passover) earlier in his ministry: the grain harvest plucked by Jesus' disciples[1]; or the (vernal) "green grass" on which the five thousand sat in the miraculous feeding accounts.[2] The fathers contended this largely (though not exclusively) by appeal to "the acceptable *year* of the Lord," preached by Jesus at Luke 4:18–19 (citing Isaiah 61:1–3).[3] The disparity has raised questions about the historical credibility of one (John) over against the others (the Synoptics and the early fathers); and this, in turn, has led to efforts among some to reconcile the two.[4]

While most of these efforts at reconciliation have sought to lengthen the Synoptic chronology to match the Johannine,[5] a bold attempt was made to do the opposite; that is, to shorten the Johannine chronology to match the

---

[1] Mark 2:23–28; cf. Matt 12:1–8; Luke 6:1–5.

[2] Mark 6:39; cf. Matt 14:19.

[3] For surveys of the broad swath of views, see Sutcliffe 1938:17–25 and Ogg 1940:62–76.

[4] See the synopses by Ogg 1962:729; Donfried 1992:1014–15.

[5] See here, especially, Turner (C.H.) 1908:406–10; Sutcliff 1938:84–112; Ogg 1940:12–25, 153–277, 289–304; Turner (H.E.W.) 1965:65–67.

Synoptic. The endeavor is most closely associated with Johannes van Bebber and Johannes Belser at the turn of the twentieth century. It has roots,
however, running at least as far back as the seventeenth century.[6] Part of
their argument appealed to suggestive (and not implausible) cues in the
Fourth Gospel's narrative: that the note about Caiaphas being high priest
"that year" (11:49; 18:13) makes no sense given the longer tenures high
priests enjoyed in the first century and, so, must refer to the single "year"
of Jesus' public ministry; and again, that Jesus' depiction of his ministry as
a "day" divided into twelve hours (9:4; 11:9–10) metaphorically stands for
the single year of his ministry, which, analogously, would have divided
into twelve months.[7]

More controversial in the contention, however, was its central premise
that the reference to "Passover" (τὸ πάσχα) at 6:4 was spurious to the
original text. That is, it was claimed that the introduction to the feast at 6:4
did not originally read, "And *the Passover*, the feast of the Jews, was
near," but rather, simply, "And the feast of the Jews, was near." As Urban
Holzmeister noted, this single mention of Passover at 6:4

> placed here in the middle of the Gospel, if it is genuine,
> clearly excludes the theory of a one year (ministry)
> and shows the ministry of Christ at least to have taken up
> a period of two years.[8]

Van Bebber, Belser and their predecessors resolved the difficulty simply
by deeming that reference a later insertion, alien to the original narrative.
To do this, they could not appeal directly to manuscript or versional traditions. As noted above, with the exception of the thirteenth century miniscule 472 (and the questionable seventeenth century Latin translation by
George of Trezibond), the whole of those traditions read τὸ πάσχα at

---

[6] Nicholas Mann 1733:156–65; Henry Browne 1844:80–94, 634–65; van Bebber
1898:24–37, 154–72 (Appendix II); 1904:70–71; and, after initial dissent (1900:35–36),
Belser 1903:160–74 (esp. pp. 169–71); 1904:159–76; 1905:196–206; 1911:425–28, 430–
37; 1914:1–3, 15–34 (esp. pp. 32–33); 1916:24–51 (esp. pp. 42–51). Also, both van Bebber and Belser together; 1907:1–45 (esp. pp. 1–4, 9–10, 12–24, 30–45). For this study I
was unable to access two earlier works in this line, Samuel Petit, *Eclogae chronologicae*
(1632) and Gerard J. Voss, *Dissertatio gemina, una de Jesu Christi genealogia, altera de
annis, quibus natus, baptizatus, mortuus* (1643). On their role in the development of the
one year hypothesis for the Fourth Gospel, see Holzmeister (1933:132–33) and Ogg
(1940:28–29). Voss is at least cited by Mann (1733:161–62).

[7] Van Bebber 1898:26–30. On this last inference, van Bebber interpreted Abraham's
joy to see Jesus' "day" at 8:56 as his witness of Jesus' ministry from the grave.

[8] Holzmeister 1933:135.

6:4.[9] Instead, recourse was made to inferences drawn from both the Fourth Gospel's narrative (internal evidence) and patristic testimony (external evidence).

The internal evidence was presented as two sides of a single coin. On the one hand, it was argued that the presence of τὸ πάσχα in the text as it stands creates problems: it presents a feast Jesus does not attend; it connotes a theme (the pascal lamb) not precisely relevant to John 6 (manna); and, read as it is with the phrase "the feast of the Jews," it duplicates the explanation of Passover already given at 2:13.[10] On the other hand, it was noticed, the absence of τὸ πάσχα makes for a more coherent reading. Without it, the imminent feast mentioned at 6:4 could be read to anticipate either the Pentecost at 5:1 (with John 5 and 6 reversed[11]) or the Feast of Tabernacles at 7:2,[12] resulting in a festal sequence that formed (more or less) a complete liturgical cycle – Passover (2:13), Pentecost ([6:4]; 5:1), Tabernacles ([6:4]; 7:2); Dedication (10:22–23), Passover (11:55).[13] Moreover, as van Bebber added (for the view that 6:4 anticipated Tabernacles at 7:2), certain features of the narrative would make better chronological sense if the incidents in chapters 4–6 came just prior to the month of Tishri (for Tabernacles) in chapter 7: specifically, the summer season suggested in the Samaritan episode (e.g., 4:6–15), the death of John the Baptist implied at 5:35 and the manna theme permeating chapter 6.[14]

As for external evidence, Nicholas Mann (and apparently Gerard J. Voss before him) argued the original absence of τὸ πάσχα at 6:4 on nothing more than bald speculation.[15] From Henry Browne (1844) onward, however, advocates made the case by drawing several inferences from certain patristic and early "heretical" sources: (1) that Ireneaus, Origen, Cyril of Alexandria and the anonymous author of *Hypotheses* did not reference a Passover at 6:4, even at junctures where their arguments would have benefited from doing so; (2) that, in their rejection of the Gospel of John, the (heretical) *Alogi* mention only two Passovers in its text; (3) that the one year theory of Jesus' public ministry, which dominated the first centuries

---

[9] See Westcott and Hort 1881–82:77–78 (Appendix); Holzmeister 1933:136; Sutcliffe 1938:27; and the discussion in Chapter 2 under '2.2 The Unnamed Feast and a Second Passover (John 5:1–6:71).'

[10] Mann 1733:161–63; van Bebber 1898:163–64; followed by Belser 1904:160.

[11] So Mann 1733:156–57, 163–64.

[12] Browne 1844:91 and van Bebber 1898:33–35, 163–69, followed by Belser 1904:170–72, 176. Van Bebber also suggested (p. 35) that, after the Dedication, Purim was implicit in the Lazarus story (11:1–53).

[13] Browne, van Bebber and Belser read 6:4 as it currently is, between 5:1 and 7:2; Mann, as already mentioned, placed 6:4 prior to 5:1.

[14] Van Bebber 1898:163–72.

[15] Mann 1733:161–63, who cites Voss.

of Christianity, could not have been sustained had Christian writers read a Passover at 6:4; and (4) that Gnostic advocacy of such a one year theory would have furnished incentive for orthodox scribes to add τὸ πάσχα to 6:4 at a later date.[16]

It lies beyond the scope of this monograph to engage this hypothesis in any detail.[17] I will at least note, however – if only as a preliminary to further work – that the reconstructed schema presented here revives the same chronological implications, but on more viable text–critical grounds. Taking the Passover at 6:4 as a 'Second Passover,' and contemplating the prior inversion of chapters 5 and 6 in the Fourth Gospel's composition history, allows Jesus' ministry to span a single year, from the Passover at 2:13 to the Passover at 11:55, without recourse to the text-critical liberties taken by van Bebber, Belser and their predecessors. As such, van Bebber's insight on Caiaphas being high priest "that year" (11:49; 18:13)[18] can still stand, but on more sturdy textual ground: it does not imply that the Fourth Evangelist mistakenly thought high priests were appointed for one year terms, but rather signifies that Caiaphas happened to be high priest during the single annum of Jesus' public ministry.

The issue, itself, requires broader treatment than can be done here: debate on the question has been vast and complex; and, as Jörg Frey has recently noted, any attempt at such harmony between John and the Synoptics must be sensitive to the compositional independence of both Johannine chronology and topography:

> Against such attempts to reconstruct an imagined, "original" work
> (that is, in this context, to harmonize the Johannine chronology
> to the Markan by inverting John 5 and 6), it is, however, advisable
> to acknowledge and evaluate the compositional independence
> of the Johannine chronology and topography – at least in view of the effect
> upon the Johannine narrative.[19]

---

[16] Browne 1844:84–92, 637; van Bebber 1898:154–63; cf. Belser 1903:58, 170–71; 1904:159–64. Even more tenuously van Bebber added that, since the "Feast of John the Baptist Beheaded" is dated to 29 August, and since, in Synoptic chronology, John's beheading immediately precedes the feeding of the five thousand (Matt 14:1–21; Mark 6:14–44), the Johannine feeding of the five thousand (John 6:1–15), itself, would have had to occur closer to the Feast of Tabernacles than it did the Feast of Passover; 1898:634–35. For a more comprehensive review, see Westcott and Hort 1881–82:77–81 (Appendix), who were suspicious but not unconvinced.

[17] Major critiques have been issued by Ioannes Maria Pfättisch (1911 [entire]); Vincenz Hartl (1917:79–121); Urban Holzmeister (1933:134–40); Edmund F. Sutcliffe (1938:26–49); and George Ogg (1940:27–60).

[18] Van Bebber 1898:26–27.

[19] Frey 2002:196n133 (parenthetical note mine).

Nevertheless, the proposal being made here might at least open the door for the matter to be revisited. Reading 6:4 as a 'Second Passover,' while surmising an earlier inversion of John 5 and 6, suggests that, at a prior phase of the Fourth Gospel's composition history, it presented a one year (rather than two or three year) *Praedicatio Domini*. Inasmuch as the Synoptic gospels may suggest – and early Christian authors certainly argued – the same, a way may present itself to find an original harmony between the three.[20]

5.2 The Resulting Schema and the Motif of Jesus' 'Hour'

5.2.1 Feasts as Temporal Benchmarks

To return to the purpose of the feasts in John, however – I note first that the sequence of named feasts reconstructed above does not represent a full liturgical calendar. The festivals in this schema, once again, list as follows:

Table 20. The Penultimate Sequence of Feasts:
The Feast at John 5:1 Between Sivan and Tishri

John 2:13	John 6:4	John 5:1	John 7:2	John 10:22	John 11:55
14 Nisan	14 'Iyyar	Sivan-Tishri	15–22 Tishri	25 Kislev	14 Nisan
Feast of Passover	Second Passover	Pentecost? Remembrance? Day of Atonement?	Feast of Tabernacles	Feast of Dedication	Feast of Passover

Were this sequence to represent a full festal year, one would expect it to include (and name) a number of other feasts and sacred days not listed: Azyma (though, as mentioned above, that feast is likely in process, albeit tacitly, at 2:23–3:21 and 20:1–23); but also, the Day of Remembrance (1 Tishri), possibly Purim (14–15 'Adar) and especially the Day of Atonement (10 Tishri). Since the Johannine sequence does not list those feasts and sacred days, however, it arguably was not meant to signify a complete liturgical cycle; and its import – as well as its purpose – may better be sought along other lines.

---

[20] By suggesting such a line of research, I do not mean to contravene the view of Gerald L. Borchert that the three Passovers in John ought to be appreciated less for their chronological implications than for the theological contribution they make to the narrative; 1993:303–16.

Among those lines – and more amenable to the selective inventory of feasts in the schema – is the use of festivals as temporal benchmarks. Besides providing occasions for collective ritual observance, feasts also (almost inadvertently) functioned as indicators of elapsing time. Their linear placement within the calendar at intervals typically one to several months apart rendered them as much apt to mark the passing of those months and seasons as they were to furnish junctures for communal commemoration. And so might it be with the feasts in this sequence. They span one annum, from Passover to Passover; and between the two, each indicates the passage of a substantial interval of time – further from the first Passover and closer to the last: the Second Passover in 'Iyyar (6:4) marks one month from the first Passover, with eleven months remaining till the last; Tabernacles in Tishri (7:2) marks six months from the first Passover, with six months till the last; and the Dedication in Kislev (10:22–23), eight months from the first Passover, with four months till the last. The feast at 5:1, being unnamed, would not register such an effect as precisely or as immediately as the others; but it would do as the narrative unfolded. Readers or hearers alighting upon the Tabernacles at 7:2, having already noted a Passover at 2:13 and a Second Passover at 6:4 – or having already read/heard the entire gospel through once – would, in retrospect, recognize that the feast at 5:1 represents the passing of another substantive interval of time between 6:4 and 7:2: if not the span between 'Iyyar (Second Passover) and Sivan (Pentecost), specifically, then at least a period lying sometime between 'Iyyar (Second Passover) and Tishri (Tabernacles).

This would explain why the Second Passover is mentioned at 6:4, even though Jesus does not go up to Jerusalem for it.[21] Though feasts did serve to beckon Jesus from Galilee to Jerusalem, typically for conflict with Judean authorities,[22] this was not their only – or even their most fundamental – purpose. They also functioned to indicate the elapsing of time, whether they (also) required Jesus' presence in Jerusalem or not. As such, 6:4 could read, "And the Passover, the feast of the Jews, was near," simply to signify the passing of a month's time since the Passover at 2:13, even though it was not a feast for which Jesus did (or, as Second Passover, needed to) make pilgrimage. Moreover, on such an understanding of the feasts, one might read the comment at 10:22–23 that "it was winter" as part of a seasonal *inclusio*, of sorts, with Jesus' words to his disciples at 4:35b, "Behold the fields, that they are white unto harvest." The latter (as interpreted here) was said during the barley harvest, heralding springtime be-

---

[21] This discussion was anticipated above, under Chapter 4, '4.3.2 The Contingent Observance of Second Passover.'

[22] So, for instance, Ernst Haenchen (1984:1.243) and C.K. Barrett (1978:251) on the feast at 5:1.

tween the First and Second Passovers and marking the beginning of Jesus' year of public ministry; the former was written about the Feast of Dedication, noting the onset of winter in late Kislev and marking the (near) end of that year of public ministry.

It is with such a function in view that the feasts in John take on a different theological import. For, in such a sequence – and serving such a purpose – they dovetail another temporal motif lacing the Fourth Gospel's narrative; that of Jesus' 'hour.'

5.2.2 Jesus' 'Hour'

The term 'hour' (ὥρα) in John denotes a number of phenomena: a literal sixty minute period (11:9–10); the time of day (1:39; 4:6, 52–53); the moment at which a transaction occurred (19:27); more metaphorically, the duration of John's ministry (5:35); and, metaphorically in a different sense, an epochal juncture in the divine plan – specifically, when worship will be "in spirit and in truth" (4:21–23), when the dead will hear the voice of the Son of God and resurrect to life or judgment (5:25, 28–29), when everyone who kills Jesus' followers will think he is offering *'avodah* (16:2–4),[23] when Jesus speaks to his disciples openly of the Father (16:25) and when those disciples scatter and leave Jesus alone (16:31–32). In fact, the use of 'hour' for the analogy of a woman in childbirth at 16:21–22 suggests that, in this last sense listed, it was considered a generic image for moments of crisis or change and, as such, could be applied to a wide range of matters.[24]

Within this last, metaphorical type of usage (and one and the same with some of the examples just cited) is the Fourth Gospel's motif of *Jesus' 'hour'* (ὥρα) or 'time' (καιρός). To recall the definition offered by Adriana Destro and Mauro Pesce, Jesus' 'hour' is "the decisive moment in which Jesus accepts his own destiny, suffers death and then experiences the resurrection and return to God."[25] This hour, it will be remembered,

---

[23] The second of the two references to 'hour' in this passage (at 16:4) reads "their hour" (ἡ ὥρα αὐτῶν) in P^{66} (apparently) ℵ (first corrector) A B L Θ 33 118 and the *Ferrar* group. That is, this 'hour' is specifically identified with those who will regard killing the disciples to be service to God.

[24] In the metaphor of the woman in labor at 16:21, "her hour" (ἡ ὥρα αὐτῆς) reads "her day" (ἡ ἡμέρα αὐτῆς) in P^{66} and D. Note, also, that, in the Greek manuscripts that attest 5:4 (A C [third corrector] L Θ Ψ 078 [apparently], *Family* 1, the *Ferrar* group and the *Majority text*), the related term καιρός appears as the object of κατά ("in its season") to describe the intervals at which the angel troubled the pool water at Bethsaida. Further, the metaphorical usage of 'hour' does not always exclude its more literal usage. C.K. Barrett (1978:545), for instance, followed by J. Edgar Bruns (1966–67:289), conflates the 'hour' of Jesus' glorification with "the sixth hour" of his crucifixion (19:14). And the same can be done with the 'hour' of Jesus' glorification and the 'hour' (as "moment") from which the Beloved Disciple takes Jesus' mother under his own care (19:27).

[25] Destro and Pesce 2000:6; see also p. 19.

arrives during the final Passover, at the close of Jesus' public ministry (12:23, 27; 13:1; 17:1). Its anticipation, however, is introduced just prior to the first Passover, during the wedding at Cana, when Jesus says to his mother, "What is there between me and you, Woman? My hour has not yet come" (οὔπω ἥκει ἡ ὥρα μου; 2:4). And, between that point and its arrival during the final Passover, Jesus and the divine plan he brings are temporally portrayed as existing in what might be called a liminal period: Jesus must avoid (7:6–8)[26] or is extraordinarily protected against (7:30; 8:20)[27] lethal harm, because "his hour (or time) had not yet come"; and certain other matters to occur or be effected at the arrival of that hour are cast as being so imminent as to have already come – specifically, the change of worship venue from temple and cult to spirit and truth (4:21–23); the vivification of the dead by the voice of the Son of God (5:25); and (during the last Passover) the abandonment of Jesus by his disciples (16:31–32):

> Jesus said to her, "Believe me, woman, an hour comes (ἔρχεται ὥρα),
> when neither in this mountain nor in Jerusalem will you worship the Father...
> But an hour comes and now is (ἀλλὰ ἔρχεται ὥρα καὶ νῦν ἐστιν),
> when the true worshippers will worship the Father in spirit and in truth;
> for, indeed, the Father seeks such who worship him." (4:21, 23)

> Truly, truly I say to you that an hour comes and now is (ὅτι ἔρχεται ὥρα
> καὶ νῦν ἐστιν[28]) when the dead will hear the voice of the Son of God
> and those who have heard will live. (5:25)

> Jesus answered them, "Do you believe? Behold, the hour is coming
> and has come (ἔρχεται ὥρα καὶ ἐλήλυθεν[29]), that you be scattered
> each to his own things, and leave me alone." (16:31–32)[30]

---

[26] When Jesus is pressured by his brothers to make pilgrimage for Tabernacles, he references the close of his ministry, saying, "My time (ὁ καιρὸς ὁ ἐμός) is not yet present but your time (ὁ δὲ καιρὸς ὁ ὑμέτερος) is always ready...I do not go up to this feast, for my time (ὁ ἐμὸς καιρός) has not yet been fulfilled"; 7:6–8.

[27] When temple officers attempt to arrest Jesus for speaking provocatively during Tabernacles, the commentary tells that, in spite of their efforts, "no one laid their hand upon him" (7:30) or "seized him" (8:20), for "his hour had not yet come" (ὅτι οὔπω ἐληλύθει ἡ ὥρα αὐτοῦ). The language is the same for both cases; though, for οὔπω at 7:30, P[66] reads οὐδέπω.

[28] The clause "and now is" (καὶ νῦν ἐστιν) is absent from ℵ (original hand).

[29] For ἐλήλυθεν, C (third corrector) D (first corrector) Θ Ψ 0250, Family 1, the Ferrar group and the Majority text read more emphatically "and now has come" (νῦν ἐλήλυθεν). Sinaiticus (ℵ [original hand]), though not reading νῦν before it, perhaps attempts a similar emphasis by repeating the subject 'the hour' (ἡ ὥρα) after it.

[30] The advance of Jesus' public ministry toward its goal is also expressed through the metaphor of "day" (ἡμέρα) crossing into "night" (νύξ). At 9:4, Jesus presages the end of his public activity, declaring, "We must work the works of the one who sent me while it is day (ἕως [or ὡς {C <original hand> L W 070 33}] ἡμέρα ἐστίν); night comes

5.2.3 Destro and Pesce Revisited

Destro and Pesce, it will be recalled, see this dynamic of Jesus' 'hour' in dialectic with the feasts in John. The anticipation of Jesus' 'hour,' in their view, represents a divinely manifested temporal mode to which the Johannine community ultimately adhered: its anticipation is introduced with Jesus' baptism (1:32–34); it arrives with the "rite of the voice from on high" (12:27–30); and, in between, its imminence envelopes and defines Jesus' ministry over against the milieu in which that ministry unfolded. That is, the anticipation of Jesus' hour "marks the rhythm of all the events of Jesus and, at times and moments, introduces that which distinguishes the conceptual picture of his movement."[31] The feasts, by contrast, represent and facilitate the aggregate of Jewish institutional rites from which the Johannine community came. As feasts they embody a temporal periodization (*tempo sociale*) to which Jesus' 'hour' (*tempo diverso*) is opposed; and, as rituals which require other rituals for their proper observance, they allow other Jewish rites to be brought into this same opposition within the narrative.[32] From the time the imminence of Jesus' 'hour' is made known at Jesus' baptism, argue Destro and Pesce, these two modes of time interact dialectically. And at the time that 'hour' arrives with the "rite from the voice from on high," its unique temporal mode draws Jesus' disciples, themselves, into itself, establishing a new periodization that is both severed from and opposed to the periodization structured by Jewish feasts (or any other calendrical rites):

(ἔρχεται νύξ), when no one can work." At 11:9–10, the same referent seems to be in view when Jesus contrasts walking in the day with stumbling in the night:

Jesus answered, "Are there not twelve hours in the day (τῆς ἡμέρας)? (D reads, "Does not the day have twelve hours?" [οὐχὶ δώδεκα ὥρας ἔχει ἡ ἡμέρα]).

If anyone walks in the day (ἐν τῇ ἡμέρᾳ), he does not stumble, for he sees the light of this world. But if anyone walks in the night (ἐν τῇ νυκτί), he does stumble, for the light is not in him." (instead of "the light is not in him" [ἐν αὐτῷ], D [original hand] reads, "the light is not in it" [ἐν αὐτῇ]; that is, "not in the night" [antecedent νυκτί]).

Further, at 13:30, the commentary connotes the same idea when it recounts that, during the meal at the conclusion of Jesus' ministry, Judas, "having taken the morsel (from Jesus), went out immediately, and it was night" (ἦν δὲ νύξ). Since 'hour' is the more dominant of the two images in the narrative, however, I speak of the dénouement of Jesus' ministry, here, under that motif.

[31] Destro and Pesce 1995a:78–79, 103–104; 1995b:87–88; 2000:6–7, 16–21, 118–20; Pesce 2001:55–56 (cf. Destro and Pesce 1997:112–26); quotation, 2000:6. For the broader discussion, see Chapter 3 under '3.3 Anthropological Theory: *'Tempo Sociale'* to the *'Tempo Diverso'* of Jesus' 'Hour,' Adriana Destro and Mauro Pesce.'

[32] Destro-Pesce 1995a:77, 79–82; 2000:5–12.

> By placing an institutive rite (the "rite of the voice from on high")
> at the beginning of the decisive and dramatic phase of Jesus' life,
> the redactor imagines a new periodization, which does not coincide
> with any other calendar or which is removed from the more habitual
> and consecrated rites of the Jewish society.
> On the contrary, it seems to be opposed to them,
> since it occurs precisely during the period of *Pesach*.[33]

By contrast to Destro and Pesce, the feasts in the hypothesis I propose here
do not function in dialectic to Jesus' 'hour,' but in service to it. Like Destro and Pesce, I understand the anticipation of that 'hour' to put Jesus in a
liminal period, from the moment it is introduced (1:32–34 or 2:4) to the
moment it finally comes (12:23). But, whereas Destro and Pesce have the
feasts in that period opposing the kind of time that 'hour' represents, I see
them, instead, assisting it – quantifying its imminence till it arrives. That
is, as Jesus' 'hour' grows so near as to be deemed already "come," the
feasts measure that ever increasing imminence concretely – from the first
Passover, at which it is introduced, to the last, at which it appears. The two
theories are not necessarily incompatible: Destro and Pesce treat the feasts
in the current state of the text, where they do not align chronologically[34]; I
consider them in a putative, earlier recension, on the premise that, in such
a phase, they did so align. But, whether it be due to successive redactional
strata or different methodological vantage points, the proposal by Destro
and Pesce and the one offered here are quite distinct in the purposes they
ascribe to the feasts: where Destro and Pesce have them in dissonance to
the imminence of Jesus' 'hour,' I see them in harmony with it.

To synthesize how this harmony works out in the narrative: Several
days after Jesus first articulates the coming of his hour to his mother at
Cana (2:4), he attends the Passover which marks one year till that hour arrives (2:13). During the barley harvest, begun after that Passover, he tells
the Samaritan woman that this hour is so imminent as to be already present
(4:23); and, not long afterward, at 6:4, the narrator notes that the Second
Passover is "near," signaling that the interval till its coming has now reduced from twelve months to eleven. As Jesus, next, communicates the
same imminence of this hour to Jerusalemites at 5:25, it is during a feast
(5:1), which, being both subsequent to the Second Passover at 6:4 yet prior
to Tabernacles at 7:2, indicates the interval to have decreased still further –
if that feast is Pentecost, to ten months; if it is less definable, some ten to
seven months. And, soon again, when Jesus must avoid (7:6–8) then es-
cape (7:30; 8:20) harm because his "time/hour had not yet come," it is near
or during "the feast of the Jews, Tabernacles" (7:2), showing the remaining

---

[33] Destro and Pesce 2000:20; italics theirs/parenthetical note mine; cf. Pesce
2001:55–56.
[34] Destro-Pesce 1995a:78, 82; 2000:6, 11–12.

time till that hour arrives now to be six months. As Jesus is found, not long afterward, "walking...in Solomon's Portico," it is during the Feast of Dedication (10:22–23), four months before the advent of the hour. And, as he enters Jerusalem for the last Passover in chapter 12, that hour finally arrives. Jesus answers the Greeks' wish for an audience at that time, saying, "The hour has come (ἐλήλυθεν ἡ ὥρα), that the Son of Man be glorified" (12:23). A moment later, he deliberates, "And what ought I say? 'Father, save me from this hour (ἐκ τῆς ὥρας ταύτης)?' But for this reason I came to this hour" (ἦλθον εἰς τὴν ὥραν ταύτην; 12:27). Before he washes the disciples' feet on the night before the pascal lambs are sacrificed, the narrator tells that he knew "that his hour had come (ὅτι ἦλθεν αὐτοῦ ἡ ὥρα[35]) that he would depart from this world to the Father" (13:1). And, in his prayer for the disciples just before his arrest, Jesus begins, "Father, the hour has come (ἐλήλυθεν ἡ ὥρα): glorify your Son, that your Son might glorify you" (17:1).

As mentioned above, this purpose for the feasts does not preclude any one or several of them serving other aims, as well, in tandem with it. Some, such as the Passovers at 6:4 and 11:55, or Tabernacles at 7:2, furnished commemorative symbolism for signs and discourse – with the Second Passover at 6:4, however, that symbolism derived, not from the slaughtering of pascal lambs, but from the giving of first manna (Exodus 16). Moreover, most feasts – all but the Passover at 6:4 – also served to bring Jesus from Galilee to Jerusalem for conflict with Judean authorities. More fundamentally, however – and earlier in the formation of the Fourth Gospel – the feasts in John exercised the theological role of quantifying the ever increasing imminence of Jesus' 'hour' from the first Passover to the last. As Jesus' glorification and return to the Father through the cross moved gradually to its culmination, the chronological sequence of feasts from Passover to Passover measured that movement in discernible intervals.

5.3 Feasts and the Current Text

In the final version of the Fourth Gospel, John 6 and 5 were inverted into their current order. The factors inducing such a change lie beyond the scope of this inquiry. They cannot be assumed to have had any relation to the feasts or Jesus' 'hour'; and, as such, require a broader context to assess than has been (or could be) constructed for this thesis. What can be traced,

---

[35] For ἦλθεν, the textual tradition also attests the perfect ἐλήλυθεν (*Majority text*), as well as synonyms ἥκει (*P*[66]) and παρῆν (D).

however, are two matters: the effects that inversion would have had on the original Johannine schema; and, conversely, the implications that earlier schema has for the narrative in its current form.

On the premise that 6:4 references a Second Passover, rather than First, the feasts now unfold as follows:

Table 21. The Current Sequence of Feasts: The Feast at John 5:1 as Unknown

John 2:13	John 5:1	John 6:4	John 7:2	John 10:22	John 11:55
14 Nisan	???	14 'Iyyar	15–22 Tishri	25 Kislev	14 Nisan
Feast of Passover	???	Second Passover	Feast of Tabernacles	Feast of Dedication	Feast of Passover

The effects this rearrangement has – both on the earlier sequence and for the new – are four: (1) the Second Passover at 6:4 remains a Second Passover; (2) the single year chronological sequence is now dismantled; (3) the feast at 5:1 has lost any moorings by which it can be identified; and (4) the temporal force of Jesus' 'hour' has been weakened. As a conclusion to this examination, I will outline each.

5.3.1 The Passover at John 6:4

First, the Second Passover at 6:4 remains a Second Passover. In the current arrangement of the feasts, one, perhaps two, of the factors that had earlier suggested it was a Second Passover no longer obtain. It is no longer immediately preceded by a(n explicit) First Passover (2:13), to which it might play the Second Passover. And it no longer appears at a juncture within an annual, chronological festal sequence, in which one could expect to find a Second Passover. The feast at 5:1 now stands between it and the prior Passover at 2:13, removing it from a point in the succession of Johannine feasts that would coincide with 'Iyyar in a single annum series.

That said, two other factors suggesting 6:4 is a Second Passover endure into the final edition. It still postdates the secular consumption of barley at 6:9 and, thus, still creates a *halakhic* tension in the narrative if read as a First Passover. And it is still couched in a manna tradition that, according to the Priestly tradition, claims Second Passover as its commemorative festival. The first giving of manna to Israel, according to Exodus 16:1, occurred "on the fifteenth day of the second month from their going out from the land of Egypt." Thus, the Passover at 6:4 should still be read as a Second Passover, not First. And, accordingly, the sign, exodus typology and Bread of Life discourse in chapter 6 should be interpreted in light of the connotations of that Second Passover, not in light of those from the First.

5.3.2 The Chronology of the Festal Sequence

Second, the feasts as a whole in John have lost their chronological sequence and, consequently, their one year span. With the feast at 5:1 now coming between the Passover at 2:13 and the Second Passover at 6:4, the feasts can no longer be read as moving sequentially through a single year's time. The only way it might have been done would be to identify the feast at 5:1 (in its current placement) as the sectarian Feast of Barley, prescribed by the Qumran sectarians and their parent group(s). As noted above, the Qumran sectarians (and their ideological forebears) scheduled the Waving of the 'Omer, not on a day within Azyma, but on the day following the first weekly Sabbath after it – in their 364-day calendar, always the twenty-sixth of the first month. In the Book of *Jubilees* (as already mentioned) this was deduced by Dominique Barthélemy, who counted a pentecontad backward over an assumed 364-day year from a Feast of Weeks/Pentecost that, from several passages, seems to date to the fifteenth day of the third month. As for the Qumran documents, themselves: *4QCalendrical Document/Mišmarot* D (4Q325) and *4QCalendrical Document C* (4Q326) put the sectarian "Feast of Barley" (מועד שורים) on that same date; as do *4QCalendrical Documents/Mišmarot A–B* (4Q320–321) and, possibly, *11QTemple Scroll*[a] (11Q19), designating it, instead, as the "Waving of the 'Omer" (הנף [ה]עו[מ]ר [יום]).[36] Assuming such a system for the Gospel of John would allow for a festal day to occur after Passover/Azyma at 2:13–3:21 had ended (14–21 Nisan), yet still between that Passover/Azyma and the Second Passover at 6:4 (14 'Iyyar); that is, at the juncture one now finds the unnamed feast at 5:1. Identifying the feast at 5:1 as such, then, would account for the (second) pilgrimage Jesus makes in chapter 5, while maintaining a chronological sequence of feasts that still extends no longer than one year:

Table 22. The Current Sequence of Feasts:
The Feast at John 5:1 as the Qumran Feast of Barley (?)

John 2:13	John 5:1	John 6:4	John 7:2	John 10:22	John 11:55
14 Nisan	26 Nisan	14 'Iyyar	15–22 Tishri	25 Kislev	14 Nisan
Feast of Passover	Feast of Barley	Second Passover	Feast of Tabernacles	Feast of Dedication	Feast of Passover

Rendering this option questionable, however, is the presence in John's festal list of the Feast of Dedication. Theories differ on the precise nature and development of the community (or communities) represented in Qumran

---

[36] See the discussion in Chapter 2, under '2.6.2 The Waving of the 'Omer.'

sectarian writings.[37]   But those that best merge historical clues from the texts with archaeological and paleographical evidence show that community to have, in some way, postured itself sharply against the Hasmoneans. The sectarians' own disenfranchisement from the Jerusalem cult likely came as a result of abuse from (and *halakhic* disputes with) Hasmonean rulers—possibly, though not necessarily, including Hasmonean claims to the high priesthood.[38] And the referent behind the adversarial sobriquet "Wicked Priest" was more likely than not one or several of the Hasmoneans.[39] On such premises, it would not be expected that, in their liturgical year, the sectarians would have included the Feast of Dedication, a festival instituted by Hasmoneans to commemorate the valor of their own reconsecration of the temple.[40] As much as been noted, recently, by Vander-Kam, who has commented on the conspicuous absence of that feast (along with Purim) from the Dead Sea Scrolls corpus.[41]

Inasmuch as the Gospel of John *does* include the Dedication among its feasts, then, it becomes problematic to associate the rest of its feasts with a sectarian conception of the liturgical year. To be sure, it is (remotely) possible that the Johannine community plotted the Hasmonean Feast of Dedication into an otherwise sectarian-type solar calendar; but this is hardly probable. As such, it becomes equally improbable that the feast at 5:1 could represent a sectarian date for the Waving of the 'Omer, however enticing the resulting scenario might be.[42]

---

[37] See the review of theories on Qumran identity and history by VanderKam 1999:488–523.

[38] So Collins 1989:159–67, 178; see, particularly, his reservations on the notion that the Hasmonean high priesthood furnished a cause for the schism (pp. 162–67).

[39]See García Martínez 1998:196–98; VanderKam 1999:501–14, 524–31; Charlesworth 2002a:25–37 (cf. idem 1980:218–24); and, now, especially, Håkan Bengtsson 2000:53–61. The theory that the references to the "Wicked Priest" in *Pesher Habakkuk* designate several ruling Hasmoneans in chronological order was first proposed by A.S. van der Woude (1982:349–59), then assimilated into the larger "Groningen Hypothesis" (see García Martínez 1988:113, 126–29; García Martínez and van der Woude 1990:536–40). Building on (and somewhat departing from) van der Woude's theory, Bengtsson argues that, though the epithet retained historical vestiges, it rather functioned as an enduring ideological gloss by which sectarians could clarify their righteous identity against any (rising) opponent; 2000:63–87, 290–97.

[40] 1 Macc 4:36–59; 2 Macc 10:1–8.

[41] VanderKam 2005:167.

[42] More tenable (though not followed here) is the suggestion of Lucetta Mowry that the feasts in John represent a reflex to (rather than application of) the Essene/sectarian calendar. Mowry builds on the conclusion of Benjamin W. Bacon that, with John 5 and 6 reversed, the feasts from the Passover at 6:4 to the Passover at 11:55 arrange themselves into a single liturgical year (see Bacon 1933:166–75, 185n5, 188–89, 192–215). Pushing further than Bacon, however, Mowry suggests that this liturgical year was woven into the Fourth Gospel amidst a post–70 Johannine encounter with refugee Essenes in Syria: the

Rather, one must conclude that, with John 5 and 6 in their current placements, the chronological sequence once governing the order of the feasts in John has been reconfigured. The feasts still move from a Passover to a Passover, but no longer do they do so *seriatim* or within a single year. Since at least thirteen months must pass between the Passover at 2:13 and the Second Passover at 6:4 – and at least another eleven between the Second Passover at 6:4 and the final Passover at 11:55 – the minimum duration of Jesus' public ministry is now, as has been thought, at least two years. And any discrepancies thought to attend the relationship of this duration to that implied in the Synoptics remain.

5.3.3 The Identity of the Unnamed Feast (John 5:1)

The third effect of inverting John 6 and 5 concerns the identity of the feast at 5:1. Specifically, the liturgical bearings by which that feast could be identified have now been removed. In the earlier festal sequence proposed here, the options for the feast at 5:1 could be delimited by balancing its necessary proximity to the Feast of Tabernacles at 7:2 against its necessary distance from that same feast. That is to say, the feast at 5:1 had to be close enough to Tabernacles to account for the acute carry over of the Sabbath controversy from chapter 5 into chapter 7; yet it had to be removed enough from Tishri to allow the practicality of two separate pilgrimages between them: one at 5:1 and one at 7:10. Since the feast at 5:1 was also preceded by the Second Passover at 6:4 (occurring in 'Iyyar), its identity was more or less constrained into only a few viable options: Pentecost, Remembrance or the Day of Atonement.

In the current sequence of feasts, however, the feast at 5:1 has been transferred to a position between chapters 4 and 6 and, thus, lies amidst a (minimal) thirteen month period required between the Passover at 2:13 and the Second Passover at 6:4. Options for its identity can be somewhat reduced by the temporal implications of 4:35, which now immediately precedes it.[43] If that verse is taken to date the Samaritan incident four months before grain harvest, the feast at 5:1 is more likely to be one of the festivals occurring between Kislev and Nisan – the Dedication (25 Kislev), Purim (14–15 'Adar) or Passover/Azyma (14–21 Nisan). If that verse, instead, is taken to put the Samaritan episode amidst the grain harvest, the feast at 5:1 is more apt to be a festival occurring between Nisan and Sivan

---

Johannine community did not adopt the Essene calendar; but, "prodded by the calendar quarrel, used the remarkable creativity of the cycle of festivals as a literary device to interpret the meaning of Christ for a Christian group living in the midst of an Essene group in Syria"; Mowry 1954:85–89, quotation p. 89. Further on the feasts in John representing the official cultic (not Qumran) calendar, see Rigato 1991:28–29.

[43] On the two temporal implications of 4:35 for narrative time, see above, under '2.2 The Unnamed Feast and a Second Passover (John 5:1–6:71).'

– Passover/Azyma or Pentecost (5–7 Sivan).[44] Even so, however, the amount of current possibilities exceeds those in the earlier schema; and these are all the more compounded by the ambiguities surrounding 4:35. The constraints that once made for a fairly secure identification of the feast at 5:1 have now been relaxed; and perhaps testimony to that effect is the wide array of theories now proposed for it.

5.3.4 The Vigor of Jesus' 'Hour'

Finally – and theologically most significant – the temporal force attending the motif of Jesus' 'hour' has been undercut. That motif, of course, carries an inherent sense of urgency, as recounted above; and, in an earlier phase, the Johannine feasts served to accentuate that urgency by quantifying the passage of a year's time in taut chronological sequence. As the 'hour' that was coming grew so near as to have already "come," the feasts marked the passing of months and seasons from Jesus' introduction of its imminence (2:4) to his declaration of its advent (12:23, 27; 13:1; 17:1): the first Passover (2:13)/twelve months; Second Passover (6:4)/eleven months; a feast between Second Passover and Tabernacles (5:1)/ten to seven months; Tabernacles (7:2)/six months; Dedication (10:22–23)/four months; and the last Passover (11:55).

With the inversion of John 6 and 5, however – and the consequent loss of chronological sequence – that temporal tautness attending the feasts has been loosened, so that, though references to Jesus 'hour' maintain a temporal momentum in and of themselves, the concrete backing of that momentum in the narrative has been diffused. Passages such as 4:21–23, 5:25 and 16:31–32 still tell that the hour which is "coming" is so imminent as to have already "arrived"; but no longer do the feasts that lace the text measure that growing proximity.

In sum, the final inversion of chapters 6 and 5 did not alter the identity of the feast at 6:4 as a Second Passover: though that feast no longer follows fast on the First Passover at 2:13 and, likewise, no longer appears where one would expect to find a Second Passover, it still postdates the secular consumption of barley at 6:9 and still forms the backdrop of a manna typology that biblically dates to 15 'Iyyar. The final inversion did, however, effect other changes in the way the feasts in John are to be read: it reconfigured their one year, chronological arrangement into a non-sequential chain, spanning at least two years; it removed the structural cues circumscribing the identity of the feast at 5:1; and, most importantly, it enervated the temporal vigor attending the theology of Jesus' 'hour.'

---

[44] If Pentecost, the year that passes between the Passover at 2:13 (14 Nisan) and the feast at 5:1 (Sivan) would be followed by another, between the feast at 5:1 and the Second Passover at 6:4 (14 'Iyyar).

Postscript

By listing these largely negative effects, I by no means intend to suggest that the final editing of the Fourth Gospel diminished an earlier (but now lost) richness in its narrative. Rather, I simply assume that, in the current form of the text, that richness occurs on a different plane than has been (or could be) investigated here – a plane that must be viewed from a vantage point other than the one used for this single monograph. If I would deduce anything from what this inquiry yields about the Gospel of John, it is, rather, that, in an earlier stage of its composition history, its structure and theology (in at least one respect) were as rich and elegant as they ultimately came to be in its final form.

5.4 Summary

The sequence of feasts reconstructed in Chapter 4 carries implications for the duration of Jesus' public ministry. By reducing the span of that ministry in the Fourth Gospel from (a minimum) two years to one – without recourse to marginal textual data – it offers a more viable hypothesis than has been done for aligning the Johannine chronology with that implied in the Synoptics and espoused by early Christian writers.

More significantly for the issue at hand, however, this reconstructed sequence further suggests a fundamental theological purpose for the feasts, related to the motif of Jesus' 'hour.' Absent several key feasts, the sequence does not represent a (full) Jewish liturgical year *per se*, but, rather, a series of temporal markers that signal the gradual passing of months and seasons: Nisan (Passover), 'Iyyar (Second Passover), Sivan-Tishri (Pentecost?, Remembrance?, the Day of Atonement?), Tishri (Tabernacles), Kislev (Dedication) to Nisan again (the last Passover). Jesus' 'hour,' for its part, culminates at the end of his public ministry; but it is anticipated, with ever intensifying urgency, from the start of that ministry. Expectation of it is introduced during the wedding at Cana (2:4); and, between that point and its arrival during the final Passover, it is cast as growing ever so near as to have essentially already come: "an hour comes and now is," Jesus says repeatedly, when worship will take place "in spirit and in truth" (4:21–23), when the dead shall "hear the voice of the Son of God and...live" (5:25) and when the disciples will "be scattered each to his own things" and leave Jesus alone (16:31–32). Since the festal sequence unfolds over this same period of time – and, inasmuch as that festal sequence, itself, represents a chronological series of temporal markers signaling the gradual passing of months and seasons – it can be inferred that, in its original design, that sequence was crafted to serve the motif of Jesus' 'hour.' Specifically, it accentuated the increasing proximity of that 'hour' by quantifying the ever diminishing interval that remained till its arrival.

With the final inversion of chapters 6 and 5, this festal sequence was dismantled and, thus, its original purpose obscured. Though the Second Passover at 6:4 remains such, the single year chronological sequence is now reconfigured, the feast at 5:1 has no moorings by which it can be identified and much of the temporal momentum driving the theology of Jesus' 'hour' has been slowed. This by no means implies that, in its composition history, the Fourth Gospel lost some of its original richness and elegance. Rather, it only suggests that such richness and elegance are now to be found in other features.

Chapter 6

Conclusion

6.1 Summary

I have argued that, in an earlier stage of the Fourth Gospel's development, its feasts served a purpose yet unnoticed. My starting points have been two: the *halakhic* problem that arises in John 6 when its Passover is read as a First Passover; and the insight of Adriana Destro and Mauro Pesce that the temporal rhythm of feasts in John interacts with the temporal rhythm of Jesus' 'hour.'

With respect to the first – the *halakhic* problem – I have noted that the barley consumption at 6:9 can legally precede an imminent Passover at 6:4 (only) if that Passover is deemed the Passover in 'Iyyar, prescribed in Numbers 9:9–14. Doing so allows the prerequisite Waving of the 'Omer to have occurred earlier in narrative time and, also, lends features to the Passover at 6:4 that fit hand-in-glove with other elements of the Johannine context. Passover in 'Iyyar is the feast implicitly associated with the manna tradition, on which John 6 largely turns. Its conditional observance accounts for Jesus' lack of pilgrimage in that chapter. And, with John 5 and 6 inverted, its placement after the Passover at 2:13 fashions the array of Johannine feasts into a liturgical scheme that suggests intent – the festivals align into a chronological sequence that spans a single annum.

Regarding the second starting point – the observation by Destro and Pesce that feasts enjoy an interface with Jesus' 'hour' – I have argued that the chronological festal sequence into which these feasts earlier fell represents a series of temporal markers that would have served the motif of Jesus' 'hour' by quantifying its growing imminence. Being absent key feasts, the schema is better understood as a series of temporal indicators than it is a full liturgical calendar; and, spanning chapters 2–12 as it does, it unfolds through the same portion of narrative in which Jesus' 'hour' is said to be coming so near as to have essentially already arrived. Destro and Pesce, who read the feasts in their current (not chronological) order, see this concurrence to be dialectical: for them, feasts represent a "*tempo sociale*" to the "*tempo diverso*" of Jesus' 'hour.'[1] I contend, by contrast, that, at least

---

[1] Destro and Pesce 1995a:103–104; 2000:6–7, 16–21, 118–20; Pesce 2001:55.

in an earlier phase of the Fourth Gospel's development, this concurrence was more harmonious; that is, that the temporal rhythm of Jewish feasts served rather than countered that of Jesus 'hour.'

This is not to deny that the feasts performed other tasks, as well, in the narrative: some furnished symbolism for signs and discourses; some lent justification for situating Jesus in Judea; and the like. Nor does it suggest that the earlier service feasts rendered to Jesus' 'hour' defines their role in the current text: the final redaction reconfigured chapters 5 and 6; and, though the Second Passover at 6:4 remains as such in that redaction, the chronological sequence of the whole has been lost and the force it once gave Jesus' 'hour' has been weakened. Rather, I more modestly contend that, alongside their other functions, feasts also clocked the coming of Jesus' 'hour.' Though that task is hidden from view in the final form of the text, it can be glimpsed through a modicum of diachronic criticism.

6.2 Further Questions

Academic studies typically conclude by raising as many questions as they (propose to) solve; and this is no exception. To the extent this thesis persuades, to that extent it carries implications requiring further investigation. Three have already been mentioned: the duration of Jesus' public ministry; the feasts in the current text; and the festal context of Jesus' Bread of Life discourse. I will elaborate on these and add a fourth – the transformation of ritual in the narrative of the Fourth Gospel.

6.2.1 The Duration of Jesus' Public Ministry

The schema of feasts reconstructed here stretches over a single annum and, thus, suggests that, in an earlier stage of its development, the Fourth Gospel gave Jesus' ministry as long a duration as is implied in the Synoptics and as was argued by early Christian writers. The coincidence is suggestive, both for the issue of John and the Synoptics and for relationship of Johannine christology to the historical Jesus. More work is required, however, than these cursory remarks can offer: the Synoptics may embody a duration for Jesus' ministry that exceeds one year; and, as Jörg Frey has noted, any attention given to the respective chronologies of John and the Synoptics must be matched by equal attention to their respective topographies.[2]

---

[2] Frey 2002:196n133.

6.2.2 The Feasts in the Current Text

According to this hypothesis, the final editor of the Fourth Gospel recon-figured the feasts from their earlier, one year chronological sequence into the order they now enjoy. In Chapter 5 (above) I sketched some of the im-plications of that reconfiguration for the feasts in the current text; and I further noted that any impairment it may have made on the older schema must be weighed against the enhancement(s) it, likewise, brought to the new one.[3]

To detect those enhancements, however, a new set of questions must be asked that was not (and could not be) addressed here. Vital among them are the following: (1) What were the theological (or other) priorities that drove the redactor to alter the earlier festal sequence and weaken its accen-tuation of Jesus' 'hour?' That is to say, what larger frame of reference is necessary to understand and appreciate the final version of John (and its feasts) on its own terms? (2) Are the narrative and theology of this final version still served by the feasts as a whole? If so, how so? And, if not, how do the (individual) feasts now function? And, further, (3) if the feasts no longer align sequentially, how do they relate and function relative to one another? Or, to put it another way, does the topical approach employed by Gale Yee[4] do better justice to the feasts in the current text than the se-quential one used in this study?

6.2.3 The Bread of Life Discourse

If the Passover at 6:4 is the Passover in 'Iyyar rather than the one in Nisan, the sign and discourse attached to it in John 6 may benefit from reassess-ment. In his classic examination of the passage in *Bread From Heaven* (1965), for instance, Peder Borgen draws analogies generously from the treatment of manna in Philo and Palestinian midrash, including *On the Life of Moses I* and *Mekilta of Rabbi Ishmael*.[5] Given the acute awareness that both these traditions (and both these works) have of Second Passover, as recounted above,[6] one might ask whether Borgen's analogies might be put on yet firmer ground (and shed yet brighter light) if they were revisited with a Second Passover, rather than First Passover, in view.

The same might be said for the Eucharistic dimension of John 6. As mentioned briefly above, if the Bread of Life discourse derives from new barley, which, itself, had been permitted for consumption by a prior Wav-

---

[3] See Chapter 5, under '5.3 Feasts and the Current Text.'

[4] See Chapter 3, under '3.1.4 Johannine *Takkanot,*' Gale A. Yee.'

[5] Borgen 1965:6–25, 38–43, 59–98.

[6] See Chapter 4, under '4.2.2.1.1 Philo Judaeus' and '4.2.2.2 Second Passover in Tan-naitic Tradition.' Note, especially, the treatments of Second Passover in Philo, *Mos.* 2.42.225–232 and *Mek.* on Exod 12:48 (*Pisḥa* 15.108–112).

ing of the 'Omer, it enjoys a ritual tie to Jesus' resurrection in chapter 20: since, in John, that resurrection, itself, occurs on the day of the Waving of the 'Omer (20:1), the resurrection becomes cast as the act which authorizes the (Eucharistic?) consumption of Jesus' "flesh" and "blood" as "Bread of Life."[7]

6.2.4 Ritual Transformation

Besides these three, one further issue might be raised, related to other rituals treated in the Fourth Gospel's narrative. If the 'hour' introduced near the first Passover (2:13) was to bring about fundamental religious changes when it arrived at the last Passover (11:55), some of those changes seem to have occurred as the feasts unfolded between the two. The term "my Father's house," for instance, which Jesus uses to describe the material temple at the first Passover (2:16) is, by the last Passover, spiritualized (14:2):

> In my Father's house are many rooms (μοναὶ πολλαί).
> Were it not so, I would have told you,
> for I go to prepare a place for you.[8]

If the "rooms" (μοναί) of this house are tantamount to the "room" (μονή) which Jesus and the Father will make with the believer (at 14:23), the new temple has become the indwelling of God in his people by the Spirit. And this seems to reflect the change of liturgical venue anticipated at 4:21–23, from worship in temple and in cult to worship "in spirit and in truth."

The same type of alteration appears to occur with ritual purity. During the wedding at Cana, the empty stone jars at 2:6–7 show ritual purity at that juncture to be the result of a physical rite effected by water. But, by Jesus' vine and branches metaphor in the Farewell Discourse, "cleanness" has become the result of a verbal act effected by Jesus' speech – "You are already clean, because of the word which I have spoken to you" (15:3).

The dynamic in question may be what Catharine Bell labels *"ritual transformation"*: not the creation of new rites *ex nihilo* (what Bell dubs "ritual invention"), but the modification of traditional rites into new forms and aims.[9] Applied to the Fourth Gospel, it seems that, in the liminal period that occurs between the first Passover, when the Jesus' 'hour' is introduced, and the last Passover, when it arrives, Jewish rituals are being gradually transformed into metaphorized counterparts; and these, in turn, form the framework for a new, distinctly Johannine (ritual) system. The idea is not unlike the "inversion" which Destro and Pesce propose to be

---

[7] See Chapter 2, '2.6.2 The Waving of the 'Omer' and Chapter 4, '4.3.2 The Contingent Observance of Second Passover.'

[8] John 14:2. Further on the first and last Passovers forming an *inclusio*, see Kerr 2002:78–79.

[9] Bell 1997:212–23; on "ritual invention," see pp. 223–42.

taking place through the narrative[10]; and, as with the three other issues listed above, so also here – much can be done (and great benefit derived) from tracing that transformation out in its full scope.

---

[10] Destro and Pesce 1995a (entire); 1995b:101–102; 2000:3–24, 118–22; Pesce 2001: 53–65. See Chapter 3, under '3.3 Anthropological Theory: *'Tempo Sociale'* to the *'Tempo Diverso.''*

Bibliography

Abbreviations follow P.H. Alexander, J.F. Kutsko, J.D. Ernest, S.A. Decker-Lucke and D.L. Petersen, eds. *The* SBL *Handbook of Style for Ancient Near Eastern, Biblical, and Early Christian Studies*. Peabody, Massachusetts: Hendrickson Publishers, 1999.

Aland, B.
  K. Aland,
  J. Karavidopoulos,
  C.M. Martini
  & B.M. Metzger
1993   *Novum Testamentum Graece*. 27th ed. Stuttgart: Deutsche
                     Bibelgesellschaft.

Aletti, J.-N.
1974   Le Discours sur le Pain de Vie (Jean 6): Problèmes de composition
                     et fonction des citations de l'Ancien Testament. *RSR* 62:169-97.

Alexander, P.S.
  & G. Vermes
1998a   4QSerekh Ha-Yaḥad: General Introduction. Pages 1-25 in *Qumran
                     Cave 4. XIX: Serekh Ha-Yaḥad and Two Related Texts*. DJD 26.
                     Oxford: Clarendon.
1998b   4QSerekh Ha-Yaḥad: 259. 4QSerekh ha-Yaḥad^e (Pls. XIV-XVI).
                     Pages 129-52 in *Qumran Cave 4. XIX: Serekh Ha-Yaḥad and Two
                     Related Texts*. DJD 26. Oxford: Clarendon.

Argyle, A.W.
1971   A Note on John 4.35. *ExpTim* 82:247-48.
Auerbach, E.
1958   Die Feste im Alten Israel. *VT* 8:1-18.
Auwers, J.-M.
1990   La Nuit de Nicodème (*Jean* 3, 2; 19, 39) ou l'Ombre du Langage.
                     RB 97:481-503.

Bacon, B.W.
1933   *The Gospel of the Hellenists*. Edited by C.H. Kraeling. New York:
                     Henry Holt and Company.
1910   *The Fourth Gospel in Research and Debate: A Series of Essays
                     on Problems Concerning the Origin and Value of the Anonymous
                     Writings Attributed to the Apostle John*. New York: Moffat,
                     Yard and Company.

Baillet, M.,
  J.T. Milik
  & R. de Vaux
  with H.W. Baker
1962   *Les "Petites Grottes" de Qumrân: Exploration de la falaise;*
                       Les grottes 2Q, 3Q, 5Q, 6Q, 7Q à 10Q; Le rouleau de cuivre.
                       DJD 3. Oxford: Clarendon.
Barrett, C.K.
1978   *The Gospel According to St. John.* 2nd edition. Philadelphia:
                       Westminster Press.
Barthélemy, D.
1952   Notes en marge de publications récentes sur les manuscrits
                       de Qumrân. *RB* 59:187-218.
Bauckham, R.
2002   The 153 Fish and the Unity of the Fourth Gospel. *Neot* 36:77-88.
Baumgarten, J.M.
1977   The Calendar of the Book of Jubilees and the Bible. Pages 101-14
                       in *Studies in Qumran Law.* SJLA 24. Leiden: Brill.
1976   *4Q Halakah^a 5,* the Law of *Ḥadash,* and the Pentecontad Calendar.
                       JJS 27:36-46.
Beasley-Murray, G.R.
1999   *John.* 2nd edition. WBC 36. Nashville: Thomas Nelson.
Beattie, D.R.G.
1994   *The Targum of Ruth: Translated, with Introduction, Apparatus,*
                       and Notes. ArBib 19. Collegeville, Minnesota: Liturgical Press.
van Bebber, J.
1904   Zur neuesten Datierung des Karfreitags. *BZ* 2:67-77.
1898   *Zur Chronologie des Lebens Jesu: Eine Exegetische Studie.*
                       Münster: Heinrich Schöningh.
van Bebber, J.
  & J. Belser
1907   Beiträge zur Erklärung des Johannesevangeliums. *TQ* 89:1-58.
Beckwith, R.T.
1996   The Date of the Crucifixion: The Misuse of Calendars and
                       Astronomy to Determine the Chronology of the Passion.
                       Pages 276-96 in *Calendar and Chronology, Jewish and Christian:*
                       Biblical, Intertestamental and Patristic Studies. AGJU 33.
                       Leiden: Brill.
Bell, C.
1997   *Ritual: Perspectives and Dimensions.* New York/Oxford: Oxford
                       University Press.
Belser, J.
1916   *Abriß des Lebens Jesu von der Taufe bis zum Tod.* Freiburg:
                       Herder.
1914   Zur Abfolge der evangelischen Geschichte. *TQ* 96:1-49.
1911   Das Johannesevangelium und seine neueste Beurteilung.
                       TQ 93:404-49.
1905   *Das Evangelium des Heiligen Johannes.* Freiburg:
                       Herder.

1904   Zu der Perikope von der Speisung der Fünftausend (Mt 14, 13-21.
                      Mk 6, 30-44. Lk 9, 10-17. Jo 6, 1-15). *BZ* 2:154-76.
1903   Zur Hypothese von der einjährigen Wirksamkeit Jesu. *BZ* 1:55-63,
                      160-74.
1900   Zur Chronologie der evangelischen Geschichte. *TQ* 82:23-42.

Ben-Dov, J.
2001   4Q319: 4QOtot (Pls. X-XIII). Pages 195-244 in *Qumran
                      Cave 4. XVI: Calendrical Texts.* Edited by S. Talmon, J. Ben-Dov
                      and U. Glessmer. DJD 21. Oxford: Clarendon Press.

Bengtsson, H.
2000   *What's in a Name?: A Study of Sobriquets in the Pesharim.* Uppsala:
                      Uppsala University.

Bernard, J.H.
1929   *A Critical and Exegetical Commentary on the Gospel according to
                      St. John.* Edited by A.H. McNeile. 2 vols. ICC. New York:
                      Charles Scribner's Sons.

Blackman, P.
1951-1956   משניות. 7 vols. London: Mishna Press, Ltd.
Blinzler, J.
1942   Review of F. Kirmis, *Kapitel V des Johannesevangeliums mit einer
                      Ausführung über die Dauer der öffentlichen Wirksamkeit Jesu,
                      den Bethesdateich und die Stellung von c. 5 zu c. 6. Klerusblatt*
                      23:203.

Boismard, M.-É.
1999   Bethzatha ou Siloé. *RB* 106:206-18.
1958   De son Ventre Couleront des Fleuves d'Eau (Jo., VII, 38).
                      RB 65:523-46.
1951   L'Évangile à quatre dimensions: Introduction à la lecture
                      de saint Jean. *LumVie* 1:94-114.

Boismard, M.-É.
  and A. Lamouille
1987   *L'Évangile de Jean.* Volume 3 of *Synopse des Quatre Évangiles
                      en Français.* New edition. Paris: Les Éditions du Cerf.

Borchert, G.L.
1993   The Passover and the Narrative Cycles in John. Pages 303-16
                      in *Perspectives on John: Methods and Interpretation in the Fourth
                      Gospel.* Edited by R.B. Sloan and M.C. Parsons. Lewiston:
                      E. Mellen Press.

Borgen, P.
1965   *Bread From Heaven: An Exegetical Study of the Concept of Manna
                      in the Gospel of John and the Writings of Philo.* SNT 10. Leiden:
                      Brill.
1963   Observations on the Midrashic Character of John 6. *ZNW* 54:232-40.
Borowski, O.
1987   *Agriculture in Iron Age Israel.* Winona Lake, Indiana:
                      Eisenbrauns.

Bousset, W.
1909   Ist das vierte Evangelium eine literarische Einheit? *TRu* 12:1-12.

Bover, J.M.
1922   "Adhuc Quattuor Menses Sunt, et Messis Venit": Ioh. 4, 35.
                       Bib 3:442-44.

Bowman, J.
1975   *The Fourth Gospel and the Jews: A Study in R. Akiba, Esther and the
                       Gospel of John.* Pittsburgh Theological Monograph Series 8.
                       Pittsburgh, Pennsylvania: Pickwick Press.
1971   The Identity and Date of the Unnamed Feast of John 5:1.
                       Pages 43-56 in *Near Eastern Studies in Honor of William Foxwell
                       Albright.* Edited by H. Goedicke. Baltimore and London:
                       Johns Hopkins Press.

Braun, F.-M.
1964   *Jean le théologien: Les grandes traditions d'Israël et l'accord
                       des Écritures selon le quatrième Évangile.* EBib 45/2. Paris:
                       J. Gabalda et Cie.
1955   L'Arrière-Fond Judaïque du Quatrième Évangile et la Communauté
                       de l'Alliance. *RB* 62:5-44.

Brown, R.E.
1966/1970   *The Gospel According to John.* 2 vols. AB 29/29A. Garden City,
                       New York: Doubleday.

Browne, H.
1844   *Ordo Sæclorum: A Treatise on the Chronology of the Holy
                       Scriptures.* London: John W. Parker.

Bruns, J.E.
1966-67   The Use of Time in the Fourth Gospel. *NTS* 13:285-90.

Bultmann, R.
1971   *The Gospel of John: A Commentary.* Translated by G.R. Beasley-
                       Murray. Philadelphia: Westminster Press. Translation of *Das
                       Evangelium des Johannes* (with the Supplement of 1966).
                       Göttingen: Vandenhoeck and Ruprecht, 1964.

Busse, U.
1991   Open Questions on John 10. Pages 6-17 in *The Shepherd Discourse
                       of John 10 and its Context: Studies by Members of the Johannine
                       Writings Seminar.* Edited by J. Beutler and R.T. Fortna.
                       SNTSMS 67. Cambridge/New York/Port Chester/Melbourne,
                       Sydney: Cambridge University Press.

Caba, J.
1974   *Dai Vangeli al Gesù Storico.* Rome: Edizioni Paoline.

Cassel, O.C.I.
  & Norris, J.P.
1871   On the Chronology of St. John V. and VI. *Journal of Philology*
                       3:107-12.

Cathcart, K.J.
  & R.P. Gordon
1989   *The Targum of the Minor Prophets: Translated, with a Critical
                       Introduction, Apparatus, and Notes.* ArBib 14. Wilmington,
                       Delaware: Michael Glazier, Inc.

Cazelles, H.
1962   Sur les origines du calendrier des Jubilés. *Bib* 43:202-12.

Charles, R.H.
1902   *The Book of Jubilees or The Little Genesis*. London: Adam and
                     Charles Black.

Charlesworth, J.H.
2002a   *The Pesharim and Qumran History: Chaos or Consensus?* Grand
                     Rapids, Michigan: William B. Eerdmans.
2002b   The Priority of John? Reflections on the Essenes and the First
                     Edition of John. Pages 73-114 in *Für und wider die Priorität*
                     des Johannesevangeliums: Symposion in Salzburg
                     am 10. März 2000. Edited by P.L. Hofrichter. Theologische Texte
                     und Studien 9. Hildescheim/Zürich/New York: Georg Olms Verlag.
1980   The Origin and Subsequent History of the Authors of the Dead Sea
                     Scrolls: Four Transitional Phases Among the Qumran Essenes.
                     RevQ 10:213-33.

Cladder, H.J.
1919   Die Jünger im Saatfeld. *TGl* 11:209-18.

Clarke, E.G.
1984   *Targum Pseudo-Jonathan of the Pentateuch: Text and Concordance*.
                     Hoboken, New Jersey: Ktav Publishing House.

Collins, J.J.
1989   The Origins of the Qumran Community: A Review of the Evidence.
                     Pages 159-78 in *To Touch the Text: Biblical and Related Studies*
                     in Honor of Joseph A. Fitzmyer, S.J. Edited by M.P. Horgan and
                     P.J. Kobelski. New York: Crossroad.

Collins, R.F.
1990   *These Things Have Been Written: Studies on the Fourth Gospel*.
                     Louvain Theological and Pastoral Monographs 2. Louvain:
                     Peeters Press/Grand Rapids, Michigan: William B. Eerdmans.
1986   Proverbial Sayings in St. John's Gospel. *MelT* 37:42-58.

Colson, F.H.
  & G.H. Whitaker
1927-1962   *Philo*. 10 vols. LCL. London: William Heinemann Ltd./Cambridge,
                     Massachusetts: Harvard University Press.

Comblin, J.
1953   La Liturgie de la Nouvelle Jérusalem (Apoc., XXI, 1—XXII, 5).
                     ETL 29:5-40.

Cothenet, É.
1993   Typologie de l'Exode dans le IVe Évangile. Pages 243-54 in
                     Tradició i traducció de la paraula: miscellània Guiu Camps.
                     Edited by F. Raurell, D. Roure and P.-R. Tragan.
                     Montserrat: Abadia de Montserrat.

Croatto, J.S.
1975   Riletture dell'Esodo nel Cap. 6 di San Giovanni. *BeO* 17:11-29.

Cullmann, O.
1969   La Samarie et les Origines de la Mission Chrétienne: Qui sont
                     les ᾿ ΆΛΛΟΙ de Jean 4.38? Pages 43-49 in *Des Sources*
                     de l'Évangile à la Formation de la Théologie Chrétienne.
                     Neuchatel: Delachaux and Niestlé.

Cuvillier, É.
1996   La Figure des Disciples en Jean 4. *NTS* 42:245-59.

Daise, M.A.
2005   "The Days of Sukkot of the Month of Kislev": The Festival
              of Dedication and the Delay of Feasts in 1QS 1:13-15. Pages 119-28
              in *Enoch and Qumran Origins: New Light on a Forgotten
              Connection.* Edited by G. Boccaccini. Grand Rapids, Michigan:
              William B. Eerdmans.
Daube, D.
1956   *The New Testament and Rabbinic Judaism.* London: University
              of London, The Athlone Press.
le Déaut, R.
1970   Une aggadah targumique et les "murmures" de Jean 6. *Bib* 51:80-83.
Destro, A.
  & M. Pesce
2000   *Come nasce una religione: Antropologia ed esegesi del Vangelo
              di Giovanni.* Percorsi 8. Rome: GLF Editori Laterza.
1997   *Antropologia delle origini cristiane.* 2nd edition. Rome: Laterza.
1995a   Dialettica di riti e costruzione del movimento nel Vangelo
              di Giovanni. Pages 77-109 in *Studi sul cristianesimo antico
              e moderno in onore di M.G. Mara.* Edited by M. Simonetti and
              P. Siniscalco. Aug 35. Rome: Institutum Patristicum
              Augustinianum.
1995b   I Riti nel Vangelo di Giovanni. Pages 85-105 in *Atti del V Simposio
              di Efeso su S. Giovanni Apostolo.* Edited by L. Padovese. Turchia:
              la Chiesa e la sua storia 8. Rome: Istituto Francescano
              de Spiritualità/Pontificio Ateneo Antoniano.
Devillers, L.
2002   *La fête de l'envoyé: La section johannique de la fête des tentes
              (Jean 7,1-10,21) et la christologie.* EBib 49. Paris:
              J. Gabalda et Cie.
1999   Une piscine peut en cacher une autre. À propos de Jean 5, 1-9a.
              RB 106:175-205.
Díez Macho, A.
1971   *Levítico.* Vol. 3 of *Neophyti 1.* Textos y Estudios 9.
              Madrid/Barcelona: Consejo Superior de Investigaciones Científicas.
Donfried, K.P.
1992   Chronology: New Testament. *ABD* 1:1011-22.
Du Rand, J.A.
1991   A Syntactical and Narratological Reading of John 10 in Coherence
              with Chapter 9. Pages 94-115 in *The Shepherd Discourse
              of John 10 and its Context: Studies by Members of the Johannine
              Writings Seminar.* Edited by J. Beutler and R.T. Fortna.
              SNTSMS 67. Cambridge/New York/Port Chester/Melbourne,
              Sydney: Cambridge University Press.
Elliger, K.
  & W. Rudolph
1983   *Biblia Hebraica Stuttgartensia.* Rev. ed. Stuttgart: Deutsche
              Bibelgesellschaft.
Ensor, P.W.
2000   The Authenticity of John 4.35. *EvQ* 72:13-21.

Enz, J.J.
1957   The Book of Exodus as a Literary Type for the Gospel of John.
                JBL 76:208-15.
Feliks, Y.
1963   החקלאות בארץ־ישראל בתקופת המשנה והתלמוד. Jerusalem:
                Magnes Press/Tel Aviv: Dvir.
Feuillet, A.
1962   Les Fleuves d'eau vive de Jo., 7, 38: Contribution à l'étude
                des rapports entre Quatrième Évangile et Apocalypse.
                Pages 107-20 in *Parole de Dieu et Sacerdoce*. Edited by E. Fischer
                and R.P.L. Bouyer. Paris: Desclée & Cie.
1960   Les thèmes bibliques majeurs du discours sur le pain de vie (Jn 6).
                NRTh 82:803-22, 918-39, 1040-62.
Finkel, A.
1974   *The Pharisees and the Teacher of Nazareth: A Study of Their*
                Background, Their Halachic and Midrashic Teachings,
                the Similarities and Differences. AGSU 4. Leiden/Köln:
                Brill.
Finkelstein, L.
1969   ספרי על ספר דברים. New York: JTSA.
Fortna, R.T.
1988   *The Fourth Gospel and Its Predecessor: From Narrative Source*
                to Present Gospel. Philadelphia: Fortress Press.
Franke, A.H.
1885   *Das Alte Testament bei Johannes: Ein Beitrag zur Erklärung und*
                Beurtheilung der johanneischen Schriften. Göttingen: Vandenhoeck
                & Ruprecht's Verlag.
Frey, J.
2002   Die "theologia crucifixi" des Johannesevangeliums. Pages 169-238
                in *Kreuzestheologie im Neuen Testament.* Edited by A. Dettwiler
                and J. Zumstein. WUNT 151. Tübingen: Mohr Siebeck.
García Martínez, F.
1998   The History of the Qumran Community in the Light of Recently
                Available Texts. Pages 194-216 in *Qumran Between the Old and*
                New Testaments. Edited by F.H. Cryer and T.L. Thompson.
                JSOTSup 290. Sheffield: Sheffield Academic Press.
1988   Qumran Origins and Early History: A Groningen Hypothesis.
                FO 25:113-36.
García Martínez, F.
  & A.S. van der Woude
1990   A "Groningen" Hypothesis of Qumran Origins and Early History.
                RevQ 14:521-41.
Gärtner, B.
1959   *John 6 and the Jewish Passover.* ConBNT 17.
                Copenhagen: Ejnar Munksgaard.
Geiger, G.
1984   Aufruf an Rückkehrende: Zum Sinn des Zitats von Ps 78,24b
                in Joh 6,31. *Bib* 65:449-64.
Giblet, J.
1965   "Et il y eut la Dedicace…": Jean 10, 22-39. *BVC* 66:17-25.

Giblin, C.H.
1983   The Miraculous Crossing of the Sea (John 6.16-21). *NTS* 29:96-103.
van Goudoever, J.
1961   *Biblical Calendars*. 2nd edition. Leiden: Brill.
Goulder, M.D.
1982   The Liturgical Origin of St. John's Gospel. Pages 205-21 in *Studia
                       Evangelica VII: Papers Presented to the Fifth International
                       Congress on Biblical Studies held at Oxford, 1973*. TUGAL 126.
                       Berlin: Akademie Verlag.
1978   *The Evangelists' Calendar: A Lectionary Explanation
                       of the Development of Scripture*. The Speaker's Lectures in Biblical
                       Studies 1972. London: SPCK.
Grelot, P.
1963   Jean, VII, 38: Eau du Rocher ou Source du Temple? *RB* 70:43-51.
1959   "De Son Ventre Couleront des Fleuves d'Eau": La Citation
                       Scripturaire de Jean, VII, 38. *RB* 66:369-74.
Grossfeld, B.
1991   *The Two Targums of Esther: Translated, with Apparatus and Notes*.
                       ArBib 18. Collegeville, Minnesota: Liturgical Press.
1988   *The Targum Onqelos to Leviticus and the Targum Onqelos
                       to Numbers: Translated, with Apparatus, and Notes*. ArBib 8.
                       Wilmington, Delaware: Michael Glazier, Inc.
Guggenheimer, H.W.
1998   *Seder Olam: The Rabbinic View of Biblical Chronology*. Northvale,
                       New Jersey/Jerusalem: Jason Aronson, Inc.
Guilding, A.
1960   *The Fourth Gospel and Jewish Worship: A Study of the Relation
                       of St. John's Gospel to the Ancient Jewish Lectionary System*.
                       Oxford: Clarendon.
Haenchen, E.
1984   *John 1-2*. Edited by R.W. Funk and U. Busse. Translated by
                       R.W. Funk. 2 vols. Hermeneia. Philadelphia: Fortress Press.
Hammer, R.
1986   *Sifre: A Tannaitic Commentary on the Book of Deuteronomy*.
                       Translated by R. Hammer. Yale Judaic Series 24. New
                       Haven/London: Yale University Press.
Hampden-Cook, E.
1923-24   The Hours of the Day in the Fourth Gospel. *ExpTim* 35:286-87.
Hanhart, K.
1977   "About the Tenth Hour"...on Nisan 15 (Jn 1,35-40).
                       Pages 335-46 in *L'Évangile de Jean: Sources, rédaction, théologie*.
                       Edited by M. de Jonge. BETL 44. Leuven: Éditions J. Duculot,
                       S.A., Gembloux and Leuven University Press.
Hanson, A.T.
1991   *The Prophetic Gospel: A Study of John and the Old Testament*.
                       Edinburgh: T. & T. Clark.
Harrington, D.J.
 & A.J. Saldarini
1987   *Targum Jonathan of the Former Prophets: Introduction, Translation
                       and Notes*. ArBib 10. Wilmington, Delaware: Michael Glazier, Inc.

Hartl, V.
1917   *Die Hypothese einer Einjährigen Wirksamkeit Jesu*. NTAbh 7.
              Münster: Verlag der Aschendorffschen Verlagsbuchhandlung.

Heinemann, J.
1968   The Triennial Lectionary Cycle. *JJS* 19:41-48.
Heising, A.
1964   Exegese und Theologie der Alt- und Neutestamentlichen
              Speisewunder. *ZKT* 86:80-96.

Hengel, M.
1989   Die Schriftauslegung des 4.Evangeliums auf dem Hintergrund
              der urchristlichen Exegese. Pages 249-88 in *"Gesetz" als Thema
              Biblischer Theologie*. Volume 4 of *Jahrbuch für Biblische Theologie
              (JBTh)*. Edited by M.A. Schökel, J.R. Donahue, P.D. Hanson,
              U. Mauser and M. Sæbø. Neukirchen-Vluyn: Neukirchener Verlag.

Holzmeister, U.
1933   *Chronologia Vitae Christi quam e Fontibus Digessit
              et ex Ordine Proposuit*. Scripta Pontificii Instituti Biblici.
              Rome: Sumptibus Pontificii Instituti Biblici.

Horovitz, H.S.
1966   ספרי דבי רב. מחברת ראשונה: ספרי על ספר במדבר
              וספרי זוטא. Jerusalem: Wahrmann Books.

Hoskyns, E.C.
1947   *The Fourth Gospel*. Edited by F.N. Davey. London:
              Faber and Faber, Ltd.

Howard, W.F.
1955   *The Fourth Gospel in Recent Criticism and Interpretation*.
              4ᵗʰ ed. Revised by C.K. Barrett. London: Epworth Press.

Hunt, B.P.W.S.
1958   *Some Johannine Problems*. London: Skeffington.
Jansen, H.L.
1985   Typology in the Gospel According to John. Pages 125-43 in
              *The Many and the One: Essays on Religion in the Graeco-Roman
              World Presented to Herman Ludin Jansen on His 80ᵗʰ Birthday*.
              Edited by P. Borgen. Trondheim: Tapir. Repr. (translated)
              from *NTT* 49 (1948):144-58.

Jaubert, A.
1991   The Calendar of Qumran and the Passion Narrative in John.
              Pages 62-75 in *John and the Dead Sea Scrolls*. Edited by
              J.H. Charlesworth. New York: Crossroad.

1965   *The Date of the Last Supper*. Staten Island, New York: Alba House.
Jeremias, J.
1966   *The Eucharistic Words of Jesus*. Translated by N. Perrin.
              New York: Charles Scribner's Sons. Translation of
              Das Abendmahlsworte Jesu. 3ʳᵈ edition. Göttingen: Vandenhoeck
              & Ruprecht, 1960.

Johnston, E.D.
1961-62   The Johannine Version of the Feeding of the Five Thousand—
              An Independent Tradition? *NTS* 8:151-54.

Kahle, P.
1927-1930   *Masoreten des Westens II.* 2 vols. BWAT 33, 50.
                   Stuttgart: Kohlhammer. Repr. Hildescheim: Olms, 1967.
Kerr, A.R.
2002   *The Temple of Jesus' Body: The Temple Theme in the Gospel
                   of John.* JSNTSup 220. Sheffield: Sheffield
                   Academic Press, Ltd.
Kirmis, F.
1940   *Kapitel V des Johannesevangeliums mit einer Ausführung
                   über die Dauer der öffentlichen Wirksamkeit Jesu,
                   den Bethesdateich und die Stellung von c. 5 zu c. 6.* Breslau:
                   Frankes Verlag und Druckerei, Otto Borgmeyer.
Klug, P.H.
1906   Das Osterfest Jo 6,4. *BZ* 4:152-63.
Kümmel, W.G.
1973   *Einleitung in das Neue Testament.* 17th newly revised edition
                   (of *Einleitung in das Neue Testament* by P. Feine and J. Behm).
                   Heidelberg: Quelle and Meyer.
Kutsch, E.
1961   Der Kalender des Jubiläenbuches und das Alte und das Neue
                   Testament. *VT* 11:39-47.
Kuzenzama, K.P.M.
1979   Jn 5-6 ou Jn 6-5? Une Question Embarrassante de Critique
                   Litteraire. *Revue Africaine de Théologie* 3:61-69.
Kysar, R.
1989   John 10:22-30. *Int* 43:66-70.
Labahn, M.
2000   *Offenbarung in Zeichen und Wort: Untersuchungen
                   zur Vorgeschichte von Joh 6, 1-25a und seiner Rezeption
                   in der Brotrede.* WUNT 2/117. Tübingen: Mohr Siebeck.
Lancaster, J.R.
  & R.L. Overstreet
1995   Jesus' Celebration of Hanukkah in John 10. *BSac* 152:318-33.
Langbrandtner, W.
1977   *Weltferner Gott oder Gott der Liebe: Der Ketzerstreit
                   in der johanneischen Kirche. Eine exegetisch-
                   religionsgeschichtliche Untersuchung mit Berücksichtigung
                   der koptisch-gnostischen Texte aus Nag-Hammadi.*
                   BBET 6. Frankfurt am Main/Bern/Las Vegas: Peter Lang.
Larson, E.,
  M.R. Lehmann
  & L. Schiffman
1999   4Q251: 4QHalakha A (Pls. III-IV). Pages 25-51 in *Qumran Cave 4.
                   XXV:Halakhic Texts.* DJD 35. Oxford: Clarendon.
Lauterbach, J.Z.
1933-35   מכילתא דרבי ישמעאל. 3 vols. Philadelphia: The Jewish
                   Publication Society of America.
Léonard, J.M.
1980   Multiplication des Pains: 2 Rois 4/42-44 et Jean 6/1-13.
                   ÉTR 55:265-70.

Lichtenstein, H.
1931-32 מגלת תענית. *HUCA* 8:318-51.
Lieberman, S.
1955-88 תוספתא: ע״פ כתב יד ווינה. 5 vols. New York:
The Jewish Theological Seminary of America.
MacGregor, G.H.C.
1928 *The Gospel of John.* MNTC. London: Hodder and Stoughton.
Maiworm, J.
1923 Die Jahreszeit am Jakobsbrunnen (Joh 4,31f.)? *TPQ* 76:93-96.
Malina, B.J.
1968 *The Palestinian Manna Tradition: The Manna Tradition
in the Palestinian Targums and its Relationship to the
New Testament Writings.* AGSU 7. Leiden: Brill.
Mann, N.
1733 *Of the True Years of the Birth and of the Death of Christ:
Two Chronological Dissertations.* London: J. Wilcox.
Manns, F.
1995 La Féte des Juifs de Jean 5,1. *Antonianum* 70:117-24.
1986 Traditions targumiques en Jean 10, 1-30. *RevScRel* 60:135-57.
Martyn, J.L.
1979 *History and Theology in the Fourth Gospel.* 2nd rev. ed. Nashville:
Abingdon.
Mayer, A.
1987-88 Elijah and Elisha in John's Signs Source. *ExpTim* 99:171-73.
McIvor, J.S.
1994 *The Targum of Chronicles: Translated, with Introduction,
Apparatus, and Notes.* ArBib 19. Collegeville, Minnesota:
Liturgical Press.
Menken, M.J.J.
1988 The Provenance and Meaning of the Old Testament Quotation in
John 6:31. *NovT* 30:39-56.
1985 *Numerical Literary Techniques in John: The Fourth Evangelist's
Use of Numbers of Words and Syllables.* NovTSup 55. Leiden:
Brill.
Menoud, P.-H.
1943 *L'Évangile de Jean d'après recherché récentes.* 2nd edition.
Cahiers Theologiques de l'Actualité Protestante 3. Paris:
Delachaux and Niestlé.
Milik, J.T.
1959 *Ten Years of Discovery in the Wilderness of Judaea.* Translated by
J. Strugnell. SBT. Naperville, Illinois: Alec R. Allenson, Inc.
1957 Le Travail d'Édition des Manuscrits du Désert de Juda. Pages 17-26
in *Volume du Congrès: Strasbourg 1956.* VTSup 4. Leiden:
Brill.
Mlakuzhyil, G.
1987 *The Christocentric Literary Structure of the Fourth Gospel.*
AnBib 117. Rome: Pontifical Biblical Institute.

Mollat, D.
1973   L'Évangile selon Saint Jean. Pages 9-227 in *L'Évangile et*
              Les Épitres de Saint Jean. 3rd edition. La Sainte Bible. Paris:
              Les Éditions du Cerf.
1960   L'Évangile selon Saint Jean. Pages 9-193 in *L'Évangile et*
              Les Épitres de Saint Jean. 2nd edition. La Sainte Bible. Paris:
              Les Éditions du Cerf.
1953   L'Évangile selon Saint Jean. Pages 9-198 in *L'Évangile et*
              Les Épitres de Saint Jean. La Sainte Bible. Paris: Les Éditions
              du Cerf.

Moreton, M.J.
1959   Feast, Sign, and Discourse in John 5. Pages 209-13 in *Studia*
              Evangelica: Papers Presented to the International Congress on
              "The Four Gospels in 1957" held at Christ Church, Oxford, 1957.
              Edited by K. Aland. TUGAL 18/5. Reihe. Berlin:
              Akademie-Verlag.

Morris, L.
1971   *The Gospel According to John: The English Text with Introduction,*
              Exposition and Notes. Grand Rapids, Michigan: William B.
              Eerdmans.
1964   *The New Testament and the Jewish Lectionaries*. London: Tyndale
              Press.

Mowry, L.
1954   The Dead Sea Scrolls and the Background for the Gospel of John.
              BA 17:78-97.

Ogg, G.
1965   The Chronology of the Last Supper. Pages 75-96 in *Historicity*
              and Chronology in the New Testament. Edited by D.E. Nineham.
              Theological Collections 6. London: SPCK.
1962   Chronology of the New Testament. Pages 728-732 in *Peake's*
              Commentary on the Bible. Edited by M. Black and H.H. Rowley.
              New York: Thomas Nelson and Sons, Ltd.
1940   *The Chronology of the Public Ministry of Jesus*. Cambridge:
              Cambridge University Press.

Öhler, M.
1997   *Elia im Neuen Testament: Untersuchungen zur Bedeutung*
              des alttestamentlichen Propheten im frühen Christentum.
              BZNW 88. Berlin/New York: Walter de Gruyter.

Okure, T.
1988   *The Johannine Approach to Mission: A Contextual Study of John*
              4:1-42. WUNT 2/31. Tübingen: J.C.B. Mohr (Paul Siebeck).

Perkin, J.R.
1966   Review of L. Morris, *The New Testament and the Jewish*
              Lectionaries. *SJT* 19:236-37.

Pesce, M.
2001   Il *Vangelo di Giovanni* e le fasi giudaiche del giovannismo.
              Alcuni aspetti. Pages 47-67 in *Verus Israel: Nuove prospettive*
              sul giudeocristianesimo. Atti del Colloquio di Torino
              (4-5 Novembre 1999). Edited by G. Filoramo and C. Gianotto.
              Brescia: Paideia.

Pfättisch, I.M.
1911   *Die Dauer der Lehrtätigkeit Jesu nach dem Evangelium des*
                     hl. Johannes. BibS(F) 16. Freiburg: Herder.
Porporato, F.X.
1929   Panem caeli dedit eis: Ps 77 (Heb. 78). *VD* 9:79-86.
Porter, J.R.
1963   The Pentateuch and the Triennial Lectionary Cycle: An Examination
                     of a Recent Theory. Pages 163-74 in *Promise and Fulfillment:*
                     Essays Presented to Professor S.H. Hooke in Celebration of His
                     Ninetieth Birthday, 21ˢᵗ January 1964. Edinburgh: T. & T. Clark.
Rahlfs, A.
1979   *Septuaginta.* 2 vols. Stuttgart: Deutsche Bibelgesellschaft.
Rahlfs, A.
J. Ziegler
& J.W. Wevers.
1931-   *Septuaginta: Vetus Testamentum Graecum. Auctoritate Societatis*
                     Litterarum Göttingensis editum. Göttingen: Vandenhoeck
                     & Ruprecht.
Richter, G.
1972   Die alttestamentlichen Zitate in der Rede vom Himmelsbrot
                     Joh 6,26 – 51a. Pages 193-279 in *Schriftauslegung: Beiträge*
                     zur Hermeneutik des Neuen Testamentes und im Neuen Testament.
                     Edited by J. Ernst. München: Ferdinand Schöningh. Repr. pages
                     199-265 in *Studien zum Johannesevangelium.* Edited by J. Hainz.
                     Biblische Untersuchungen 13. Regensberg: Friedrich Pustet, 1977.
Rigato, M.-L.
1991   "Era Festa Dei Giudei" (Gv 5,1). Quale? *RevistB* 39:25-29.
Robinson, B.P.
1965   Christ as a Northern Prophet in St John. *Scr* 17:104-108.
Ruddick, C.T.
1967-68   Feeding and Sacrifice: The Old Testament Background of the Fourth
                     Gospel. *ExpTim* 79:340-41.
Sahlin, H.
1950   *Zur Typologie des Johannesevangeliums.* UUA 4. Uppsala:
                     A.-B. Lundequistska Bokhandeln/Leipzig: Otto Harrassowitz.
Saxby, H.
1992   The Time-Scheme in the Gospel of John. *ExpTim* 104:9-13.
Schnackenburg, R.
1968   *The Gospel According to St. John.* Translated by K. Smyth. 3 vols.
                     New York: Crossroad. Translation of *Das Johannesevangelium.*
                     3 vols. HTKNT IV. Freiburg: Herder, 1965.
Schürer, E.
1973   *The History of the Jewish People in the Age of Jesus Christ*
                     (175 B.C.-A.D. 135). Revised and Edited by G. Vermes and
                     F. Millar. 3 vols. Edinburgh: T. & T. Clark Ltd.
Scott, W.R.
1993   The Booths of Ancient Israel's Autumn Festival. Ph.D. diss.,
                     The Johns Hopkins University.
Segal, J.B.
1957   Intercalation and the Hebrew Calendar. *VT* 7:250-307.

Segalla, G.
1992   *Evangelo e Vangeli: Quattro Evangelisti, Quattro Vangeli,*
                       Quattro Destinatari. Bologna: Centro Editoriale Dehoniano.

Shachter, J.
 & H. Freedman
1935   *Sanhedrin.* Volume 4/5 of *The Babylonian Talmud: Seder Neziḳin.*
                       London: Soncino.

Shorter, M.
1972-73   The Position of Chapter VI in the Fourth Gospel. *ExpTim*
                       84:181-83.

Skehan, P.W.
1958   The Date of the Last Supper. *CBQ* 20:192-99.

Smith, Jr., D.M.
1981   B.W. Bacon on John and Mark. *PRSt* 8:201-18.

Smith, R.H.
1962   Exodus Typology in the Fourth Gospel. *JBL* 81:329-42.

Sperber, A.
1968   תרגום לכתובים .Volume 4a of כתבי הקדש בארמית‎. Leiden:
                       Brill.

1962   תרגום יונתן לנביאים אחרונים. Volume 3 of
                       כתבי הקדש בארמית. Leiden: Brill.

1959a   תרגום אונקלוס לתורה. Volume 1 of כתבי הקדש בארמית.
                       Leiden: Brill.

1959b   תרגום יונתן לנביאים ראשונים. Volume 2 of
                       כתבי הקדש בארמית. Leiden: Brill.

Sutcliffe, E.F.
1938   *A Two Year Public Ministry Defended.* The Bellarmine Series 1.
                       London: Burns, Oates & Washbourne, Ltd.

Talbert, C.H.
1993   Worship in the Fourth Gospel and in its Milieu. Pages 337-56
                       in *Perspectives on John: Methods and Interpretation in the
                       Fourth Gospel.* Edited by R.B. Sloan and M.C. Parsons.
                       Lewiston: E. Mellen Press.

Talmon, S.
2001   לוח המועדים בשנת החמה של עדת היחד על פי רשימת שירי
                       דוד במגילת המזמורים ממערה 11 XXVII (11QPsᵃ). Pages
                       204-19 in *Fifty Years of Dead Sea Scrolls Research: Studies
                       in Memory of Jacob Licht.* Edited by G. Brin and B. Nitzan.
                       Jerusalem: Yad Ben-Zvi Press.

Talmon, S.
 with J. Ben-Dov
2001a   4Q320-330, 337, 394 1-2: Introduction. Pages 1-36 in *Qumran Cave
                       4. XVI: Calendrical Texts.* Edited by S. Talmon, J. Ben-Dov and
                       U. Glessmer. DJD 21. Oxford: Clarendon Press.
2001b   4Q320: 4QCalendrical Document/Mishmarot A (Pls. I-II). Pages
                       37-63 in *Qumran Cave 4. XVI: Calendrical Texts.* Edited by
                       S. Talmon, J. Ben-Dov and U. Glessmer. DJD 21. Oxford:
                       Clarendon Press.

2001c   4Q321: 4QCalendrical Document/Mishmarot B (Pls. III-IV). Pages
                 65 -79 in *Qumran Cave 4. XVI: Calendrical Texts*. Edited by
                 S. Talmon, J. Ben-Dov and U. Glessmer. DJD 21. Oxford:
                 Clarendon Press.
2001d   4Q325: 4QCalendrical Document/Mishmarot D (Pl. VII). Pages
                 123-31 in *Qumran Cave 4. XVI: Calendrical Texts*. Edited by
                 S. Talmon, J. Ben-Dov and U. Glessmer. DJD 21. Oxford:
                 Clarendon Press.
2001e   4Q326: 4QCalendrical Document C (Pl. VII). Pages 133-38
                 in *Qumran Cave 4. XVI: Calendrical Texts*. Edited by S. Talmon,
                 J. Ben-Dov and U. Glessmer. DJD 21. Oxford: Clarendon Press.

Thackeray, H. St. J.
1957   *Jewish Antiquities, Books I-IV*. Vol. 4 of *Josephus*. 9 vols.
                 London: William Heinemann Ltd./Cambridge, Massachusetts:
                 Harvard University Press.

Theobald, M.
1997   Schriftzitate im "Lebensbrot"–Dialog Jesu (Joh 6): Ein Paradigma
                 für den Schriftgebrauch des Vierten Evangelisten. Pages 327-66
                 in *The Scriptures in the Gospels*. Edited by C.M. Tuckett.
                 BETL 131. Leuven: Leuven University Press/Uitgeverij Peeters.

Tov, E.
2002   *The Texts From the Judaean Desert: Indices and an Introduction
                 to the* Discoveries in the Judaean Desert *Series*. DJD 39.
                 Oxford: Clarendon.

Trench, G.H.
1918   *A Study of St. John's Gospel*. London: John Murray.

Turner, C.H.
1908   Chronology of the New Testament. Pages 403-25 in *A Dictionary
                 of the Bible Dealing with Language, Literature, and Contents
                 Including the Biblical Theology*. Edited by J. Hastings. New York:
                 Charles Scribner's Sons/Edinburgh: T. & T. Clark.

Turner, H.E.W.
1965   The Chronological Framework of the Ministry. Pages 59-74
                 in *Historicity and Chronology in the New Testament*. Edited by
                 D.E. Nineham. Theological Collections 6. London: SPCK.

Ubbink, J.Th.
1922   Jh 5_1: "Een Feest" of "Het (Paasch)feest"? *Nieuwe theologische
                 Studiën* 5:131-36.

Vallauri, E.
1985   ...Alzati gli Occhi... (Lc. 6,20; Giov. 6,5). *BeO* 27:163-69.

Valletta, T.R.
1991   The "Bread of Life" Discourse in the Context of Exodus Typology.
                 Pages 129-43 in *Proceedings of the Eastern Great Lakes and
                 Midwest Biblical Society*. Volume 11. Grand Rapids, Michigan:
                 Eastern Great Lakes Biblical Society.

VanderKam, J.C.
2005   Response: Jubilees and Enoch. Pages 162-70 in *Enoch and Qumran
                 Origins: New Light on a Forgotten Connection*. Edited by
                 G. Boccaccini. Grand Rapids, Michigan: William B. Eerdmans.

1999	Identity and History of the Community. Pages 487-533 in Vol. 2 of *The Dead Sea Scrolls After Fifty Years: A Comprehensive Assessment*. Leiden/Boston/Köln: Brill.
1998	*Calendars in the Dead Sea Scrolls: Measuring Time*. Literature of the Dead Sea Scrolls. London and New York: Routledge.
1992	Dedication, Feast of. *ABD* 2:123-25.
1990	John 10 and the Feast of Dedication. Pages 203-14 in *Of Scribes and Scrolls: Studies on the Hebrew Bible, Intertestamental Judaism, and Christian Origins Presented to John Strugnell on the Occasion of His Sixtieth Birthday*. Edited by H.W. Attridge, J.J. Collins and T.H. Tobin. Lanham, Maryland: University Press of America.
1987	Hanukkah: Its Timing and Significance According to 1 and 2 Maccabees. *JSP* 1:23-40.
1979	The Origin, Character, and Early History of the 364-Day Solar Calendar: A Reassessment of Jaubert's Hypotheses. *CBQ* 41:390-411.

Vermes, G.
1969	"He is the Bread": *Targum Neofiti* Exodus 16:15. Pages 256-63 in *Neotestamentica et Semitica: Studies in Honour of Matthew Black*. Edited by E.E. Ellis and M. Wilcox. Edinburgh: T. & T. Clark.

Vogelstein, H.
1894	*Die Landwirtschaft in Palästina zur Zeit der Mišnah. Teil I: Der Getreidebau*. Breslau: Graß, Barth & Company (W. Friedrich).

Vogt, E.
1955	Antiquum Kalendarium Sacerdotale. *Bib* 36:403-408.

Watson, W.G.E.
1970	Antecedents of a New Testament Proverb. *VT* 20:368-70.

Weiss, I.H.
1946	‏ספרא דבי רב הוא ספר תורת כהנים.‏ New York, New York: Om Publishing Company.

Wendt, H.H.
1902	*The Gospel According to St. John: An Inquiry into Its Genesis and Historical Value*. Translated by E. Lummis. Edinburgh: T. & T. Clark.

Westcott, B.F.
1954	*The Gospel According to St. John: The Authorized Version with Introduction and Notes*. 2 vols. Grand Rapids, Michigan: William B. Eerdmans.

Westcott, B.F.
  & F.J.A. Hort
1881-82	*The New Testament in the Original Greek*. 2 vols. New York: Harper & Brothers.

Williford, D.D.
1981	A Study of the Religious Feasts as Background for the Organization and Message of the Gospel of John. Ph.D. diss., Southwestern Baptist Theological Seminary.

Wise, M.O.
1990	*A Critical Study of the Temple Scroll from Qumran Cave 11*. SAOC 49. Chicago, Illinois: Oriental Institute of the University of Chicago.

van der Woude, A.S.
1982   Wicked Priest or Wicked Priests? Reflections on the Identification
               of the Wicked Priest in the Habakkuk Commentary. *JJS* 33:349-59.
Wright, G.E.
1955   Israelite Daily Life. *BA* 18:50-79.
Yadin, Y.
1977/1983   *The Temple Scroll.* 3 vols. Jerusalem: Israel Exploration Society,
               The Institute of Archaeology of the Hebrew University of Jerusalem,
               The Shrine of the Book.
Yee, G.A.
1989   *Jewish Feasts and the Gospel of John.* Zacchaeus Studies:
               New Testament. Wilmington, Delaware: Michael Glazier.
Ziegler, J.
1983   *Isaias.* Vol. 14 of *Septuaginta: Vetus Testamentum Graecum.*
               Auctoritate Societatis Litterarum Göttingensis editum.
               Göttingen: Vandenhoeck & Ruprecht.
Zohary, M.
1982   *Plants of the Bible: A Complete Handbook to All the Plants with 200
               Full-Color Plates Taken in the Natural Habitat.* London: Cambridge
               University Press.
Zuckermandel, M.S.
   with S. Lieberman
1937   תוספתא: על פי כתבי יד ערפורט ווינה. 2nd edition. Jerusalem:
               Bamberger and Wahrmann.

Index of Ancient Sources

2. Septuagint (including Old Testament Apocrypha)

Index of Modern Authors

Index of Subjects

Wissenschaftliche Untersuchungen zum Neuen Testament

Alphabetical Index of the First and Second Series

Ådna, Jostein: Jesu Stellung zum Tempel.
2000. *Vol. II/119.*
Ådna, Jostein (Ed.): The Formation of the
Early Church. 2005. *Vol. 183.*
– and *Kvalbein, Hans* (Ed.): The Mission of
the Early Church to Jews and Gentiles.
2000. *Vol. 127.*
Alkier, Stefan: Wunder und Wirklichkeit in
den Briefen des Apostels Paulus. 2001.
Vol. 134.
Anderson, Paul N.: The Christology of the
Fourth Gospel. 1996. *Vol. II/78.*
Appold, Mark L.: The Oneness Motif in the
Fourth Gospel. 1976. *Vol. II/1.*
Arnold, Clinton E.: The Colossian
Syncretism. 1995. *Vol. II/77.*
Ascough, Richard S.: Paul's Macedonian
Associations. 2003. *Vol. II/161.*
Asiedu-Peprah, Martin: Johannine Sabbath
Conflicts As Juridical Controversy. 2001.
Vol. II/132.
Aune, David E.: Apocalypticism, Prophecy
and Magic in Early Christianity. 2006.
Vol. 199.
Avemarie, Friedrich: Die Tauferzählungen der
Apostelgeschichte. 2002. *Vol. 139.*
Avemarie, Friedrich and *Hermann
Lichtenberger* (Ed.): Auferstehung –
Ressurection. 2001. *Vol. 135.*
– Bund und Tora. 1996. *Vol. 92.*
Baarlink, Heinrich: Verkündigtes Heil. 2004.
Vol. 168.
Bachmann, Michael: Sünder oder Übertreter.
1992. *Vol. 59.*
Bachmann, Michael (Ed.): Lutherische und
Neue Paulusperspektive. 2005. *Vol. 182.*
Back, Frances: Verwandlung durch Offenba-
rung bei Paulus. 2002. *Vol. II/153.*
Baker, William R.: Personal Speech-Ethics in
the Epistle of James. 1995. *Vol. II/68.*
Bakke, Odd Magne: 'Concord and Peace'.
2001. *Vol. II/143.*
Baldwin, Matthew C.: Whose *Acts of Peter*?
2005. *Vol. II/196.*
Balla, Peter: Challenges to New Testament
Theology. 1997. *Vol. II/95.*
– The Child-Parent Relationship in the New
Testament and its Environment. 2003.
Vol. 155.

Bammel, Ernst: Judaica. Vol. I 1986. *Vol. 37.*
– Vol. II 1997. *Vol. 91.*
Bash, Anthony: Ambassadors for Christ. 1997.
Vol. II/92.
Bauernfeind, Otto: Kommentar und Studien
zur Apostelgeschichte. 1980. *Vol. 22.*
Baum, Armin Daniel: Pseudepigraphie und
literarische Fälschung im frühen Christen-
tum. 2001. *Vol. II/138.*
Bayer, Hans Friedrich: Jesus' Predictions of
Vindication and Resurrection. 1986.
Vol. II/20.
Becker, Eve-Marie: Das Markus-Evangelium
im Rahmen antiker Historiographie.
2006. *Vol. 194.*
Becker, Eve-Marie and *Peter Pilhofer* (Ed.):
Biographie und Persönlichkeit des Paulus.
2005. *Vol. 187.*
Becker, Michael: Wunder und Wundertäter
im früh-rabbinischen Judentum. 2002.
Vol. II/144.
Becker, Michael and *Markus Öhler* (Ed.): Apo-
kalyptik als Herausforderung neutesta-
mentlicher Theologie. 2006. *Vol. II/214.*
Bell, Richard H.: The Irrevocable Call of God.
2005. *Vol. 184.*
– No One Seeks for God. 1998. *Vol. 106.*
– Provoked to Jealousy. 1994. *Vol. II/63.*
Bennema, Cornelis: The Power of Saving
Wisdom. 2002. *Vol. II/148.*
Bergman, Jan: see *Kieffer, René*
Bergmeier, Roland: Das Gesetz im Römerbrief
und andere Studien zum Neuen Testament.
2000. *Vol. 121.*
Bernett, Monika: Der Kaiserkult in Judäa
unter den Herodiern und Römern. 2007.
Vol. 203.
Betz, Otto: Jesus, der Messias Israels. 1987.
Vol. 42.
– Jesus, der Herr der Kirche. 1990. *Vol. 52.*
Beyschlag, Karlmann: Simon Magus und die
christliche Gnosis. 1974. *Vol. 16.*
Bittner, Wolfgang J.: Jesu Zeichen im Johan-
nesevangelium. 1987. *Vol. II/26.*
Bjerkelund, Carl J.: Tauta Egeneto. 1987.
Vol. 40.
Blackburn, Barry Lee: Theios Aner and the
Markan Miracle Traditions. 1991.
Vol. II/40.

Bock, Darrell L.: Blasphemy and Exaltation in Judaism and the Final Examination of Jesus. 1998. *Vol. II/106.*

Bockmuehl, Markus N.A.: Revelation and Mystery in Ancient Judaism and Pauline Christianity. 1990. *Vol. II/36.*

Bøe, Sverre: Gog and Magog. 2001. *Vol. II/135.*

Böhlig, Alexander: Gnosis und Synkretismus. Vol. 1 1989. *Vol. 47* – Vol. 2 1989. *Vol. 48.*

Böhm, Martina: Samarien und die Samaritai bei Lukas. 1999. *Vol. II/111.*

Böttrich, Christfried: Weltweisheit – Menschheitsethik – Urkult. 1992. *Vol. II/50.*

Bolyki, János: Jesu Tischgemeinschaften. 1997. *Vol. II/96.*

Bosman, Philip: Conscience in Philo and Paul. 2003. *Vol. II/166.*

Bovon, François: Studies in Early Christianity. 2003. *Vol. 161.*

Brändl, Martin: Der Agon bei Paulus. 2006. *Vol. II/222.*

Breytenbach, Cilliers: see *Frey, Jörg.*

Brocke, Christoph vom: Thessaloniki – Stadt des Kassander und Gemeinde des Paulus. 2001. *Vol. II/125.*

Brunson, Andrew: Psalm 118 in the Gospel of John. 2003. *Vol. II/158.*

Büchli, Jörg: Der Poimandres – ein paganisiertes Evangelium. 1987. *Vol. II/27.*

Bühner, Jan A.: Der Gesandte und sein Weg im 4. Evangelium. 1977. *Vol. II/2.*

Burchard, Christoph: Untersuchungen zu Joseph und Aseneth. 1965. *Vol. 8.*

– Studien zur Theologie, Sprache und Umwelt des Neuen Testaments. Ed. by D. Sänger. 1998. *Vol. 107.*

Burnett, Richard: Karl Barth's Theological Exegesis. 2001. *Vol. II/145.*

Byron, John: Slavery Metaphors in Early Judaism and Pauline Christianity. 2003. *Vol. II/162.*

Byrskog, Samuel: Story as History – History as Story. 2000. *Vol. 123.*

Cancik, Hubert (Ed.): Markus-Philologie. 1984. *Vol. 33.*

Capes, David B.: Old Testament Yaweh Texts in Paul's Christology. 1992. *Vol. II/47.*

Caragounis, Chrys C.: The Development of Greek and the New Testament. 2004. *Vol. 167.*

– The Son of Man. 1986. *Vol. 38.*

– see *Fridrichsen, Anton.*

Carleton Paget, James: The Epistle of Barnabas. 1994. *Vol. II/64.*

Carson, D.A., O'Brien, Peter T. and *Mark Seifrid* (Ed.): Justification and Variegated Nomism.

Vol. 1: The Complexities of Second Temple Judaism. 2001. *Vol. II/140.*

Vol. 2: The Paradoxes of Paul. 2004. *Vol. II/181.*

Chae, Young Sam: Jesus as the Eschatological Davidic Shepherd. 2006. *Vol. II/216.*

Chester, Andrew: Messiah and Exaltation. 2007. *Vol. 207.*

Ciampa, Roy E.: The Presence and Function of Scripture in Galatians 1 and 2. 1998. *Vol. II/102.*

Classen, Carl Joachim: Rhetorical Criticsm of the New Testament. 2000. *Vol. 128.*

Colpe, Carsten: Iranier – Aramäer – Hebräer – Hellenen. 2003. *Vol. 154.*

Crump, David: Jesus the Intercessor. 1992. *Vol. II/49.*

Dahl, Nils Alstrup: Studies in Ephesians. 2000. *Vol. 131.*

Daise, Michael A.: Feasts in John. 2007. *Vol. 229.*

Deines, Roland: Die Gerechtigkeit der Tora im Reich des Messias. 2004. *Vol. 177.*

– Jüdische Steingefäße und pharisäische Frömmigkeit. 1993. *Vol. II/52.*

– Die Pharisäer. 1997. *Vol. 101.*

Deines, Roland and *Karl-Wilhelm Niebuhr* (Ed.): Philo und das Neue Testament. 2004. *Vol. 172.*

Dennis, John A.: Jesus' Death and the Gathering of True Israel. 2006. *Vol. 217.*

Dettwiler, Andreas and *Jean Zumstein* (Ed.): Kreuzestheologie im Neuen Testament. 2002. *Vol. 151.*

Dickson, John P.: Mission-Commitment in Ancient Judaism and in the Pauline Communities. 2003. *Vol. II/159.*

Dietzfelbinger, Christian: Der Abschied des Kommenden. 1997. *Vol. 95.*

Dimitrov, Ivan Z., James D.G. Dunn, Ulrich Luz and *Karl-Wilhelm Niebuhr* (Ed.): Das Alte Testament als christliche Bibel in orthodoxer und westlicher Sicht. 2004. *Vol. 174.*

Dobbeler, Axel von: Glaube als Teilhabe. 1987. *Vol. II/22.*

Dryden, J. de Waal: Theology and Ethics in 1 Peter. 2006. *Vol. II/209.*

Du Toit, David S.: Theios Anthropos. 1997. *Vol. II/91.*

Dübbers, Michael: Christologie und Existenz im Kolosserbrief. 2005. *Vol. II/191.*

Dunn, James D.G.: The New Perspective on Paul. 2005. *Vol. 185.*

Dunn, James D.G. (Ed.): Jews and Christians. 1992. *Vol. 66.*

– Paul and the Mosaic Law. 1996. *Vol. 89.*

– see *Dimitrov, Ivan Z.*

–, *Hans Klein, Ulrich Luz* and *Vasile Mihoc* (Ed.)*:* Auslegung der Bibel in orthodoxer und westlicher Perspektive. 2000. *Vol. 130.*

Ebel, Eva: Die Attraktivität früher christlicher Gemeinden. 2004. *Vol. II/178.*

Ebertz, Michael N.: Das Charisma des Gekreuzigten. 1987. *Vol. 45.*

Eckstein, Hans-Joachim: Der Begriff Syneidesis bei Paulus. 1983. *Vol. II/10.*

– Verheißung und Gesetz. 1996. *Vol. 86.*

Ego, Beate: Im Himmel wie auf Erden. 1989. *Vol. II/34.*

Ego, Beate, Armin Lange and *Peter Pilhofer (Ed.):* Gemeinde ohne Tempel – Community without Temple. 1999. *Vol. 118.*

– and *Helmut Merkel* (Ed.): Religiöses Lernen in der biblischen, frühjüdischen und frühchristlichen Überlieferung. 2005. *Vol. 180.*

Eisen, Ute E.: see *Paulsen, Henning.*

Elledge, C.D.: Life after Death in Early Judaism. 2006. *Vol. II/208.*

Ellis, E. Earle: Prophecy and Hermeneutic in Early Christianity. 1978. *Vol. 18.*

– The Old Testament in Early Christianity. 1991. *Vol. 54.*

Endo, Masanobu: Creation and Christology. 2002. *Vol. 149.*

Ennulat, Andreas: Die 'Minor Agreements'. 1994. *Vol. II/62.*

Ensor, Peter W.: Jesus and His 'Works'. 1996. *Vol. II/85.*

Eskola, Timo: Messiah and the Throne. 2001. *Vol. II/142.*

– Theodicy and Predestination in Pauline Soteriology. 1998. *Vol. II/100.*

Fatehi, Mehrdad: The Spirit's Relation to the Risen Lord in Paul. 2000. *Vol. II/128.*

Feldmeier, Reinhard: Die Krisis des Gottessohnes. 1987. *Vol. II/21.*

– Die Christen als Fremde. 1992. *Vol. 64.*

Feldmeier, Reinhard and *Ulrich Heckel* (Ed.): Die Heiden. 1994. *Vol. 70.*

Fletcher-Louis, Crispin H.T.: Luke-Acts: Angels, Christology and Soteriology. 1997. *Vol. II/94.*

Förster, Niclas: Marcus Magus. 1999. *Vol. 114.*

Forbes, Christopher Brian: Prophecy and Inspired Speech in Early Christianity and its Hellenistic Environment. 1995. *Vol. II/75.*

Fornberg, Tord: see *Fridrichsen, Anton.*

Fossum, Jarl E.: The Name of God and the Angel of the Lord. 1985. *Vol. 36.*

Foster, Paul: Community, Law and Mission in Matthew's Gospel. *Vol. II/177.*

Fotopoulos, John: Food Offered to Idols in Roman Corinth. 2003. *Vol. II/151.*

Frenschkowski, Marco: Offenbarung und Epiphanie. Vol. 1 1995. *Vol. II/79* – Vol. 2 1997. *Vol. II/80.*

Frey, Jörg: Eugen Drewermann und die biblische Exegese. 1995. *Vol. II/71.*

– Die johanneische Eschatologie. Vol. I. 1997. *Vol. 96.* – Vol. II. 1998. *Vol. 110.* – Vol. III. 2000. *Vol. 117.*

Frey, Jörg and *Cilliers Breytenbach* (Ed.): Aufgabe und Durchführung einer Theologie des Neuen Testaments. 2007. *Vol. 205.*

– and *Udo Schnelle (Ed.):* Kontexte des Johannesevangeliums. 2004. *Vol. 175.*

– and *Jens Schröter* (Ed.): Deutungen des Todes Jesu im Neuen Testament. 2005. *Vol. 181.*

–, *Jan G. van der Watt,* and *Ruben Zimmermann* (Ed.): Imagery in the Gospel of John. 2006. *Vol. 200.*

Freyne, Sean: Galilee and Gospel. 2000. *Vol. 125.*

Fridrichsen, Anton: Exegetical Writings. Edited by C.C. Caragounis and T. Fornberg. 1994. *Vol. 76.*

Gäbel, Georg: Die Kulttheologie des Hebräerbriefes. 2006. *Vol. II/212.*

Gäckle, Volker: Die Starken und die Schwachen in Korinth und in Rom. 2005. *Vol. 200.*

Garlington, Don B.: 'The Obedience of Faith'. 1991. *Vol. II/38.*

– Faith, Obedience, and Perseverance. 1994. *Vol. 79.*

Garnet, Paul: Salvation and Atonement in the Qumran Scrolls. 1977. *Vol. II/3.*

Gemünden, Petra von (Ed.): see *Weissenrieder, Annette.*

Gese, Michael: Das Vermächtnis des Apostels. 1997. *Vol. II/99.*

Gheorghita, Radu: The Role of the Septuagint in Hebrews. 2003. *Vol. II/160.*

Gordley, Matthew E.: The Colossian Hymn in Context. 2007. *Vol. II/228.*

Gräbe, Petrus J.: The Power of God in Paul's Letters. 2000. *Vol. II/123.*

Gräßer, Erich: Der Alte Bund im Neuen. 1985. *Vol. 35.*

– Forschungen zur Apostelgeschichte. 2001. *Vol. 137.*

Green, Joel B.: The Death of Jesus. 1988. *Vol. II/33.*

Gregg, Brian Han: The Historical Jesus and the Final Judgment Sayings in Q. 2005. *Vol. II/207.*

Gregory, Andrew: The Reception of Luke and Acts in the Period before Irenaeus. 2003. *Vol. II/169.*

Grindheim, Sigurd: The Crux of Election. 2005. *Vol. II/202.*

Gundry, Robert H.: The Old is Better. 2005. *Vol. 178.*

Gundry Volf, Judith M.: Paul and Perseverance. 1990. *Vol. II/37.*

Häußer, Detlef: Christusbekenntnis und Jesusüberlieferung bei Paulus. 2006. *Vol. 210.*

Hafemann, Scott J.: Suffering and the Spirit. 1986. *Vol. II/19.*

– Paul, Moses, and the History of Israel. 1995. *Vol. 81.*

Hahn, Ferdinand: Studien zum Neuen Testament.
Vol. I: Grundsatzfragen, Jesusforschung, Evangelien. 2006. *Vol. 191.*
Vol. II: Bekenntnisbildung und Theologie in urchristlicher Zeit. 2006. *Vol. 192.*

Hahn, Johannes (Ed.): Zerstörungen des Jerusalemer Tempels. 2002. *Vol. 147.*

Hamid-Khani, Saeed: Relevation and Concealment of Christ. 2000. *Vol. II/120.*

Hannah, Darrel D.: Michael and Christ. 1999. *Vol. II/109.*

Harrison, James R.: Paul's Language of Grace in Its Graeco-Roman Context. 2003. *Vol. II/172.*

Hartman, Lars: Text-Centered New Testament Studies. Ed. von D. Hellholm. 1997. *Vol. 102.*

Hartog, Paul: Polycarp and the New Testament. 2001. *Vol. II/134.*

Heckel, Theo K.: Der Innere Mensch. 1993. *Vol. II/53.*

– Vom Evangelium des Markus zum viergestaltigen Evangelium. 1999. *Vol. 120.*

Heckel, Ulrich: Kraft in Schwachheit. 1993. *Vol. II/56.*

– Der Segen im Neuen Testament. 2002. *Vol. 150.*

– see *Feldmeier, Reinhard.*

– see *Hengel, Martin.*

Heiligenthal, Roman: Werke als Zeichen. 1983. *Vol. II/9.*

Hellholm, D.: see *Hartman, Lars.*

Hemer, Colin J.: The Book of Acts in the Setting of Hellenistic History. 1989. *Vol. 49.*

Hengel, Martin: Judentum und Hellenismus. 1969, ³1988. *Vol. 10.*

– Die johanneische Frage. 1993. *Vol. 67.*

– Judaica et Hellenistica. Kleine Schriften I. 1996. *Vol. 90.*

– Judaica, Hellenistica et Christiana. Kleine Schriften II. 1999. *Vol. 109.*

– Paulus und Jakobus. Kleine Schriften III. 2002. *Vol. 141.*

– Studien zur Christologie. Kleine Schriften IV. 2006. *Vol. 201.*

– and *Anna Maria Schwemer:* Paulus zwischen Damaskus und Antiochien. 1998. *Vol. 108.*

– Der messianische Anspruch Jesu und die Anfänge der Christologie. 2001. *Vol. 138.*

Hengel, Martin and *Ulrich Heckel* (Ed.): Paulus und das antike Judentum. 1991. *Vol. 58.*

– and *Hermut Löhr* (Ed.): Schriftauslegung im antiken Judentum und im Urchristentum. 1994. *Vol. 73.*

– and *Anna Maria Schwemer* (Ed.): Königsherrschaft Gottes und himmlischer Kult. 1991. *Vol. 55.*

– Die Septuaginta. 1994. *Vol. 72.*

–, *Siegfried Mittmann* and *Anna Maria Schwemer* (Ed.): La Cité de Dieu / Die Stadt Gottes. 2000. *Vol. 129.*

Hentschel, Anni: Diakonia im Neuen Testament. 2007. *Vol. 226.*

Hernández Jr., Juan: Scribal Habits and Theological Influence in the Apocalypse. 2006. *Vol. II/218.*

Herrenbrück, Fritz: Jesus und die Zöllner. 1990. *Vol. II/41.*

Herzer, Jens: Paulus oder Petrus? 1998. *Vol. 103.*

Hill, Charles E.: From the Lost Teaching of Polycarp. 2005. *Vol. 186.*

Hoegen-Rohls, Christina: Der nachösterliche Johannes. 1996. *Vol. II/84.*

Hoffmann, Matthias Reinhard: The Destroyer and the Lamb. 2005. *Vol. II/203.*

Hofius, Otfried: Katapausis. 1970. *Vol. 11.*

– Der Vorhang vor dem Thron Gottes. 1972. *Vol. 14.*

– Der Christushymnus Philipper 2,6-11. 1976, ²1991. *Vol. 17.*

– Paulusstudien. 1989, ²1994. *Vol. 51.*

– Neutestamentliche Studien. 2000. *Vol. 132.*

– Paulusstudien II. 2002. *Vol. 143.*

– and *Hans-Christian Kammler:* Johannesstudien. 1996. *Vol. 88.*

Holtz, Traugott: Geschichte und Theologie des Urchristentums. 1991. *Vol. 57.*

Hommel, Hildebrecht: Sebasmata.
Vol. 1 1983. *Vol. 31.*
Vol. 2 1984. *Vol. 32.*

Horbury, William: Herodian Judaism and New Testament Study. 2006. *Vol. 193.*

Horst, Pieter W. van der: Jews and Christians in Their Graeco-Roman Context. 2006. *Vol. 196.*

Hvalvik, Reidar: The Struggle for Scripture and Covenant. 1996. *Vol. II/82.*

Jauhiainen, Marko: The Use of Zechariah in Revelation. 2005. *Vol. II/199.*

Jensen, Morten H.: Herod Antipas in Galilee. 2006. *Vol. II/215.*

Johns, Loren L.: The Lamb Christology of the Apocalypse of John. 2003. *Vol. II/167.*

Jossa, Giorgio: Jews or Christians? 2006. *Vol. 202.*

Joubert, Stephan: Paul as Benefactor. 2000. *Vol. II/124.*

Jungbauer, Harry: „Ehre Vater und Mutter". 2002. *Vol. II/146.*

Kähler, Christoph: Jesu Gleichnisse als Poesie und Therapie. 1995. *Vol. 78.*

Kamlah, Ehrhard: Die Form der katalogischen Paränese im Neuen Testament. 1964. *Vol. 7.*

Kammler, Hans-Christian: Christologie und Eschatologie. 2000. *Vol. 126.*

– Kreuz und Weisheit. 2003. *Vol. 159.*

– see *Hofius, Otfried.*

Kelhoffer, James A.: The Diet of John the Baptist. 2005. *Vol. 176.*

– Miracle and Mission. 1999. *Vol. II/112.*

Kelley, Nicole: Knowledge and Religious Authority in the Pseudo-Clementines. 2006. *Vol. II/213.*

Kieffer, René and *Jan Bergman (Ed.):* La Main de Dieu / Die Hand Gottes. 1997. *Vol. 94.*

Kierspel, Lars: The Jews and the World in the Fourth Gospel. 2006. *Vol. 220.*

Kim, Seyoon: The Origin of Paul's Gospel. 1981, ²1984. *Vol. II/4.*

– Paul and the New Perspective. 2002. *Vol. 140.*

– "The 'Son of Man'" as the Son of God. 1983. *Vol. 30.*

Klauck, Hans-Josef: Religion und Gesellschaft im frühen Christentum. 2003. *Vol. 152.*

Klein, Hans: see *Dunn, James D.G.*

Kleinknecht, Karl Th.: Der leidende Gerechtfertigte. 1984, ²1988. *Vol. II/13.*

Klinghardt, Matthias: Gesetz und Volk Gottes. 1988. *Vol. II/32.*

Kloppenborg, John S.: The Tenants in the Vineyard. 2006. *Vol. 195.*

Koch, Michael: Drachenkampf und Sonnenfrau. 2004. *Vol. II/184.*

Koch, Stefan: Rechtliche Regelung von Konflikten im frühen Christentum. 2004. *Vol. II/174.*

Köhler, Wolf-Dietrich: Rezeption des Matthäusevangeliums in der Zeit vor Irenäus. 1987. *Vol. II/24.*

Köhn, Andreas: Der Neutestamentler Ernst Lohmeyer. 2004. *Vol. II/180.*

Kooten, George H. van: Cosmic Christology in Paul and the Pauline School. 2003. *Vol. II/171.*

Korn, Manfred: Die Geschichte Jesu in veränderter Zeit. 1993. *Vol. II/51.*

Koskenniemi, Erkki: Apollonios von Tyana in der neutestamentlichen Exegese. 1994. *Vol. II/61.*

– The Old Testament Miracle-Workers in Early Judaism. 2005. *Vol. II/206.*

Kraus, Thomas J.: Sprache, Stil und historischer Ort des zweiten Petrusbriefes. 2001. *Vol. II/136.*

Kraus, Wolfgang: Das Volk Gottes. 1996. *Vol. 85.*

Kraus, Wolfgang and *Karl-Wilhelm Niebuhr* (Ed.): Frühjudentum und Neues Testament im Horizont Biblischer Theologie. 2003. *Vol. 162.*

– see *Walter, Nikolaus.*

Kreplin, Matthias: Das Selbstverständnis Jesu. 2001. *Vol. II/141.*

Kuhn, Karl G.: Achtzehngebet und Vaterunser und der Reim. 1950. *Vol. 1.*

Kvalbein, Hans: see *Ådna, Jostein.*

Kwon, Yon-Gyong: Eschatology in Galatians. 2004. *Vol. II/183.*

Laansma, Jon: I Will Give You Rest. 1997. *Vol. II/98.*

Labahn, Michael: Offenbarung in Zeichen und Wort. 2000. *Vol. II/117.*

Lambers-Petry, Doris: see *Tomson, Peter J.*

Lange, Armin: see *Ego, Beate.*

Lampe, Peter: Die stadtrömischen Christen in den ersten beiden Jahrhunderten. 1987, ²1989. *Vol. II/18.*

Landmesser, Christof: Wahrheit als Grundbegriff neutestamentlicher Wissenschaft. 1999. *Vol. 113.*

– Jüngerberufung und Zuwendung zu Gott. 2000. *Vol. 133.*

Lau, Andrew: Manifest in Flesh. 1996. *Vol. II/86.*

Lawrence, Louise: An Ethnography of the Gospel of Matthew. 2003. *Vol. II/165.*

Lee, Aquila H.I.: From Messiah to Preexistent Son. 2005. *Vol. II/192.*

Lee, Pilchan: The New Jerusalem in the Book of Relevation. 2000. *Vol. II/129.*

Lichtenberger, Hermann: Das Ich Adams und das Ich der Menschheit. 2004. *Vol. 164.*

– see *Avemarie, Friedrich.*

Lierman, John: The New Testament Moses. 2004. *Vol. II/173.*

– (Ed.): Challenging Perspectives on the Gospel of John. 2006. *Vol. II/219.*

Lieu, Samuel N.C.: Manichaeism in the Later Roman Empire and Medieval China. ²1992. *Vol. 63.*

Lindgård, Fredrik: Paul's Line of Thought in 2 Corinthians 4:16-5:10. 2004. *Vol. II/189.*

Loader, William R.G.: Jesus' Attitude Towards the Law. 1997. *Vol. II/97.*

Löhr, Gebhard: Verherrlichung Gottes durch Philosophie. 1997. *Vol. 97.*

Löhr, Hermut: Studien zum frühchristlichen und frühjüdischen Gebet. 2003. *Vol. 160.*
– see *Hengel, Martin.*

Löhr, Winrich Alfried: Basilides und seine Schule. 1995. *Vol. 83.*

Luomanen, Petri: Entering the Kingdom of Heaven. 1998. *Vol. II/101.*

Luz, Ulrich: see *Dunn, James D.G.*

Mackay, Ian D.: John's Raltionship with Mark. 2004. *Vol. II/182.*

Mackie, Scott D.: Eschatology and Exhortation in the Epistle to the Hebrews. 2006. *Vol. II/223.*

Maier, Gerhard: Mensch und freier Wille. 1971. *Vol. 12.*
– Die Johannesoffenbarung und die Kirche. 1981. *Vol. 25.*

Markschies, Christoph: Valentinus Gnosticus? 1992. *Vol. 65.*

Marshall, Peter: Enmity in Corinth: Social Conventions in Paul's Relations with the Corinthians. 1987. *Vol. II/23.*

Mayer, Annemarie: Sprache der Einheit im Epheserbrief und in der Ökumene. 2002. *Vol. II/150.*

Mayordomo, Moisés: Argumentiert Paulus logisch? 2005. *Vol. 188.*

McDonough, Sean M.: YHWH at Patmos: Rev. 1:4 in its Hellenistic and Early Jewish Setting. 1999. *Vol. II/107.*

McDowell, Markus: Prayers of Jewish Women. 2006. *Vol. II/211.*

McGlynn, Moyna: Divine Judgement and Divine Benevolence in the Book of Wisdom. 2001. *Vol. II/139.*

Meade, David G.: Pseudonymity and Canon. 1986. *Vol. 39.*

Meadors, Edward P.: Jesus the Messianic Herald of Salvation. 1995. *Vol. II/72.*

Meißner, Stefan: Die Heimholung des Ketzers. 1996. *Vol. II/87.*

Mell, Ulrich: Die „anderen" Winzer. 1994. *Vol. 77.*
– see *Sänger, Dieter.*

Mengel, Berthold: Studien zum Philipperbrief. 1982. *Vol. II/8.*

Merkel, Helmut: Die Widersprüche zwischen den Evangelien. 1971. *Vol. 13.*

– see *Ego, Beate.*

Merklein, Helmut: Studien zu Jesus und Paulus. Vol. 1 1987. *Vol. 43.* – Vol. 2 1998. *Vol. 105.*

Metzdorf, Christina: Die Tempelaktion Jesu. 2003. *Vol. II/168.*

Metzler, Karin: Der griechische Begriff des Verzeihens. 1991. *Vol. II/44.*

Metzner, Rainer: Die Rezeption des Matthäusevangeliums im 1. Petrusbrief. 1995. *Vol. II/74.*
– Das Verständnis der Sünde im Johannesevangelium. 2000. *Vol. 122.*

Mihoc, Vasile: see *Dunn, James D.G..*

Mineshige, Kiyoshi: Besitzverzicht und Almosen bei Lukas. 2003. *Vol. II/163.*

Mittmann, Siegfried: see *Hengel, Martin.*

Mittmann-Richert, Ulrike: Magnifikat und Benediktus. 1996. *Vol. II/90.*

Mournet, Terence C.: Oral Tradition and Literary Dependency. 2005. *Vol. II/195.*

Mußner, Franz: Jesus von Nazareth im Umfeld Israels und der Urkirche. Ed. von M. Theobald. 1998. *Vol. 111.*

Mutschler, Bernhard: Das Corpus Johanneum bei Irenäus von Lyon. 2005. *Vol. 189.*

Niebuhr, Karl-Wilhelm: Gesetz und Paränese. 1987. *Vol. II/28.*
– Heidenapostel aus Israel. 1992. *Vol. 62.*
– see *Deines, Roland*
– see *Dimitrov, Ivan Z.*
– see *Kraus, Wolfgang*

Nielsen, Anders E.: "Until it is Fullfilled". 2000. *Vol. II/126.*

Nissen, Andreas: Gott und der Nächste im antiken Judentum. 1974. *Vol. 15.*

Noack, Christian: Gottesbewußtsein. 2000. *Vol. II/116.*

Noormann, Rolf: Irenäus als Paulusinterpret. 1994. *Vol. II/66.*

Novakovic, Lidija: Messiah, the Healer of the Sick. 2003. *Vol. II/170.*

Obermann, Andreas: Die christologische Erfüllung der Schrift im Johannesevangelium. 1996. *Vol. II/83.*

Öhler, Markus: Barnabas. 2003. *Vol. 156.*
– see *Becker, Michael*

Okure, Teresa: The Johannine Approach to Mission. 1988. *Vol. II/31.*

Onuki, Takashi: Heil und Erlösung. 2004. *Vol. 165.*

Oropeza, B. J.: Paul and Apostasy. 2000. *Vol. II/115.*

Ostmeyer, Karl-Heinrich: Kommunikation mit Gott und Christus. 2006. *Vol. 197.*
– Taufe und Typos. 2000. *Vol. II/118.*

Paulsen, Henning: Studien zur Literatur und Geschichte des frühen Christentums. Ed. von Ute E. Eisen. 1997. *Vol. 99.*

Pao, David W.: Acts and the Isaianic New Exodus. 2000. *Vol. II/130.*

Park, Eung Chun: The Mission Discourse in Matthew's Interpretation. 1995. *Vol. II/81.*

Park, Joseph S.: Conceptions of Afterlife in Jewish Insriptions. 2000. *Vol. II/121.*

Pate, C. Marvin: The Reverse of the Curse. 2000. *Vol. II/114.*

Pearce, Sarah J.K.: The Land of the Body. 2007. *Vol. 208.*

Peres, Imre: Griechische Grabinschriften und neutestamentliche Eschatologie. 2003. *Vol. 157.*

Philip, Finny: The Origins of Pauline Pneumatology. 2005. *Vol. II/194.*

Philonenko, Marc (Ed.): Le Trône de Dieu. 1993. *Vol. 69.*

Pilhofer, Peter: Presbyteron Kreitton. 1990. *Vol. II/39.*

– Philippi. Vol. 1 1995. *Vol. 87.* – Vol. 2 2000. *Vol. 119.*

– Die frühen Christen und ihre Welt. 2002. *Vol. 145.*

– see *Becker, Eve-Marie.*

– see *Ego, Beate.*

Pitre, Brant: Jesus, the Tribulation, and the End of the Exile. 2005. *Vol. II/204.*

Plümacher, Eckhard: Geschichte und Geschichten. 2004. *Vol. 170.*

Pöhlmann, Wolfgang: Der Verlorene Sohn und das Haus. 1993. *Vol. 68.*

Pokorný, Petr and *Josef B. Souèek:* Bibelauslegung als Theologie. 1997. *Vol. 100.*

– and *Jan Roskovec* (Ed.): Philosophical Hermeneutics and Biblical Exegesis. 2002. *Vol. 153.*

Popkes, Enno Edzard: Die Theologie der Liebe Gottes in den johanneischen Schriften. 2005. *Vol. II/197.*

Porter, Stanley E.: The Paul of Acts. 1999. *Vol. 115.*

Prieur, Alexander: Die Verkündigung der Gottesherrschaft. 1996. *Vol. II/89.*

Probst, Hermann: Paulus und der Brief. 1991. *Vol. II/45.*

Räisänen, Heikki: Paul and the Law. 1983, ²1987. *Vol. 29.*

Rehkopf, Friedrich: Die lukanische Sonderquelle. 1959. *Vol. 5.*

Rein, Matthias: Die Heilung des Blindgeborenen (Joh 9). 1995. *Vol. II/73.*

Reinmuth, Eckart: Pseudo-Philo und Lukas. 1994. *Vol. 74.*

Reiser, Marius: Syntax und Stil des Markusevangeliums. 1984. *Vol. II/11.*

Rhodes, James N.: The Epistle of Barnabas and the Deuteronomic Tradition. 2004. *Vol. II/188.*

Richards, E. Randolph: The Secretary in the Letters of Paul. 1991. *Vol. II/42.*

Riesner, Rainer: Jesus als Lehrer. 1981, ³1988. *Vol. II/7.*

– Die Frühzeit des Apostels Paulus. 1994. *Vol. 71.*

Rissi, Mathias: Die Theologie des Hebräerbriefs. 1987. *Vol. 41.*

Roskovec, Jan: see *Pokorný, Petr.*

Röhser, Günter: Metaphorik und Personifikation der Sünde. 1987. *Vol. II/25.*

Rose, Christian: Die Wolke der Zeugen. 1994. *Vol. II/60.*

Rothschild, Clare K.: Baptist Traditions and Q. 2005. *Vol. 190.*

– Luke Acts and the Rhetoric of History. 2004. *Vol. II/175.*

Rüegger, Hans-Ulrich: Verstehen, was Markus erzählt. 2002. *Vol. II/155.*

Rüger, Hans Peter: Die Weisheitsschrift aus der Kairoer Geniza. 1991. *Vol. 53.*

Sänger, Dieter: Antikes Judentum und die Mysterien. 1980. *Vol. II/5.*

– Die Verkündigung des Gekreuzigten und Israel. 1994. *Vol. 75.*

– see *Burchard, Christoph*

– and *Ulrich Mell* (Hrsg.): Paulus und Johannes. 2006. *Vol. 198.*

Salier, Willis Hedley: The Rhetorical Impact of the Semeia in the Gospel of John. 2004. *Vol. II/186.*

Salzmann, Jorg Christian: Lehren und Ermahnen. 1994. *Vol. II/59.*

Sandnes, Karl Olav: Paul – One of the Prophets? 1991. *Vol. II/43.*

Sato, Migaku: Q und Prophetie. 1988. *Vol. II/29.*

Schäfer, Ruth: Paulus bis zum Apostelkonzil. 2004. *Vol. II/179.*

Schaper, Joachim: Eschatology in the Greek Psalter. 1995. *Vol. II/76.*

Schimanowski, Gottfried: Die himmlische Liturgie in der Apokalypse des Johannes. 2002. *Vol. II/154.*

– Weisheit und Messias. 1985. *Vol. II/17.*

Schlichting, Günter: Ein jüdisches Leben Jesu. 1982. *Vol. 24.*

Schließer, Benjamin: Abraham's Faith in Romans 4. 2007. *Vol. II/224.*

Schnabel, Eckhard J.: Law and Wisdom from Ben Sira to Paul. 1985. *Vol. II/16.*

Schnelle, Udo: see *Frey, Jörg.*

Schröter, Jens: Von Jesus zum Neuen Testament. 2007. *Vol. 204.*
– see *Frey, Jörg.*
Schutter, William L.: Hermeneutic and Composition in I Peter. 1989. *Vol. II/30.*
Schwartz, Daniel R.: Studies in the Jewish Background of Christianity. 1992. *Vol. 60.*
Schwemer, Anna Maria: see *Hengel, Martin*
Scott, Ian W.: Implicit Epistemology in the Letters of Paul. 2005. *Vol. II/205.*
Scott, James M.: Adoption as Sons of God. 1992. *Vol. II/48.*
– Paul and the Nations. 1995. *Vol. 84.*
Shum, Shiu-Lun: Paul's Use of Isaiah in Romans. 2002. *Vol. II/156.*
Siegert, Folker: Drei hellenistisch-jüdische Predigten. Teil I 1980. *Vol. 20* – Teil II 1992. *Vol. 61.*
– Nag-Hammadi-Register. 1982. *Vol. 26.*
– Argumentation bei Paulus. 1985. *Vol. 34.*
– Philon von Alexandrien. 1988. *Vol. 46.*
Simon, Marcel: Le christianisme antique et son contexte religieux I/II. 1981. *Vol. 23.*
Snodgrass, Klyne: The Parable of the Wicked Tenants. 1983. *Vol. 27.*
Söding, Thomas: Das Wort vom Kreuz. 1997. *Vol. 93.*
– see *Thüsing, Wilhelm.*
Sommer, Urs: Die Passionsgeschichte des Markusevangeliums. 1993. *Vol. II/58.*
Souèek, Josef B.: see *Pokorný, Petr.*
Spangenberg, Volker: Herrlichkeit des Neuen Bundes. 1993. *Vol. II/55.*
Spanje, T.E. van: Inconsistency in Paul? 1999. *Vol. II/110.*
Speyer, Wolfgang: Frühes Christentum im antiken Strahlungsfeld. Vol. I: 1989. *Vol. 50.*
– Vol. II: 1999. *Vol. 116.*
Stadelmann, Helge: Ben Sira als Schriftgelehrter. 1980. *Vol. II/6.*
Stenschke, Christoph W.: Luke's Portrait of Gentiles Prior to Their Coming to Faith. *Vol. II/108.*
Sterck-Degueldre, Jean-Pierre: Eine Frau namens Lydia. 2004. *Vol. II/176.*
Stettler, Christian: Der Kolosserhymnus. 2000. *Vol. II/131.*
Stettler, Hanna: Die Christologie der Pastoralbriefe. 1998. *Vol. II/105.*
Stökl Ben Ezra, Daniel: The Impact of Yom Kippur on Early Christianity. 2003. *Vol. 163.*
Strobel, August: Die Stunde der Wahrheit. 1980. *Vol. 21.*
Stroumsa, Guy G.: Barbarian Philosophy. 1999. *Vol. 112.*
Stuckenbruck, Loren T.: Angel Veneration and Christology. 1995. *Vol. II/70.*

Stuhlmacher, Peter (Ed.): Das Evangelium und die Evangelien. 1983. *Vol. 28.*
– Biblische Theologie und Evangelium. 2002. *Vol. 146.*
Sung, Chong-Hyon: Vergebung der Sünden. 1993. *Vol. II/57.*
Tajra, Harry W.: The Trial of St. Paul. 1989. *Vol. II/35.*
– The Martyrdom of St.Paul. 1994. *Vol. II/67.*
Theißen, Gerd: Studien zur Soziologie des Urchristentums. 1979, ³1989. *Vol. 19.*
Theobald, Michael: Studien zum Römerbrief. 2001. *Vol. 136.*
Theobald, Michael: see *Mußner, Franz.*
Thornton, Claus-Jürgen: Der Zeuge des Zeugen. 1991. *Vol. 56.*
Thüsing, Wilhelm: Studien zur neutestamentlichen Theologie. Ed. von Thomas Söding. 1995. *Vol. 82.*
Thurén, Lauri: Derhethorizing Paul. 2000. *Vol. 124.*
Tolmie, D. Francois: Persuading the Galatians. 2005. *Vol. II/190.*
Tomson, Peter J. and *Doris Lambers-Petry* (Ed.): The Image of the Judaeo-Christians in Ancient Jewish and Christian Literature. 2003. *Vol. 158.*
Trebilco, Paul: The Early Christians in Ephesus from Paul to Ignatius. 2004. *Vol. 166.*
Treloar, Geoffrey R.: Lightfoot the Historian. 1998. *Vol. II/103.*
Tsuji, Manabu: Glaube zwischen Vollkommenheit und Verweltlichung. 1997. *Vol. II/93.*
Twelftree, Graham H.: Jesus the Exorcist. 1993. *Vol. II/54.*
Ulrichs, Karl Friedrich: Christusglaube. 2007. *Vol. II/227.*
Urban, Christina: Das Menschenbild nach dem Johannesevangelium. 2001. *Vol. II/137.*
Visotzky, Burton L.: Fathers of the World. 1995. *Vol. 80.*
Vollenweider, Samuel: Horizonte neutestamentlicher Christologie. 2002. *Vol. 144.*
Vos, Johan S.: Die Kunst der Argumentation bei Paulus. 2002. *Vol. 149.*
Wagener, Ulrike: Die Ordnung des „Hauses Gottes". 1994. *Vol. II/65.*
Wahlen, Clinton: Jesus and the Impurity of Spirits in the Synoptic Gospels. 2004. *Vol. II/185.*
Walker, Donald D.: Paul's Offer of Leniency (2 Cor 10:1). 2002. *Vol. II/152.*
Walter, Nikolaus: Praeparatio Evangelica. Ed. von Wolfgang Kraus und Florian Wilk. 1997. *Vol. 98.*

Wander, Bernd: Gottesfürchtige und Sympathisanten. 1998. *Vol. 104.*

Waters, Guy: The End of Deuteronomy in the Epistles of Paul. 2006. *Vol. 221.*

Watt, Jan G. van der: see *Frey, Jörg*

Watts, Rikki: Isaiah's New Exodus and Mark. 1997. *Vol. II/88.*

Wedderburn, A.J.M.: Baptism and Resurrection. 1987. *Vol. 44.*

Wegner, Uwe: Der Hauptmann von Kafarnaum. 1985. *Vol. II/14.*

Weissenrieder, Annette: Images of Illness in the Gospel of Luke. 2003. Vol. II/164.

−, *Friederike Wendt* and *Petra von Gemünden* (Ed.): Picturing the New Testament. 2005. *Vol. II/193.*

Welck, Christian: Erzählte ‚Zeichen'. 1994. *Vol. II/69.*

Wendt, Friederike (Ed.): see *Weissenrieder, Annette.*

Wiarda, Timothy: Peter in the Gospels. 2000. *Vol. II/127.*

Wifstrand, Albert: Epochs and Styles. 2005. *Vol. 179.*

Wilk, Florian: see *Walter, Nikolaus.*

Williams, Catrin H.: I am He. 2000. *Vol. II/113.*

Wilson, Todd A.: The Curse of the Law and the Crisis in Galatia. 2007. *Vol. II/225.*

Wilson, Walter T.: Love without Pretense. 1991. *Vol. II/46.*

Wischmeyer, Oda: Von Ben Sira zu Paulus. 2004. *Vol. 173.*

Wisdom, Jeffrey: Blessing for the Nations and the Curse of the Law. 2001. *Vol. II/133.*

Wold, Benjamin G.: Women, Men, and Angels. 2005. *Vol. II/2001.*

Wright, Archie T.: The Origin of Evil Spirits. 2005. *Vol. II/198.*

Wucherpfennig, Ansgar: Heracleon Philologus. 2002. *Vol. 142.*

Yeung, Maureen: Faith in Jesus and Paul. 2002. *Vol. II/147.*

Zimmermann, Alfred E.: Die urchristlichen Lehrer. 1984, ²1988. *Vol. II/12.*

Zimmermann, Johannes: Messianische Texte aus Qumran. 1998. *Vol. II/104.*

Zimmermann, Ruben: Christologie der Bilder im Johannesevangelium. 2004. *Vol. 171.*

− Geschlechtermetaphorik und Gottesverhältnis. 2001. *Vol. II/122.*

− see *Frey, Jörg*

Zumstein, Jean: see *Dettwiler, Andreas*

Zwiep, Arie W.: Judas and the Choice of Matthias. 2004. *Vol. II/187.*

For a complete catalogue please write to the publisher
Mohr Siebeck • P.O. Box 2030 • D–72010 Tübingen/Germany
Up-to-date information on the internet at www.mohr.de